Documents on North East India

Documents on North East India

Compiled by
Jaideep Saikia

Institute for Defence Studies and Analyses, New Delhi

SHIPRA

(2022 PoD, First Published in India in 2010)

Rs. 1600; US$ 64

ISBN: 978-81-7541-579-9

2025 Impression, PoD

Documents on North East India

Published by:
SHIPRA PUBLICATIONS
LG 18-19, Pankaj Central Market,
I.P. Ext., Patparganj, Delhi 110092
91 11 47322068; 96500 28065, 9810522367
info@shiprapublication.com
www.shiprapublication.com

Preface

An important manner in which historiography can achieve clearer representation is by perusal of official documents that have been scripted over a period of time-especially if it pertains to a particular theme. Were one to-for instance-seek an examination of the genesis and progression of World War II, it would be worthwhile to read the treaty that was concluded between the Allies and the Germans in the Hall of Mirrors in the Palace of Versailles on 28 June 1919, the "Pact of Steel" signed between Germany and Italy on 22 May 1939 that "united" the two nations military alliance "by the inner affinity of their ideologies", or for the matter the Ribbentrop-Molotov Agreement that was inked on 20 August 1939. Analyses of such documents-if it is husbanded by a generic comprehension of the backdrop in which these were initialed-could act as veritable waypoints that led up to the war, and pave way for a sounder understanding of the matrix that had governed a particular period in history.

Official documents-to paraphrase Mahatma Gandhi when he sought to define history-could be characterised as "a record of an interruption of the course of nature." Indeed, such documents are the only authentic records that history possess-rest of the account are usually subject to varying interpretations, with historians and analysts culling description from, by and large, indefinite and unverifiable sources. While pre-history by its very usage prevents sound entry of authenticity and casts it to the realm of "pieces" and "imprecise designs", the historical records that characterise medieval ages are usually hagiographies, chronicled in a manner that suited the patron. Indeed, with the advent of modern methodologies the imprecision or eulogy should have disappeared from historical writings, but that has not entirely been the case. Certain historians have allowed bias to colour the ink with which they document history, not necessarily by fabricating fact-for that would probably be no longer possible-but by viewing the past from differing ideological stations, keeping thereby the door ajar for misinterpretation and ambiguity.

Indeed, such ambiguity can characterise even official treaties, with differing interpretations obfuscating the actual. This was seen, for instance, in the agreement concluded between Great Britain and Tibet in 1914 in Simla, which as the author of India's China War, Neville Maxwell states ended "with two participants in what was meant to be a tripartite conference openly signing a secret declaration; with one text of a draft convention initialed by all three parties, another initialed by two, and a map initialed by all three." Official documents can lead to confusion as well, as has been the case in the Simla agreement of 1914. Indeed, the documents of Simla 1914 and the attendant contending interpretations continue to exercise a powerful influence on Indo-China relationship.

But, despite the misrepresentation that occasionally arise out of black-and-white treaties and official documents, the fact of the matter is that such documents can at least be recalled for adjudication, and in order to stand the scrutiny of historians and legal interpreters-an aspect that an incident in history-perhaps noted only by a chronicler-cannot be subjected to. Official documents, therefore, are the pages that bind history in the most explicit manner possible. Indeed, as aforesaid, even such documents can at times be subjected to misinterpretation, but as has been seen the devil lies in interpretation and not in invalid construal or misrepresentation of history. Moreover, differences could also occur as a result of the nature of the document that two or more sides are party to. It is, therefore, important to differentiate between a treaty, an agreement and an accord, although on occasions the distinction between these are slender. For instance, a treaty is a "formal agreement" between two or more countries, and is generally used when the two countries have clear sovereign status-despite the fact that a treaty may be imposed upon a country by another country, as was the case in the Treaty of Versailles. An agreement, too, may have all the ingredients of a treaty, but is seen to be used in cases when two or more parties "consent" to a course of action, the emphasis being that one or more parties dilute the event by scaling the episode down from a high-sounding "treaty", the usage of which would have elevated the lesser party to a position that would not be in the interest of the party that normally scripts the "agreement". After all, treaties do take place between people as well, especially for the purchase of property, but they are normally termed "agreement". An "accord", on the other hand, is a less condescending term that is used between two or more parties, employed primarily in order to exhibit a sense of parity, and normally after an aggrieved party has been assuaged and after it has been able to appropriate special considerations from another party. Official documents, naturally, also take the shape of acts, promulgations and white papers, among many others in the genre.

The compilation that makes up this assemblage are not only of the varying shades of documents as has been sought to be described above, but those that pertain exclusively to the North East, a region that came to be prefixed to India with the signing of a treaty, its outlying principalities united into the composite whole that presently makes up the region by a variety of agreements. Several accords and agreements have been anvilled from time to time in order to keep that unity intact. It is also a constituency that has been provided special laws, ostensibly for efficient governance, but the terms of a few of which continue to be bitterly contested by a certain section of the region's populace. The North East is also a region whose history attends at once to legend, folklore and hagiography, and when perceived from the prism of the sub-continent's history takes a bend that meanders into uncharted territory.

Early chroniclers that accompanied invaders and military adventurers into the present North East have documented the region in a variety of ways, much of which (as aforesaid) have a bias towards the patron on whose behest the campaigns were recorded. For instance, historians studying the Mughal wars in Assam have found that reading a single chronicle provides only a version of the times gone by. This aspect has been brought out brilliantly by the celebrated Assamese historian, Suryya Kumar Bhuyan in his editorial preface to the medieval Persian chronicle, Baharistan-I-Ghaybi, an account of the Mughal wars in Assam, Cooch Behar, Bengal, Bihar and Orissa during the reigns of Jahangir and Shahjahan, by Mirza Nathan. Commenting on this important aspect, Bhuyan states, "the Persian tawarikh are as invaluable for the history of the Muslim wars as their Assamese counterparts the Buranjis; for where can we get a better opportunity for arriving at truth except in these contemporaneous accounts preserved by the two protagonists of the conflicts-the Assamese and the Mughals? Events and personalities dimly narrated or portrayed in the one are elaborated in the other; matters left out in one source as trite and commonplace are described in the other with epical vigour." Indeed, Mirza Nathan-incidentally not a scholar of the genre of Al-Beruni, the author of Ta'rikhu'l-Hind, but a general in the payroll of Jahangir-seems to be quite clear in his objective when he wrote Baharistan-I-Ghaybi. He states, "as it occurred to the mind of this most insignificant one that if a small portion of the events which took place during the prosperous reign of the greatest Sultan and the greatest Khaqan of the world, Nuru'd-Din Muhammad Jahangir Badshah Ghazi, be put into writing, (then) the imprint of that auspicious writing will remain on the pages of time..."Similarly, the task of chronicling the reigns of different Ahom monarchs fell on the Deodhais, who were commissioned by the rulers to write the Buranjis. Needless to say, that the Buranjis, too, would have the same tenor as that of the Tawarikhs, or perhaps even the Bakhars of the Marathas.

While it is not a matter of any contest that readers would certainly be interested in studying early and medieval North Eastern history, the fact of the matter-as has been explained above-is that the documents that are being forwarded in this compilation have been chosen because they bear a mark of authenticity on their pages. However, that is not to say that earlier chronicles such as the Tawarikh and the Buranji are bereft of realistic accounts. But, as historian Bhuyan had opined, ambiguities sometimes mar such writing. Indeed, it is such considerations that led the compiler to include in the collection documents that do not go back too far into antiquity. The Treaty of Yandaboo, signed between the British and the king of present Myanmar on 24 February 1826 is the earliest document in the compilation. The document is interesting for a number of reasons. While the most important feature of the treaty was the inclusion of Assam with British India, a continuing aspect of debate pertains to the United Liberation Front of Asom's (ULFA) argument that Assam be granted sovereignty as it was never a part of India and it was only as a result of the Treaty of Yandaboo that a third party (Burma) handed over Assam to the British. ULFA argues that since the Assamese were not party to the treaty, the sovereign status of the state, as it pertained before it came under "temporary" control of the Burmese (The Burmese occupied Assam for four years between 1822 to1826), should have been restored with the leaving of the British in 1947. The ULFA's logic in its own words are, "Assam, presently under the occupation of Indian rule, was independent from the ancient times...(the Assamese) defended their independence successfully resisting the invasions of the mighty Mughals seventeen times. However, consequent to the Yandaboo Treaty signed between Man (Burma, now Myanmar) and British on 24 February 1826, Assam ultimately became a British colony. After that the peoples engaged in struggle against the British to restore the lost independence. At that time the 'liberation struggle of Assam' was united with the Indian freedom struggle under the principle of 'line of united struggle'. Assam should have established an independent state, just after the British left the South Asian continent, like the establishment of independent countries such as India, Pakistan and Myanmar. However, the British-created leadership of independent India turned Assam into a colony of India through intrigue and conspiracy. So Assam became dependent again."

ULFA's disputation has not only led to a 30-year insurrection, but also a surfeit of arguments for or against its contention. The most prominent line that is taken by the theoreticians of the organisation is the so-called "distinctiveness" of Assam from India, culling selective instances from history, geography, anthropology and economics, and, of course, that of centrist exploitation. Some of the points that have been put forward include physical traits like "yellowish colour, short nose, flat face, scattered beard etc as being representative features of Assamese people". Another rather interesting aspect that "showcases" the difference is the claim that anthropologists have discovered Haemoglobin-E in the blood samples of native communities of Assam, which is absent in the blood samples of other communities in India. Yet another instance pertains to the food habit. It is argued that in Assam the people of the upper caste are non-vegetarians, while those of India are strict vegetarians. It has also been attempted to distinguish the "Assamese people" from the "people of India" by stating that all the languages of Assam are of the Tibeto-Burman language family, when in fact the Assamese language in which the supporters of ULFA propound such theories itself is from the Indo-Aryan tree. While it is not one of the brief of the compiler to put forward value judgments to such theses, the only point that would be made is that distinctiveness does not necessarily demonstrate a case for political apartness. At any rate, critics of ULFA have been able to draw equally from history to exhibit Assam's proximate ties with India, and as a result the unity that binds the state to the nation.

But it must be said that "New Delhi's simplistic assessment of the situation in Assam and its problems has helped the ULFA ideology to survive despite its inherent weaknesses". An important passage from Udayon Misra's The Periphery Strikes Back: Challenges to the Nation-State in Assam and Nagaland is being liberally quoted in order to elucidate the point. Misra writes, "If the ULFA manner of functioning, its random resort to kidnappings and killings have resulted in narrowing its support base, then the manner in which the security forces have been conducting themselves, the tell-tale pictures of torture of suspected ultras, the rapes and molestations, not to speak of the countless custodial and "encounter" deaths have all greatly helped to keep the anti-Delhi and anti-India mood alive. This, despite the fact that for most Assamese even today the goal of independence from India is neither acceptable nor desirable."

Some of the documents in the collection-if read alongside the backdrop that accompanied them-might also provide an access to the motivation for some of the insurgencies that have erupted in the region. The "Manipur Merger Agreement", by which the "land of emeralds" was annexed to the Dominion of India on 15 October 1949, for instance, has an interesting background. On September 1949, the Governor of Assam, Sri Prakasa invited the king of Manipur, Bodh Chandra for a meeting in Shillong. On 18 September 1949, the very first day the two met, the governor presented the maharaja with a pre-drafted document whereby Manipur would be merged with India. Bodh Chandra was asked to sign the agreement which he refused. He offered instead to confer with his council of ministers. The monarch on return to his "Redlands" residence in the hill station found that the Indian army had surrounded the premises. He had been placed under house arrest. Finally, on 21 September 1949, Bodh Chandra signed the "Merger Agreement." Under the terms of the agreement Manipur would be put under Indian rule from October 1949. The agreement was kept secret until 15 October 1949. The same day an order was passed dissolving the Manipur state assembly and the elected council of ministers. Following the dissolution of the assembly, a member of the dissolved council of ministers, Hijam Irabot Singh, went under ground. Although Irabot Singh died six years later, in 1955, the seeds of dissent that he had sown developed into full-blown insurgency by the early 1960s. Today, Manipur is the most disturbed province in the North East with the state accounting for 47 per cent of the insurgency related violence in the region.

Among the scores of documents that have shaped the region's destiny, the "Assam Accord (Memorandum of Settlement)" stands out as a determining one. The Accord was signed-rather hurriedly, some observers maintain-in the early hours of 15 August 1985 in order to facilitate its inclusion in the prime minister of India's address to the nation from the ramparts of Red Fort later in the morning. The document signed by members of the All Assam Students' Union (AASU), the All Assam Gana Sangram Parishad (AAGSP) and representatives of the governments of India and Assam came after an agitation by the Assamese against illegal migration from Bangladesh.

However, the accord provisions have not been fully implemented even after the passage of 24 years. The most glaring aspect pertains to the question of illegal migration from Bangladesh. Not only has the influx from the erstwhile East Pakistan into the North East increased, but the "search for lebensraum" in the region has been fortified by the entry of Islamist militants from Bangladesh-the latter utilising the demographic jungles of Assam and thereabouts both as a gateway to the rest of India in order to perpetrate terror and as "pull-back" area afterwards. Political insouciance and patronage for such ingress have been touted to be the correct explanation for the malaise, but it would interest the reader to discover that the Illegal Migrants (Determination by Tribunal) (IM (DT)) Act, 1983 (included in the collection), a piece of legislation that was the centre of protracted debate for over 20 years, and which was struck down by the Supreme Court of India as ultra vires, found only passing mention in the Assam Accord. Appending it as the last clause in the section on Foreigners Issue, the accord merely records that the "Government will give due consideration to certain difficulties expressed by the AASU/AAGSP regarding the implementation of the Illegal Migrants (Determination by Tribunals) Act, 1983." Is it that the agitation leaders had not fathomed-in the wee hours of 15 August 1985-the manner in which the IM (DT) Act would subvert the very essence of the six-year long agitation? Indeed, under the IM (DT) Act, the onus of establishing nationality rests not on the illegal migrant, or the Government, but on the private individual who must pay a fee to lodge a complaint and do so under a stipulated jurisdiction. Such provisions made it virtually impossible to detect and deport illegal migrants. Striking down the IM (DT) Act, the Supreme Court of India in its landmark judgment had ruled that "a deep analysis of the IM (DT) Act and the rules made thereunder would reveal that they have been purposely so enacted or made so as to give shelter or protection to illegal migrants who came to Assam from Bangladesh on or after 25th March, 1971 rather than to identify and deport them."

Indeed, it is hoped that passages that relate to ULFA, Manipur and the Assam Accord-as was discussed above-would set the mood for a reading of the compilation; and instill a sense of inquisitiveness in the reader to unravel the background in which not only such treaties were concluded, but the debate that it has set into motion about the North East. In most parts, the rest of the documents that have been included in the book have similar flavours. Therefore, whether it is the Naga-Akbar Hydari Accord of June 1947, the Governor of Assam's submission to the President of India on the question of illegal migration, the ceasefire ground rules between Government of India and National Socialist Council of Nagalim-Isaac-Muivah; almost all the documents spew as a result of a feeling of "distinctiveness" among the people of the North East, and the endeavour on the part of New Delhi to assuage such sentiment. The compilation also includes a beautiful speech by former Indian president, Dr. S. Radhakrishnan on the occasion of the inauguration of the state of Nagaland on 1 December 1963. The head of state had said, "Indian society has always been a multi-lingual, multi-racial and multi-religious one, having a variety of racial and ethnic groups...the rule of law and government by the consent of the governed are essence of democracy. Government must be the custodian of the general welfare of its people and not of any special interest. The Government must capture the hearts and minds of the people. The administrators must exercise the human, the healing touch in their relations with the people and should not deprive the Naga of their innocent joys, their songs and dances, their feasts and festivals which are not repugnant to our moral sense. It must be understood that emotional integration is as important as development initiative that takes place to economically improve the region."

The effort that has been put to collect the documents that are bound in the covers of this compilation would not go waste were the reader to not only gain some historical insight into the North East-an expanse that is not only an integral part of India-but also were she to view the region with charity and imbibe what the philosopher-statesman in Dr.

Radhakrishnan meant when he affirmed, on the granting of statehood to Nagaland, "Understanding and friendship help to build a society where hatred and violence tend to disrupt it. Let us avoid the latter and adopt the former. On this auspicious day I make an appeal to all the Naga people: let all past rancour and misunderstanding be forgotten and let a new chapter of progress, prosperity and goodwill be written on the page which opens today." The appeal, it is certain, were as much for rest of India as it was for the Nagas and other North Eastern Indians.

1 July 2010 **Jaideep Saikia**

Compiler's Note

The documents that have been included in the collection have been assembled from open source material-from appendices in books, websites and sources that date back to the nineteenth century. The compiler of the anthology respectfully acknowledges the original sources from which the documents have been culled. The intent and purpose of the compilation is only to provide wide circulation to certain crucial documents that have shaped North East India in a number of ways, and in order to be able to aid scholarship that is appropriately beginning to examine the region. The fact that individual and express authorization for publication of the documents from the original scriveners of the documents has not been taken does not in any manner minimises either the accreditation to the original creation or the design of the unique documents. Indeed, in all the cases only the architects are to be credited, and the publisher and the compiler can at best be recognised for bringing together a set of select documents that pertain to a region that has not yet been suitably assayed for correct evaluation and study.

The compilation is not exhaustive, and the selection that makes up the book has been chosen primarily with the issue of India's national security in mind. Indeed, some of the documents are not exclusive to the North East, but have a bearing on the region nonetheless.

The compiler is grateful to the Institute for Defence Studies and Analyses, New Delhi. The compilation would not have seen the light of day were it not for the institute's support.

Contents

List of Abbreviations

AAGSP	:	All Assam Gana Sangram Parishad
AASU	:	All Assam Students' Union
ABNES	:	Akhil Bharat Nepali Ekta Samaj
ABSU	:	All Bodo Students' Union
ACR	:	Annual Confidential Report
APCOCA	:	Arunachal Pradesh Control of Organised Crime Act
BAC	:	Bodoland Autonomous Council
BEC	:	Bodoland Executive Council
BOPs	:	Border Out-Posts
BPAC	:	Bodo Peoples' Action Committee
BSF	:	Border Security Force
BTC	:	Bodo Territorial Council
CFMG	:	Ceasefire Monitoring Group
CID	:	Criminal Investigation Department
Cr.PC	:	Criminal Procedure Code
CWD	:	Central Works Department
DEM	:	Dukhtaran-e-Millat
DG	:	Director General
DIGP	:	Deputy Inspector General of Police
HuJ	:	Harkat-ul-Jihad
HuM	:	Harkat-ul-Mujahideen
IAS	:	Indian Administrative Service
ICC	:	Indian Citizenship Certificates
ICS	:	Indian Civil Service
ILAA	:	Islamic Liberation Army of Assam
IM (DT)	:	Illegal Migrants (Determination by Tribunals) Act
IPS	:	Indian Police Service
ISI	:	Inter Services Intelligence
ISS	:	Islamic Sevak Sangha
J&K	:	Jammu & Kashmir
JIC	:	Joint Intelligence Committee
JUUEH	:	Jamaat-Ul-Ulema-E-Hind
KCP	:	Kangleipak Communist Party
KYKL	:	Kanglei Yaol Kana Lup
LoC	:	Line-of-Control

LTTE	:	Liberation Tigers of Tamil Eelam
MCC	:	Maoist Communist Centre
MLA	:	Member of Legislative Assembly
MLTA	:	Muslim Liberation Tigers of Assam
MNF	:	Mizo National Front
MPLF	:	Manipur Peoples' Liberation Front
MULFA	:	Muslim United Liberation Front of Assam
MVF	:	Muslim Volunteer Force
NDFB	:	National Democratic Front of Bodoland
NEFA	:	North East Frontier Agency
NFG	:	Nagaland Federal Government
NGO	:	Non-Governmental Organisation
NNC	:	Naga National Council
NPC	:	Naga Peoples' Convention
NRC	:	National Register of Citizens
NSCN-IM	:	National Socialist Council of Nagalim-Isaac Muivah
NSCN-K	:	National Socialist Council of Nagalim-Khaplang
NWFP	:	North West Frontier Province
PIA	:	Pakistan International Airlines
PIP	:	Prevention of Infiltration from Pakistan
PLA	:	Peoples' Liberation Army
PoK	:	Pakistan-occupied Kashmir
POTO	:	Prevention of Terrorism Ordinance
PREPAK	:	Peoples' Revolutionary Party of Kangleipak
PULF	:	Peoples' United Liberation Front
PWD	:	Public Works Department
RAW	:	Research and Analysis Wing
SC	:	Scheduled Caste
SDO	:	Sub Divisional Officer
SP	:	Superintendent of Police
SSB	:	Special Services Bureau
ST	:	Scheduled Tribe
TADA	:	Terrorist and Disruptive Activities
TNLA	:	Tamil Nadu Liberation Army
TNRT	:	Tamil National Retrieval Troops
TNV	:	Tripura National Volunteers
ULFA	:	United Liberation Front of Asom
UMLFA	:	United Muslim Liberation Front of Assam
UNLF	:	United National Liberation Front
UP	:	Uttar Pradesh
URPA	:	United Reformation Protest of Assam
USSR	:	Union of Soviet Socialist Republic

Treaty of Yandaboo

[The Treaty was concluded between the King of Ava (present Myanmar and thereabouts) and the British on 24 February 1826. Under the aegis of the Treaty, Assam was handed over by Burma (which was "temporarily" in control of Assam) to the British. It would be of interest to note to the reader that the United Liberation Front of Asom has prefaced its demand for a sovereign Assam on the basis of this Treaty, stating that Assam was not a part of India before the Treaty and should, therefore, be reinstated to it independent status after the departure of the British]

TREATY of PEACE between the HONOURABLE EAST INDIA COMPANY on the one part, and HIS MAJESTY the KING of AVA on the other, settled MAJOR-GENERAL SIR ARCHIBALD CAMPBELL, K.C.B., and K.C.T.S., COMMANDING the EXPEDITION, and SENIOR COMMISSIONER in PEGU and AVA; THOMAS CAMPBELL ROBERTSON, ESQ., CIVIL COMMISSIONER in PEGU and AVA; and HENRY DUCIE CHAD, ESQ., CAPTAIN, COMMANDING BRITANNIC MAJESTY'S and the HONOURABLE COMPANY'S NAVAL FORCE, on the part of the Honourable Company; and by MENGYEE-MAHA-MEN-KYAN-TEN WOONGYEE, LORD of LAYKAING, and MENGYEE-MARA-HLAH-THUO-HAH-THOO-ATWEN-WOON, LORD of the REVENUE, on the part of the King of Ava; who have each communicated to the other their full powers, agreed to and executed at Yandaboo in the Kingdom of Ava, on this Twenty-fourth day of February, in the year of Our Lord One Thousand Eight Hundred and Twenty-six, corresponding with the Fourth day of the decrease of the Moon Taboung, in the year One Thousand One Hundred and Eighty-seven Gaudma Era, 1826.

Article 1

There shall be perpetual peace and friendship between the Honourable Company on the one part, and His Majesty the King of Ava on the other.

Article 2

His Majesty the King of Ava renounces all claims upon, and will abstain from all future interference with, the principality of Assam and its dependencies, and also with the contiguous petty States of Cachar and

Jyntia. With regard to Munnipoor it is stipulated, that should Ghumbheer Sing desire to return to that country, he shall be recognized by the King of Ava as Rajah thereof.

Article 3

To prevent all future disputes respecting the boundary line between the two great Nations, the British Government will retain the conquered Provinces of Arracan, including the four divisions of Arracan, Ramree, Cheduba, and Sandoway, and His Majesty the King of Ava cedes all right thereto. The Unnoupectoumien or Arakan Mountains (known in Arakan by the name of the Yeomatoung or Pokhingloung Range) will henceforth form the boundary between the two great Nations on that side. Any doubts regarding the said line of demarcation will be settled by Commissioners appointed by the respective governments for that purpose, such Commissioners from both powers to be of suitable and corresponding rank.

Article 4

His Majesty the King of Ava cedes to the British Government the conquered Provinces of Yeh, Tavoy, and Mergui and Tenasserim, with the islands and dependencies thereunto appertaining, taking the Salween River as the line of demarcation on that frontier; any doubts regarding their boundaries will be settled as specified in the concluding part of Article third.

Article 5

In proof of the sincere disposition of the Burmese Government to maintain the relations of peace and amity between the Nations, and as part indemnification to the British Government for the expenses of the War, His Majesty the King of Ava agrees to pay the sum of one crore of Rupees.

Article 6

No person whatever, whether native or foreign, is hereafter to be molested by either party, on account of the part which the map have taken or have been compelled to take in the present war.

Article 7

In order to cultivate and improve the relations of amity and peace hereby established between the two governments, it is agreed that accredited ministers, retaining an escort or safeguard of fifty men, from each shall reside at the Durbar of the other, who shall be permitted to purchase, or to build a suitable place of residence, of permanent materials; and a Commercial Treaty, upon principles of reciprocal advantage, will be entered into by the two high contracting powers.

Article 8

All public and private debts contracted by either government, or by the subjects of either government, with the others previous to the war, to be recognized and liquidated upon the same principles of honour and good faith as if hostilities had not taken place between the two Nations, and no advantage shall be taken by either party of the period that may have elapsed since the debts were incurred, or in consequence of the war; and according to the universal law of Nations, it is further stipulated, that the property of all British subjects who may die in the dominions of His Majesty the King of Ava., shall, in the absence of legal heirs, be placed in the hands of the British Resident or Consul in the said dominions, who will dispose of the same according to the tenor of the British law. In like manner the property of Burmese subjects dying under the same circumstances, in and part of the British dominions, shall be made over to the minister or other authority delegated by His Burmese Majesty to the Supreme Government of India.

Article 9

The King of Ava will abolish all exactions upon British ships or vessels in Burman ports, that are not required from Burmah ships or vessels in British port nor shall ships or vessels, the property of British subjects, whether European or Indian, entering the Rangoon River or other Burman ports, be required to land their guns, or unship their rudders, or to do any other act not required of Burmese ships or vessels in British ports.

Article 10

The good and faithful Ally of the British Government, His Majesty the King of Siam, having taken a part in the present War, will, to the fullest extent, as far as regards His Majesty and his subjects, be included in the above Treaty.

Article 11

This Treaty to be ratified by the Burmese authorities competent in the like cases, and the Ratification to be accompanied by all British, whether Europe or Native, American, and other prisoners, who will be delivered over to the British Commissioners; the British Commissioners on their part engaging that the said Treaty shall be ratified by the Right Honourable the Governor General in Council, and the Ratification shall be delivered to His Majesty the King of Ava in four months, or sooner if possible, and all the Burmese prisoners shall, in like manner be delivered over to their own Government as soon as they arrive from Bengal.

Archibald Campbell

Largeen Meonja
Woonghee

T.C. Robertson
Civil Commissioner

Seal of the Lotoo

HY. D. Chads
Captain, Royal Navy

Shwagum Woon
Atawoon

Additional Article

The British Commissioners being most anxiously desirous to manifest the sincerity of their wish for peace, and to make the immediate execution of the fifth Article of this Treaty as little irksome or inconvenient as possible to His Majesty the King of Ava, consent to the following arrangements, with respect to the division of the sum total, as specified in the Article before referred to, into instalments, *viz.*, upon the payment of twenty-five lacks of Rupees, or one-fourth of the sum total (the other Articles of the Treaty being executed), the Army will retire to Rangoon. Upon the further payment of a similar sum at that place within one hundred days from this date, with the proviso as above, the Army will evacuate the dominions of His Majesty the King of Ava with the least possible delay, leaving the remaining moiety of the sum total to be paid by equal annual instalments in two years, from this Twenty-fourth day of February 1826 A.D., through the Consul or Resident in Ava or Pegu, on the part of the Honourable the East India Company.

Archibald Campbell

Largeen Meonja
Woonghee

T.C. Robertson
Civil Commissioner

Seal of the Lotoo

Hy. D. Chads
Captain, Royal Navy

Shwagum Woon
Atawoon

Ratified by the Governor General in Council, at Fort William in Bengal, this Eleventh day of April, in the Year of our Lord One Thousand Eight Hundred and Twenty-six

Amherst
Combermere
J.H. Harington
W.B. Bayley

Foreigners Act

[Enacted in 1946, the pre-constitution Foreigners' Act continues to determine the rules of citizenship and matters relating to naturalisation etc in India]

The term "foreigner" according to the definitions given in the Foreigners Act, 1946 and the Registration of Foreigners Act, 1949, "means a person who is not a citizen of India". According to this definition, a person, who is not a citizen of India as defined in the Citizenship Act, 1955 and who had not acquired Indian Citizenship under the Naturalisation Act, 1926 as amended up-to-date including a person who had acquired citizenship under the Pakistan Citizenship Act, 1957, is a foreigner

A person who is not a citizen of India at the commencement of the constitution of India (i.e. on 26.1.50) or is deemed not to be so under article 5, 6 and 7 of the constitution can be treated as a foreigner unless subsequently he acquires or has acquired citizenship of this country under the provisions of the Citizenship Act.

Articles 5, 6 and 7 of the Constitution of India read as follows:

CITIZENSHIP

5. Citizenship at the Commencement of the Constitution: At the commencement of this constitution every person who has his domicile in the territory of India and

(a) Who was born in the territory of India; or
(b) Either of whose parents was born in the territory of India; or
(c) Who has been ordinarily resident in the territory of India for not less than five years immediately preceding such commencement, shall be a citizen of India.

6. Rights of Citizenship of Certain Person who have Migrated to India from Pakistan: Notwithstanding anything in Article 5, a person who has migrated to the territory of India from the territory now included in Pakistan shall be deemed to be citizen of India at the commencement of this constitution if

(a) He or either of his parents or any of his grandparents was born in

India as defined in the Government of India Act, 1935 (as originally enacted); and

(b) (i) In the case where such person has so migrated before the nineteenth day of July1948, he has been ordinarily resident in the territory of India since the date of his migration; or

(ii) In the case where such person has so migrated on or after the nineteenth day of July, 1948, he has been registered as a citizen of India by an officer appointed in that behalf by the Government of the Dominion of India on an application made by him therefore to such officer before the commencement of this constitution in the form and manner prescribed by that Government:

Provided that no person no person shall be registered unless he has been resident in the territory of India for at least six months immediately preceding the date of his application.

7. Rights of Citizenship of Certain Migrants to Pakistan: Notwithstanding anything in article 5 and 6, a person who has after the first day of March 1947, migrated from the territory of India to the territory now included in Pakistan shall not be citizen of India:

Provided that nothing in this article shall apply to a person who, after having so migrated to the territory now included in Pakistan, has returned to the territory of India under a permit for resettlement or permanent return issued by or under the authority of any law and every such person shall for the purpose of clause (b) of Article 6 be deemed to have migrated to the territory of India after the nineteenth day of July1948.

Sections 3 to 7 of the Citizenship Act are as under:

Section 3. Citizenship by Birth

(1) Except as provided in Sub-section (2) of this section, every person born in India on or after the 26th January 1950 shall be a citizen of India by birth.

(2) A person shall not be such a citizen by virtue of this section if at the time of his birth—

(a) His father possesses such immunity from suits and legal processes as is accorded to an envoy of a foreign power accredited to the President of India and is not a citizen of India; or

(b) His father is an enemy alien and a birth occurs in a place then under occupation by the enemy.

Section 4. Citizenship by Descent

(1) A person born outside India on or after the 26th January 1950 shall be a citizen of India by descent if his father is a citizen of India at the time of birth:

Provided that if the father of such a person was citizen of India by descent only that person shall not be a citizen of India by virtue of this section unless

(a) His birth is registered at an Indian consulate within one years of its occurrence or the commencement of this Act, whichever is latter, or with the permission of the Central Government after the expiry of the said period; or his father is at the time of his birth, in service under Government of India.

(2) If the central Government so directs, a birth shall be deemed for the purposes of this section to have been registered with its permission, notwithstanding that its permission was not obtained before the registration.

(3) For the purposes of the proviso to sub-section (1) any male person born outside undivided India who was, or, was deemed to be, a citizen of India at the commencement of the constitution shall be deemed to be, a citizen of India at the commencement of the constitution shall be deemed to be a citizen of India by descent only.

Section 5. Citizenship by Registration

(1) Subject to the provision of this and such conditions and restrictions as may be prescribed, the prescribed authority may, on application made in this behalf, register as a citizen of India any person who is not already such citizen by virtue of the constitutions of this act and belongs to any of the following categories:

(a) Person of Indian origin who are ordinarily resident in India and have been so resident for six months immediately before making an application for registration;

(b) Persons of Indian origin who are ordinarily resident in any country or place outside undivided India;

(c) Women who are, or have been, married to citizens of India;

(d) Minor children of persons who are citizens of India;

(e) Persons of full age and capacity who are citizens of a country specified in the First Schedule:

Provided that in prescribing the conditions and restrictions subject to which persons of any such country may be registered as a citizens of India under this clause, the central Government shall have due regard to the conditions subject to which citizens of India may, by law or practice of that country become citizens of that country by registration.

Explanation:

(1) For the purpose of this sub-section, a person shall be deemed to be of Indian origin if he or either of his parents, or any of his grandparents was born in undivided India.

(2) No person being of full age shall be registered as a citizen of India under sub-section (1) until he has taken the oath of allegiance in the form specified in the Second Schedule.

(3) No person who has renounced, or has been deprived of, his Indian citizenship has terminated under this Act shall be registered as a citizen of India under sub-section (1) except by order of the central Government.

(4) The Central Government may, if satisfied that there are special circumstances justifying such registration, cause any minor to be registered as a citizen of India.

(5) A person registered under this section shall be a citizen of India by registration as from the date on which he is so registered; and a person registered under the provisions of clause (b)(ii) of article 6 or article 8 of the Constitution shall be deemed to be a citizen of India by registration as from the commencement of the Constitution or the date on which he was so registered, whichever may be later.

Section 6. Citizenship by Naturalisation

(1) Where an application is made in the prescribed manner by any person of full age and capacity who is not a citizen of a country specified in the First schedule for the grant of a certificate of naturalisation to him, the Central Government may, if satisfied that the applicant is qualified for naturalisation under the provisions of the Third Schedule, grant to him a certificate of naturalisation:

Provided that, if in the opinion of the Central Government, the applicant is a person who has rendered distinguished service to the cause of science, philosophy, art, literature, world peace or human progress generally, it may waive all or any of the conditions specified in the Third Schedule.

(2) The person to whom a certificate of naturalisation is granted under subsection (1) shall, on taking the oath of allegiance in the form specified in the Second Schedule, be a citizen of India by naturalisation as from the date on which that certificate is granted.

Section 7. Citizenship by Incorporation of Territory

If any territory becomes a part of India, the Central Government may, by order notified in the official gazette, specify the persons who shall be citizens of India by reason of their connection with that territory; and those persons shall be citizens of India as from the date to be specified in the order.

The first Schedule to the Citizenship Act includes amongst other countries Pakistan also.

Thus a person who has not acquired citizenship or who is not a citizen under Article 5 to 8 of the Constitution and the above quoted provisions of the Citizenship Act is a foreigner.

Section 3 of the Foreigners Act empowers the central Government to make orders for prohibiting, regulating or restricting the entry of foreigners into India or their departure of their presence or continued present in India. In exercise of this power, the central Government has made different orders, namely, Foreigners Order, 1958; Foreigners (Restriction on Movement) Order, 1960; Foreigners (Internment) Order, 1962; Foreigners (Tribunals) Order, 1964 and Foreigners (Restriction on Pakistani Nationals) Order, 1965, besides other orders. The power conferred upon the Central Government under section 3 of the Foreigners Act for passing deportation orders and to restrict and regulate the movement stays and employment of foreigners has also been entrusted to the State Government of Assam along with other state Governments by a notification dated 15th March 1962 (S.O.802 dated 15 March 1962). Thus the government of Assam is empowered under the law not only to make deportation orders against foreigners, but also to constitute tribunals for determination of the question as to whether a person is or is not a foreigner within the meaning of the Foreigners Act, and also to make other orders regulating or restricting the movement of foreigners. By another notification the central Government (vide notification No.S.O.804 dated 15 March 1962) the Superintendents of Police were entrusted with the powers and functions of the central Government in making orders of deportation etc. under Section 3 of the Foreigners Act and the power and functions so entrusted were to be exercised in respect of Pakistani nationals in compliance with general or special directions issued by the Government of Assam and the Central Government such powers also conferred upon Deputy Inspector General of police, CID, Assam, the Superintendent of police and the Deputy Commissioners (in-charge of police) to discharge the functions of the Central Government. The aforesaid notification, besides others, fully empowered the state Government of Assam and its officers to deport foreigners from Assam.

Section 2. Power to Order Expulsion of Certain Immigrants

If the central Government is of opinion that any person or class of persons, having been ordinarily resident in any place outside India, has or have, whether before or after the commencement of this Act, come into Assam and that the stay of such person or class of persons in Assam is detrimental to the interests of the general public of India or of any section thereof or any Scheduled Tribe in Assam, the central Government may, by order:

(a) Direct such person or class of persons to remove himself or themselves from India or Assam within such time and by such route as may be specified in the order; and

(b) Give such further directions in regard to his or their removal from India or Assam as it may consider necessary or expedient:

Provided that nothing in this Section shall apply to any person, who, on account of civil disturbances or the fear of such disturbances in any area now forming part of Pakistan has been displaced from or has left his place of residence in such area and who has been subsequently residing in Assam.

Note: "Very serious economic and law and order problems were created in the State of Assam as a result of large-scale immigration of people from East Bengal. It was to meet this situation that this enactment was passed."

Section 3. Delegation of Power

The central Government may, by notification in the Official Gazette, direct that the powers and duties conferred or imposed on it by Section 2 shall, subject to such conditions, if any, as may be specified in the notification, be exercised or discharged also by:

(a) Any officer subordinate to the Central Government.

(b) The Government of Assam or any officer subordinate to that Government.

The power under section 3 of the Act was to be exercised by the Superintendents of police under the Government of Assam, conferred by notification issued by the Central Government. The Act is still in force but hardly implemented.

The Passport Act and the Rules framed thereunder prohibit entry of foreign nationals into India without a valid passport, the contravention of which punishable with imprisonment. But strangely enough although entry without a passport is punishable, yet overstaying in India by a foreigner after the expiry of the period limited by the Passport is not an offence under the Passport Act and the Rules.

The Naga-Akbar Hydari Accord

[A 9-point accord was signed between the then Governor of Assam, Sir Akbar Hydari and the representatives of the Naga National Council at Kohima after three days of deliberation on the eve of India's independence]

Tribes Represented at Discussions on the 26th, 27th and 28th June 1947 at Kohima

- Western Angamis
- Eastern Angamis
- Kukis
- Kacha Nagas (Mzemi)
- Rengmas
- Semas
- Lothas
- Aos
- Sangtams
- Changs

HEADS OF PROPOSED UNDERSTANDING

That the right of the Nagas to develop themselves according to their freely expressed wishes is recognized.

1. Judicial

All cases whether civil or criminal arising between Nagas in the Naga Hills will be disposed of by duly constituted Naga Courts according to Naga customary law or such law as may be introduced with the consent of duly recognized Naga representative organizations: save that where a sentence of transportation or death has been passed there will be a right of appeal to the Governor.

In cases arising between Nagas and non-Nagas in (a) Kohima and Mokokchung town areas, and (b) in the neighbouring plains districts, the judge if not a Naga will be assisted by a Naga assessor.

2. Executive

The general principle is accepted that what the Naga Council is prepared to pay for, the Naga Council should control. This principle will apply equally to the work done as well as the staff employed.

While the District Officer will be appointed at the discretion of the Governor, Subdivisions of the Naga Hills should be administered by a Sub-divisional Council with a full time executive President paid by Naga Council who would be responsible to the District Officer for all matters falling within the latter's responsibility, and to the Naga Council for all matters falling within their responsibility.

In regard to:

(a) *Agriculture*: The Naga Council will exercise all the powers now vested in the District Officer.

(b) *C.W.D.*: The Naga Council would take over full control.

(c) *Education and Forest Department*: The Naga Council is prepared to pay for all the services and staff.

3. Legislative

That no laws passed by the Provincial or Central Legislature which would materially affect the terms of this agreement or the religious practices of the Nagas shall have legal force in the Naga Hills without the consent of the Naga Council. In cases of dispute as to whether any law did so affect this agreement the matter would be referred by the Naga Council to the Governor who would then direct that the law in question should not have legal force in the Naga Hills pending the decision of the Central Government.

4. Land

That land with all its resources in the Naga Hills should not be alienated to a non-Naga without the consent of the Naga Council.

5. Taxation

That the Naga Council will be responsible for the imposition, collection, and expenditure of land revenue and house tax and of such other taxes as may be imposed by the Naga Council.

6. Boundaries

That present administrative divisions should be modified so as (1) to bring back into the Naga Hills District all the forests transferred to the Sibsagar and Nowgong Districts in the past, and (2) to bring under one unified administrative unit as far as possible all Nagas. All the areas so included would be within the scope of the present proposed agreement. No areas should be transferred out of the Naga Hills without the consent of the Naga Council.

7. Arms Act

The Deputy Commissioner will act on the advice of the Naga Council in accordance with the provisions of the Arms Act.

8. Regulations

The Chin Hills regulations and the Bengal Eastern Frontier Regulations will remain in force.

9. Period of Agreement

The Governor of Assam as the Agent of the Government of the Indian Union will have a special responsibility for a period of 10 years to ensure the observance of the agreement, at the end of this period the Naga Council will be asked whether they require the above agreement to be extended for a further period or a new agreement regarding the future of Naga people arrived at.

Instrument of Accession [Tripura]

[*By signing the Instrument, Kanchan Prabha Devi, Maharani Regent of Tripura State, ceded Tripura, on 13 August 1947, to the Dominion of India. Louis Mountbatten, Governor General of India signed the Instrument on behalf of the Dominion*]

Whereas, the Indian Independence Act, 1947 provides that as from the fifteenth day of August, 1947 there shall be set up an Independent Dominion known as INDIA, and that the Government of India Act, 1935 shall with such omissions, additions, adaptations and modification as the Governor General may by order specify to be applicable to the Dominion of India.

And whereas the Government of India Act, 1935 as so adapted by the Governor General provides that an Indian state may accede to the dominion of India by an Instrument of Accession executed by the ruler thereof.

Now therefore I, Kanchan Prabha Devi, Maharani Regent of Tripura state in the exercise of my sovereignty in and over my said State do hereby execute this my Instrument of Accession and I hereby declare that I accede to the Dominion of India with the intent that the Governor General of India, the Dominion legislature, the Federal Court and other Dominion authority established for the purposes of the Dominion shall, by virtue of this my Instrument of Accession but subject always to the terms thereof, and for the purposes only of the Dominion exercise in relation to the State of TRIPURA (hereinafter referred to as 'the State') such functions as may be vested in them by or under the Government of India Act, 1935, as in force in the Dominion of India on the 15th day of August, 1947 (which Act as so in force is hereinafter referred to as 'the Act'), and I further declare that the Dominion of India may, through such agency or agencies and in such manner, as it thinks fit to exercise in relation to the administration of civil and criminal justice in this State all such powers, authorities and jurisdiction as were at any time exercisable by His Majesty's representative for the exercise of the functions of the Crown in its relations with Indian States.

2. I hereby assume the obligation of ensuring that due effect is given to the provisions of the Act within this State so far as they are applicable therein by virtue of this my Instrument of Accession.

3. Without prejudice to the provisions of paragraph 1, I accept the

matters specified in the schedule hereto as the matters with respect to which the Dominion Legislature may make laws for this State.

4. I hereby declare that I accede to the Dominion of India on the assurance that if an agreement is made between the Governor General and the Ruler of this State whereby any function in relation to the administration in this State of any law of dominion legislature shall be exercised by the Ruler of this State, then any such agreement shall be deemed to form part of this Instrument and shall be construed and have effect accordingly.

5. The terms of this my Instrument of Accession shall not be varied by any amendment of the Act or of the Indian Independence Act, 1947, unless such amendment is accepted by me by an Instrument supplementary to this Instrument.

6. Nothing in this Instrument shall empower the Dominion Legislature to make any law for this State authorising the compulsory acquisition of land for any purpose, but I hereby undertake that should the Dominion for purpose of a Dominion law which applies in this State deem it necessary to acquire any land, I will at their request provide the land at their expense or if the land belongs to me transfer it to them on such terms as may be agreed, or in default of agreement, determined by an arbitrator to be appointed by the Chief Justice of Delhi.

7. Nothing in this Instrument shall be deemed to commit me in any way to acceptance of any future Constitution of India or to fetter my discretion to enter into an arrangement with the Government of India under any such future Constitution.

8. Nothing in this Instrument affects the continuance of my sovereignty in and over this State, or save as provided by or under this Instrument, the exercise of any owners, authority and rights now enjoyed by me as Ruler of this State or the validity of any law at present in force in this state.

9. I hereby declare that I have executed this Instrument on behalf of this State and that any reference in this Instrument to me or to the Ruler of the State is to be construed as including a reference to my heirs and successors. Given under my hand this 13th day of August, Nineteen hundred and forty seven.

Sd/-
Kanchan Prabha Devi
Maharani Regent of Tripura

I do hereby accept this Instrument of Accession. Dated this 13th day of August, Nineteen hundred and forty seven.

Sd/-
Louis Mountbatten
Governor General of India.

SCHEDULE

The matters with respect to which the Dominion legislature may make laws for this State.

A. Defence

1. The naval, military and air force of the Dominion and any other armed forces raised or maintained by the Dominion, any armed forces, including forces raised or maintained by an Acceding state, which are attached to, or operating with, any of the armed forces of the Dominion.
2. Naval, military and air force works, administration of cantonment area.
3. Arms, Firearms, ammunition.
4. Explosives.

B. External Affairs

1. External affairs, the implementing of treaties and agreements with other countries, including the surrender of criminals and accused persons to parts of His Majesty's Dominion outside India.
2. Admission into, and emigration and expulsion from, India, including in relation thereto the regulation of the movements in India or persons who are not British subjects domiciled in India or subjects of any acceding State, pilgrimages to places beyond India.
3. Naturalisation.

C. Communication

1. Posts and Telegraphs, including telephone, wireless broadcasting and other like forms of communication.
2. Federal railway, the regulation of all railways other than minor railways in respect of safety, maximum and minimum rates and fares, station and service terminal changes, interchange of traffic and the responsibility of railways administrations as carrier of goods and passengers, the regulation of minor railways in respect of safety and responsibility of the administration of such railways as carriers of goods and passengers.
3. Maritime shipping and navigation, including shipping and navigation on tidal waters, admiralty jurisdiction.
4. Port quarantine.
5. Major ports, that is to say, the declaration and administration of the ports, and the constitution and powers of port authorities therein.

6. Aircraft and Air navigation, the provision of aerodromes regulation and organization of Air traffic and of aerodromes.
7. Lighthouses, including lightships, beacons and other provisions for the safety of shipping and aircraft.
8. Carriage of passengers and goods by sea or by air.
9. Extension of the powers and jurisdiction of members of the police force belonging to any unit to railway area outside that unit.

D. Ancillary

1. Elections to the Dominion Legislature, subject to the provisions of the Act and of any order made thereunder.
2. Offence against laws with respect to any of the aforesaid matters.
3. Inquiries and statistics for the purpose of any of the aforesaid matters.
4. Jurisdiction and powers of all courts with respect to any of the aforesaid matters, but except with the consent of the Ruler of the acceding state, not so as to confer any Jurisdiction and powers upon any courts other courts ordinarily exercising jurisdiction in or in relation to that State.

Manipur State Constitution Act

[*The Act was enacted by the Maharaja of Manipur, Bodh Chandra Singh in 1947 for the governance of Manipur*]

Whereas it is expedient to enact a law for the governance of the Manipur State, His Highness the Maharajah of Manipur is pleased to enact as follows:

CHAPTER I

1. Title—This Act shall be called the Manipur State Constitution Act, 1947.

2. Extent and Application—This Act shall extend to the whole of the Manipur State inclusive of the Hill Areas saving that it shall not apply in any matter where a specific reservation of powers is made to any Authority in the Hills under the provisions of the Manipur State Hill (Administration) Regulation, 1947.

3. Government of the State by His Highness the Maharajah—The territories for the time being and hereafter vested in the Maharajah are governed by and in the name of the Maharajah. All right, authority and jurisdiction which appertain or are incidental to the Government of such territories are exercisable by the Maharajah subject to the provision of this Act.

4. Succession—Succession to the throne shall be governed by the law of Primogeniture provided that the heir must be the legitimate son of a marriage recognised by the Council of Ministers. In the event of failure of heirs in the direct male line, His Highness the Maharajah shall, after consultation with the Council of Ministers and the Assembly, designate his heir.

5. Attainment of Majority—The Maharajah or his heir shall be taken to attain majority at the age of 21 years.

6. Council or Regency—(a) Where by reason of the Maharajah being a minor or where by reason of any mental defect or grave bodily sickness as a result of which the Maharaja becomes permanently incapable of exercising his powers, the Council of Ministers shall take steps to set up a Council of Regency which shall exercise those powers in the State and shall continue in office for such time as the Council may determine.

(b) Notwithstanding the provision of Sub-Section (a) above, the Maharajah in consultation with the Council of Ministers may, at any time or for any reason which may appear suitable, set up a Council of Regency to exercise his functions.

(c) A Council of Regency set up under Sub-Section (a) and (b) above, may comprise of one or more persons as may seem desirable. The Regent or Council of Regency shall before taking office be required to take an Oath before the State Assembly to be loyal to the State and to observe faithfully the Constitution and Laws.

(d) Wherein any event it shall be necessary to set up a Council of Regency either for the reasons laid down in Sub-Sections (a) and (b) above or for any other reason or where for any reason the Maharajah has become incapable of exercising his powers before such regency can be set up, the Council of Ministers shall take whatever steps may be necessary for the Governance of the State till such time as the Regency is created.

7. Failure of Heirs and Disputed Succession—(a) In the event of failure of Heirs in the direct male line and the failure of the Maharajah to designate his Heir under section 4 above, a joint extraordinary session of the State Assembly and the Council of Ministers shall immediately be convened and shall remain in closed and continuous session till it shall have determined by a 75 per cent majority of the members present and voting, the person to whom the throne shall pass.

(b) Where for any reason the succession to the throne is disputed, the Council of Ministers shall, on the death of the Ruler, take such steps as may immediately be necessary for the good governance of the State and shall refer the matter under dispute to the Chief Court for the decision. Where any party is aggrieved by the decision of the Chief Court, and appeal shall lie to such authority as may be determined hereafter.

8. The Maharajah's Prerogatives—(a) All family matters which are the Maharajah's sole concern as head of the Ruling family, all matters which are his sole concern as the Defender of Faith and all matters connected with Titles, Honours and Palace ceremonial shall be deemed to fall within the Maharajah's personal prerogative and in such matters the Maharajah shall exercise full discretion subject to the provisions of the Constitution and the Laws of the State.

The Maharajah's prerogative shall not, however, be taken to comprise any matter wherein the legitimate interests of the State administration or a civil right sustainable in a court of law is involved. It will be within the prerogative of the Maharajah to remit punishment and pardon offenders subject to the provisions of the Manipur State Courts Act provided that this prerogative shall not prejudice the right of any individual to compensation.

(b) It shall be the prerogative of the Maharajah and the Maharani that neither may be made answerable at Law or subject to any legal proceeding in the State Courts. Their persons and property shall be inviolable.

(c) Notwithstanding Section 8 (b) above, it shall be lawful for the State Council in consultation with the Chief Court to draw up a Statement of charges against the Maharajah or the Maharani where it is proved beyond all possible doubt that the Maharajah or the Maharani has been guilty of Murder or any other heinous offence or of any extreme Political Crime against the provisions of the Constitution.

(d) On a statement of charges being drawn up under clause (c) above, the Council shall present it before the Maharajah or the Maharani and require satisfaction. Should satisfaction be not forthcoming the Council may refer the matter to such Authority as may be determined hereafter.

CHAPTER II
DEFINITIONS

9. In this act and the Rules issued thereunder unless there is something repugnant to the subject or the context:

(a) State shall mean the Manipur State comprising the whole territory of Manipur as delineated in the maps of the Survey of India current at the date of this.

(b) The Maharajah means His Highness the Maharajah of Manipur, the constitutional Head of the State.

(c) Chief Minister means the Office entrusted with the Chief Executive Function of the State.

(d) Minister means a member of the Council of Minister appointed under this Act by name or by virtue of his office to administer certain branches of the State Administration and to perform the duties and exercise the power imposed and conferred upon a Minister by this Act and Rules framed thereunder.

(e) Council means the State Council of Ministers constituted under this Act.

(f) Assembly means the State Assembly as constituted under this Act.

(g) Gazette means the Official journal of the State by means of which important orders, notices, communiqués, etc., are published.

(h) Speaker means the President of the Assembly and includes the Deputy Speaker in the absence of the Speaker or in the absence of both, a member voted to the chair.

(i) Civil List means the appropriation of funds for the expenses of the Ruling Family and the Privy Purse of the Ruler.

(j) Privy Purse means such portion of the Civil List as is appropriated exclusively for the personal expenses of Maharajah.
(k) Revenue includes all receipts of the State from State assets, from all lands, Forest, Taxes, Fines, Penalties, Forfeitures, Escheats, Lapse and other sources.
(l) Rules means any Rule issued under this Act.
(m) Fundamental Rights shall mean those rights which the State People shall enjoy as of right under this Act.
(n) The pronoun "he" and its derivatives are used of any person whether male or female.

CHAPTER III
THE EXECUTIVE

10. Council of Ministers—

(a) Subject to the provisions of this Act and subject also to the provisions of the Rules for the Administration of the Manipur State the Executive Authority of the State is delegated to and shall vest in the Council of Ministers.
(b) Where under this Act or the Rules for the Administration or the State, it is requisite that the approval of the Maharajah shall be taken to any measure, the Chief Minister shall seek the approval of the Maharajah in person or in writing and shall obtain the Maharajah's orders thereon. Should in any case the Maharajah's approval be withheld, the Maharajah shall be pleased to inform the Chief Minister in person or in writing and to communicate his reasons for withholding such approval in writing to the council.
(c) The Council of Ministers shall consist of the Chief Minister and six other Ministers.
(d) The six Ministers on the Council shall be elected by the State Assembly subject to the proviso that two of these Ministers shall be representatives of the Hill people of the State elected in such manner as shall be laid down in the Rules of Business of the State Assembly.

The Chief Minister shall be appointed by the Maharajah in consultation with the elected Ministers on the Council.
(e) The Chief Minister and Ministers shall receive letters of appointment over the seal of Maharajah.
(f) The Chief Minister in consultation with the Ministers shall allot portfolios.

11. The Chief Ministers shall be the President of the Council and the Vice President shall be appointed by the Council.

12. The Council of Ministers shall have a common seal and shall be jointly responsible to the Maharajah for the administration of the State.

13. The Council of Ministers and the Ministers individually shall exercise such powers and functions as may be assigned to them by or under this Act or by or under the Rules for the Administration of the State.

14. The quorum necessary for the transaction of business at a meeting of the Council shall not be less than three excluding the President.

15. The Chief Minister and Ministers shall, on taking Office, swear an oath of loyalty and allegiance to the Maharajah in the following form:

> *"I (Name of Minister) having been appointed as a Member of the Manipur State Council, do solemnly swear that I will be loyal and faithful and bear true allegiance to the Maharajah, his heirs and successors and that I will faithfully discharge the duties laid on me under this Act."*

16. A Minister of the Council shall not be removable from office except in accordance with the provisions of the Chapter IV below.

CHAPTER IV
THE STATE ASSEMBLY

17. There shall be constituted a State Assembly. The Assembly shall be elected for a period of three years and shall comprise Representatives freely elected by the people on an adult franchise and on the principle of Joint Electorate. Elections shall be in such manner and by such franchise as may be laid down under the Rules for the elections to the State Assembly provided always that the Representatives returnable from General, Hill and Mahamadan Constituencies shall be in the ratios of 30:18:3 respectively with an additional two seats for the Representatives of educational and commercial interests.

18. The State Assembly may debate all matters concerning the Government and well being of the State which, in the opinion of five Members of the Assembly, it is in the public interest to debate. The Assembly shall tender such advice to the Council of Ministers in any matter in which a majority of the Members present, are agreed on the advice which shall be tendered provided that no matter touching the Maharajah's Prerogative shall be debated and provided that the Maharajah may on the advice of the Council, veto debate on may matter where such course shall in the public interest be necessary.

19. The State Assembly shall not tender advice to the Council on any matter which is of primary concern to the Hill people unless such advice has the support of a majority of the Hill Representatives in the Assembly.

20. Subject to the provisions of this Act, the Assembly may make rules for regulating its proceedings and the conduct of Business.

21. Where in any case it is required to pass a veto of no confidence against a Minister of the Council for his individual acts, a motion of no confidence, signed by not less than ten Members of the Assembly and laying out in detail, the facts giving rise to the motion, may with the permission of the Speaker of the Assembly be moved. If such motion shall receive the support of at least 75 per cent of the Members present and voting, it shall be forwarded through the Chief Minister to the Maharajah, who, unless there appear strong and valid reasons to the contrary which shall be recorded in writing, shall after consultation with the Chief Minister require the Minister against whom the motion has been passed to resign.

22. Wherein any case the State Council or the Maharajah is in the special circumstances of any case, unable to accept the advice of the Assembly, the Maharajah or the Council as the case may be, shall communicate in writing the reasons which have led to such course and shall give facilities for personal discussion of the matter with a representative or representatives deputed by the Assembly.

23. Subject to the provisions of this Act and the Rules framed under it for the disposal of the Assembly business, there shall be Freedom of Speech in the Assembly and no member shall be liable to any proceedings in any court in respect of any speech or vote given by him in the Assembly or a committee thereof and no person shall be liable in respect of any publication by or under the authority of the Assembly of any report, paper, vote or proceedings.

24. No member of the Assembly shall be liable to arrest or detention in prison under a civil process:

(a) If he is a member of the Assembly, during the continuance of the Assembly.
(b) If he is a member of any committee of the Assembly, during the continuance of the meeting of the Committee.

25. The elected Ministers, the Speaker, Deputy Speaker and members of the Assembly shall receive such emoluments as may be determined from time to time by the Assembly.

CHAPTER V
THE LAW MAKING AUTHORITY

26. The Law Making Authority in the State shall consist of the Maharajah in Council in collaboration with the State Assembly acting under Section 18, above.

27. When the Council or the Assembly consider that a law should be enacted the Council shall cause a Bill to be drafted, which shall be laid

before the Assembly and a reasonable time shall be given for consideration thereof. The Council shall then cause to be made such alternations or amendments as may be deemed necessary in the light of the advice tendered by the Assembly and the Chief Minister shall submit the Bill in its final form for the assent of the Maharajah.

28. On the receipt of the Maharajah's Assent the Bill shall be published in the State Gazette and shall become an Act having the force of law.

29. Should the Maharajah in any case with his Assent to a Bill that Bill shall lapse as if it had not been passed. If the Assent of the Maharajah is not forthcoming with one calendar month of the Bill being submitted to him he shall be deemed to have with held his assent.

30. Where the Assent of the Maharajah to any Bill is withheld, the Council may cause the same Bill to be introduced in the next session of the Assembly and if passed without amendment by a 75 per cent majority of the Assembly, the Bill shall be certified over the Seal of the Council and shall become law.

31. Nothing in this Chapter shall be deemed to derogate from the absolute right of the Maharajah in Council to promulgate, in emergency cases, orders having the force of law without previous reference to the Assembly where the public interest in their opinion demands that such order shall be promulgated provided that the first opportunity shall be taken of laying the order before the Assembly for consideration. Any such order shall not have the force of law for period of more than six months.

CHAPTER VI
FINANCE

32. The Revenue of the State and such other receipts as may accrue from whatever source, less such reasonable percentage of the total real Revenue as may be reserved for the Civil List, are placed at the disposal of the Council for expenditure on the Government of the State in the manner prescribed by State Account Rules saving that in every year a sum representing not less than 17 per cent of the average real revenue of the State for the preceding three years shall be allocated for expenditure on the welfare and administration of the Hill people.

33. The Minister in charge of Finance shall prepare an Annual Budget showing the estimated receipts and expenditure for the ensuing year classified under the prescribed heads of account and shall submit it to that Assembly within fifteen days of its meeting for the Budget session along with a statement of account for the previous year.

34. The Assembly shall after considering the Budget, submit it with their recommendation to the Council, who, having made such modifications may be deemed necessary shall submit it to the Maharajah for approval.

Where any delay occurs in the granting of Assent to the Budget by the Maharajah and were such Assent has not been obtained by the first day of the financial year, provisional effect should be given to the Budget as passed by the Assembly and funds shall be drawn against its provision as if it had received Assent.

35. The Maharajah's Civil List shall be fixed at a figure equal to 10 per cent of the real revenues of the State over the preceding three years, provided that no extraordinary revenues shall be taken into account when determining this amount and provided that no State revenue in excess of Rupees twenty lakh shall be taken into account in any one year. The appropriations to the Maharajah's Civil List shall be non-votable and shall not be the subject of debate in the Assembly.

36. No tax whatsoever shall be shown in the budget and no tax shall be collected by any officer of the State or by any person unless such tax has been imposed by due process of Law.

37 (a) There shall be a State Auditor who shall be appointed by the Maharajah in Council on a nomination to be made by the Comptroller of Audit, Assam, or such other officer as may be deemed suitable. Such nominee shall be employed on contract for a period of not less than five years and shall be removable only by the Maharajah in Council in consultation with the authority making the nomination.

(b) The conditions of Service of the State Auditor shall be such as may be prescribed by the Maharajah in Council provided always that he shall not be eligible for any office of profit in the State after his retirement.

(c) The Auditor shall exercise such powers and perform such duties as may be laid down in the State Account Rules.

CHAPTER VII
HILL PEOPLE

38. The Council shall be responsible for the welfare and the good administration of the Hill people of the State and shall provide such funds for this purpose as may, subject to the provision of Section 32 above, be deemed necessary, provided that the local authorities in the Hill shall exercise such powers of Local Self Government as may be laid down in the Manipur State Hill (Administration) Regulation 1947.

CHAPTER VIII
THE SERVICES

39. The Council shall issue Rules regulating the Conditions of Service in the Departments of the State.

40. A Manipur State Appointments Board shall be constituted and the Council shall issue Rules regulating the constitution, functions and procedure of the Board. The Board shall consist of not less than three members, one of whom must be a Hillman and a Chairman and shall be final authority in all matters connected with appointments and promotions to the State Service except in so far as specific powers may be reserved under this Act or the Rules for the Administration of the State.

CHAPTER IX
THE JUDICATURE

41. (a) There shall be a complete separation of the Judiciary from the Executive.

(b) The judicature of the State shall be as laid down in the Manipur State Courts Act, 1947.

42. The Chief Justice of the State and two Puisne Judges shall be appointed by the Maharajah in Council under the Royal Seal and shall hold office until the age of 65 years provided that:

(a) A Judge may resign his office.

(b) A Judge may be removed from his office by the Maharajah in Council only on the grounds of misbehaviour of infirmity of body or mind.

43. A person shall not be appointed as a Judge of the Chief Court unless he:

(a) be a graduate in law and has held Judicial Office at least for five years, or

(b) is a barrister qualified in England of five years' standing, or

(c) has for at least five years held Judicial Office in British India in a post not inferior to that of a Subordinate Judge, or

(d) has for at least a period of ten years been a pleader of any High Court or the Manipur Chief Court, or

(e) be a person recognised as having a special capacity for the exercise of judicial functions.

CHAPTER X
FUNDAMENTAL RIGHTS AND DUTIES OF CITIZENSHIP

44. All citizens shall be equal before the law. Titles and other privileges of birth shall not be recognised in the eyes of law.

45. The liberty of the individual shall be guaranteed. No person may be subjected to any judicial interrogation or placed under arrest or be in any other way deprived of his liberty, save as provided by law.

46. No person shall be tried save by a competent Court.

47. No person may be tried except by a competent Court who shall give full opportunity to such person to defend himself by all means.

48. All penalties shall be as determined by law.

49. Capital punishment may not be inflicted for purely political crimes.

50. No citizen may be banished from the State, expelled from one part of the country to another, and obliged to reside in a specific place save in such cases may be expressly determined by law.

51. Every dwelling shall be inviolable save under express provision of law.

52. There shall be guaranteed to all people justice, social, economic and political; equality of status, of opportunity and before the law; freedom of thought, expression of belief, faith, worship, vocation, association, and action, subject to law and public morality.

53. The practice of Arts and Sciences shall be unrestricted and shall enjoy the protection and support of the State.

54. Without any prejudice to the communities concerned, public institutions shall be opened to all citizens of the State.

55. (a) All officials of the State or of a local Government shall be answerable before the law for their individual and unlawful actions.

(b) Where damage is caused to an individual by the act of an official of the State or an official of a Local Government, such an individual may sue the State before the Chief Court and may seek redress save where such damage has been caused by a bonafide act of a State servant in pursuance of a policy duly laid down by a Competent Authority.

CHAPTER XI
GENERAL CLAUSES

56. Any provision of this Act may be subject to amendment by the Maharajah in Council provided that such amendment is laid before the Assembly and receive the support of at least 80 per cent of the members of the State Assembly present and voting, when such amendment is debated.

57. Where in any case circumstances arise which prevent the proper operation in law or in spirit of this Constitution Act, the Council may at their discretion refer the matter for decision to such authority outside the State as may be decided hereafter and the decision of that authority shall be binding.

58. The Court language of the State shall be Manipuri or English.

Bodh Chandra Singh
Maharajah of Manipur

Manipur Merger Agreement

[By the agreement, the Maharaja of Manipur ceded Manipur to the Dominion of India on 15 October 1949, and gave full and exclusive authority, jurisdiction and powers for and in relation to the governance of Manipur and agreed to transfer the administration of the State to the Dominion of India]

Agreement made this twenty first day of September 1949 between the Governor General of India and his Highness, the Maharajah of Manipur.

Whereas in the best interests of the State of Manipur as well as of the Dominion of India it is desirable to provide for the administration of the said State by or under the authority of the Dominion Government.

It is hereby agreed as follows:

Article I

His Highness the Maharajah of Manipur hereby cedes to the Dominion Government full and exclusive authority, jurisdiction and powers for and in relation to the governance of the State and agrees to transfer the administration of the State to the Dominion Government on the fifteenth day of October 1949 (there in after referred to as "the said day"). As from the said day the Dominion Government will be competent to exercise the said powers, authority and jurisdiction in such manner and through such agency as it may think fit.

Article II

His Highness the Maharajah shall continue to enjoy the same personal rights, privileges, dignities, titles, authority over religious observances, customs, usages, rites and ceremonies and institutions in charge of the same in the State, which he would have enjoyed had this agreement not been made.

Article III

His highness the Maharajah shall with effect from the said day be entitled to receive for his lifetime from the revenue of the State annually for his Privy Purse the sum of Rupees three lakh free of all taxes. This amount is intended to cover all the expenses of the Ruler and his family, including expenses on account of his personal staff and armed guards, maintenance of his residences, marriages and other ceremonies, etc. and the allowances to the Ruler's relations who on the date of execution of this agreement were in receipt of such allowances from the revenues of the State, and will neither be increased nor reduced for any reason whatsoever. The Government of India undertake that the said sum of Rupees three lakh shall be paid to His Highness the Maharajah in four equal installments in advances at the beginning of each quarter from the State treasury or at such other treasury as may be specified by the Government of India.

Article IV

His Highness the Maharajah shall be entitled to the full ownership, use and enjoyment of all private properties (as distinct from State properties) belonging to him on the date of this agreement. His Highness the Maharajah will furnish to the dominion Government before the first January 1950, an inventory of all the immovable property, securities and cash balance held by him as such private property. If any dispute arises as to whether any item of property is the private property of his highness the Maharajah or State property, it shall be referred to a Judicial Officer qualified to be appointed as a High Court Judge, and the decision of that officer shall be final and binding on both parties. Provided that his Highness the Maharajah's right to the use of the residences known as "Redlands" and "Les Chatalettes" in Shillong, and the property in the town of Gauhati known as "Manipuri Basti" shall not be questioned.

Article V

All the members of His Highness's family shall be entitled to all the personal rights, privileges, dignities and titles enjoyed by them whether within or outside the territories of the State, immediately before the 15th August 1947.

Article VI

The Dominion Government guarantees the succession, according to law and custom, to the *gaddi* of the State and to his highness, the Maharajah's personal rights, privileges, dignities, titles, authority over religious observances, customs usages, rites and ceremonies and institutions in charge of the same in the State.

Article VII

No enquiry shall be made by or under the authority of the Government of India, and no proceedings shall lie in any Court in Manipur, against His highness the Maharajah whether in a personal capacity or otherwise in respect of anything done or omitted to be done by him or under his authority during the period of his administration of that State.

Article VIII

The Government of India hereby guarantees either the continuance in service of the permanent members of the Public Services of Manipur on conditions which will be not less advantageous than those on which they were serving before the date on which the administration of Manipur is made over to the Government of India or the payment of reasonable compensation.

The Government of India further guarantees the continuance of pensions and leave salaries sanctioned by His Highness the Maharajah to servants of the State who have retired or proceeded on leave preparatory to retirement, before the date on which the Administration of Manipur is made over to the Government of India.

The Government of India shall also undertake to make suitable provisions for the employment of Manipuris in the various branches of Public Services, and in every way encourage Manipuris to join them. They also undertake to preserve various laws, customs and conventions prevailing in the State pertaining to the social, economic and religious life of the people.

Article IX

Except with the previous sanction of the Government of India no proceedings, civil or criminal shall be instituted against any person in respect of any act done or purporting to be done in the execution of his duties as a servant of the State before the day on which the administration is made over to the Government of India.

In confirmation whereof Mr. Vapal Pangunni Menon, Adviser to the Government of India in the Ministry of States, has appended his signature on behalf and with the authority of the Governor General of India and His Highness Maharajah Bodh Chandra Singh, Maharajah of Manipur has appended his signature on behalf of himself, his heirs and successors.

Bodh Chandra Singh
Maharajah of Manipur

V.P. Menon	**Sri Prakasa**
Adviser to the Government of India	**Governor of Assam**
Ministry of States	**Shillong**

21 September 1949

The Immigrants (Expulsion from Assam) Act

[*The Act was enacted to "expel" persons or class of persons from India or Assam if their stay in Assam was considered detrimental to the interest of the general public. This Act came into force in 1950, and in the backdrop of migration from East Pakistan in the years immediately following the partition of India in 1947*]

Be it enacted by Parliament as follows:

1. (1) This Act may be called the Immigrants (Expulsion from Assam) Act, 1950.

(2) It extends to the whole of India.

2. If the Central Government is of opinion that any person or class of persons, having been ordinarily resident in any place outside India, has or have, whether before or after the commencement of this Act, come into Assam and that the stay of such person or class of persons in Assam is detrimental to the interests of the general public or any section thereof or of any Scheduled Tribe in Assam, the Central Government may by order

(a) direct such persons or class of persons to remove himself or themselves from India or Assam within such time and by such route as may be specified in the order; and

(b) give such further directions in regard to his or their removal from India or Assam as it my consider necessary or expedient:

Provided that nothing in this section shall apply to any person who on account of civil disturbances or the fear of such disturbances in any area now forming part of Pakistan has been displaced from or has left his place of residence in such area and who has been subsequently residing in Assam.

3. The Central Government may, by notification in the Official Gazette, direct that the powers and duties conferred or imposed on it by Section 2 shall, subject to such conditions, if any, as may be specified in the notification, be exercised or discharged also by

(a) Any officer subordinate to the Central Government;

(b) The Government of Assam, Meghalaya or any officer subordinate to that Government.

4. Any authority empowered by or in pursuance of the provisions of this Act to exercise any power may, in addition to any other action expressly

provided for in this Act, take or cause to be taken such steps, and use or cause to be used such force, as may in its opinion be reasonably necessary for the effective exercise of such power.

5. Any person who

(a) Contravenes or attempts to contravene or abets the contravention of any other made under section 2, or

(b) Fails to comply with any direction given by any such order, or

(c) Harbours any person who has contravened any order made under section 2 or has failed to comply with any direction given by any such order shall be punishable with imprisonment which may extend to three years and shall also be liable to fine.

6. No suit, prosecution or other legal proceedings shall lie against any person for anything which in good faith is done or intended to be done under this Act.

7. In this Act, except in section 3, references to Assam shall be construed as including also a reference to the State of Meghalaya and Nagaland and the Union territories of Arunachal Pradesh and Mizoram.

Sixth Schedule
[Articles 244(2) and 275(1)]

[*The Sixth Schedule of the Constitution provided for special provisions for the administration of tribal areas in undivided Assam. The formation of the autonomous councils in the North East are governed by the Sixth Schedule*]

1. Autonomous Districts and Autonomous Regions: (1) Subject to the provisions of this paragraph, the tribal areas in each item of Part A of the table appended to paragraph 20 of this Schedule shall be an autonomous district.

(2) If there are different Scheduled Tribes in an autonomous district, the Governor may, by public notification, divide the area or areas inhabited by them into autonomous regions.

(3) The Governor may, by public notification

(a) Include any area in Part A of the said table;

(b) Exclude any area from Part A of the said table;

(c) Create a new autonomous district;

(d) Increase the area of any autonomous district;

(e) Diminish the area of any autonomous district;

(f) Unite two or, more autonomous districts or parts thereof so as to form one autonomous district;

(g) Define the boundaries of any autonomous district. Provided that no order shall be made by the Governor under clauses (c), (d), (e) and (f) of this sub-paragraph except after consideration of the report of a Commission appointed under sub paragraph (1) of paragraph 14 of this Schedule.

2. Constitution of District Councils and Regional Councils: (1) There shall be a District Council for each autonomous district consisting of not more than twenty-four members, of whom not less than three-fourths shall be elected on the basis of adult suffrage.

(2) There shall be separate Regional Council for each area constituted and autonomous region under sub-paragraph (2) of paragraph 1 of this Schedule.

(3) Each District Council and each Regional Council shall be a body corporate by the name respectively of "the District Council of (name of

district)" and "the Regional Council of (name of region)", shall have perpetual succession and a common seal and shall by the said name sue and be sued.

(4) Subject to the provisions of this Schedule, the administration of an autonomous district shall, in so far as it is not vested under this Schedule in any Regional Council within such district, the vested in the District Council for such district and the administration of an autonomous region shall be vested in the Regional Council for such region.

(5) In an autonomous district with Regional Councils, the District Council shall have only such powers with respect to the areas under the authority of the Regional Council as may be delegated to it by the Regional Council in addition to the powers conferred on it by this Schedule with respect to such areas.

(6) The Governor shall make rules for the first constitution of District Councils and Regional Councils in consultations with the existing tribal Councils or other representative tribal organisations within the autonomous districts or regions concerned and such rules shall provide for:

(a) The composition of the District Councils and Regional Councils and the allocation of seats therein;
(b) The delimitation of territorial constituencies for the purpose of elections to those Councils;
(c) The qualifications for voting at such election and the preparation of electoral rolls therefore;
(d) The qualifications for being elected at such elections as member of such Councils;
(e) The term of office of members of such Councils;
(f) Any other matter relating to or connected with elections or nomination to such councils;
(g) The procedure and the conduct of business in the District and Regional Councils;
(h) The appointment of officers and staff of the District and Regional Councils.

(7) The District or the Regional Council may after its first constitution make rules with regard to the matters specified in sub-paragraph (6) of this paragraph and may also make rules regulating:

(a) The formation of subordinate local Councils or Boards and their procedure and the conduct of their business; and
(b) Generally all matters relating to the transaction of business pertaining to the administration of the district or region, as the case may be:

Provided that until rules are made by the District or the Regional Council under this sub-paragraph the rules made by the Governor under sub-paragraph (6) of this paragraph shall have effect in respect of election to, the officers and staff or and the procedure and tile conduct of business in each such Council:

Provided further that the Deputy Commissioner or the Sub-Divisional Officer, as the case may be, of the North Cachar and Mikir Hills shall be the Chairman co-officio of the District Council in respect of the territories included in items 5 and 6 respectively of Part A of the table appended to paragraph 20 of this Schedule and shall have power for a period of six year after the first constitution of the District Council subject to the control of the Governor, to annul or modify any resolution or decision of the District Councillor to issue such instructions to the District Council, as he may consider appropriate, and the District Council shall comply with every such instruction issued.

3. Powers of the District Council and Regional Councils to Make Laws: (1) The Regional Council for an autonomous region in respect of all areas within such region and the District Council for an autonomous district in respect of all area with in the district except those which are under the authority of Regional Councils if any within the district shall have power to make laws with respect to:

(a) The allotment, occupation or use or the setting apart, of land, other than any and which is reserved forest for the purposes of agriculture or grazing or for residential or other nor-agricultural purposes or for any other purpose likely to promote the interests of the inhabitants of any village or town;

Provided that nothing in such laws shall prevent the compulsory acquisition of any land, whether occupied or unoccupied, for public purposes by the Government of Assam in accordance with the law for the time being in force authorising such acquisition;

(b) The management of any forest not being a reserved forest;
(c) The use of any canal or watercourse for the purpose of agriculture;
(d) The regulation of the practice of "Jhum" or other forms of shifting cultivation;
(e) The establishment of village or town committees or council and their powers;
(f) Any other matter relating to village or town administration including village or town police and public health and sanitation;
(g) The appointment or succession of Chiefs or Head-men;
(h) The inheritance of property;

(i) Marriage;
(j) Social customs

(2) In this paragraph, a "reserved forest" means any area, which is a reserved forest under the Assam Forest Regulation, 1891, or under any other law for the time being in force in area in question.

(3) All laws made under this paragraph shall be submitted forthwith to the Governor and, until assented to by him, shall have no effect.

4. Administration of Justice in Autonomous Districts and Autonomous Regions: (1) The Regional Council for an autonomous region in respect of areas within such region and the District Council for an autonomous district in respect of areas within the district other than those which are under the authority of the Regional Councils, if any, within the district may constitute village councils or courts for the trial of suits and cases between the parties all of whom belong to Scheduled Tribes within such areas, other than suits and cases to which the provisions of sub-paragraph (1) of paragraph 5 of this Schedule apply, to the exclusion of any court in the State and may appoint suitable persons to be members of such village councils or presiding officers of such courts, and may also appoint such officers as may be necessary for the administration of the laws made under paragraph 3 of this Schedule.

(2) Notwithstanding anything in this Constitution, the Regional Council for an autonomous region or any court constituted in that behalf by the Regional Council or, if in respect of any area within an autonomous district there is no Regional Council, the District Council for such district or any court, constituted in that behalf by the District Council, shall exercise the powers of a court of appeal in respect of all suits and cases tribals by a village council or court constituted under sub-paragraph (1) of this paragraph within such region or area, as the case may be, other than those to which the provisions of sub-paragraph (1) of paragraph 5 of this Schedule apply, and no other court except the High Court and the Supreme Court shall have jurisdiction over such suits or cases,

(3) The High Court of Assam shall have and exercise such jurisdiction over the suits and cases to which the provisions of sub-paragraph (2) of this paragraph apply as the Governor may from time to time by order specify.

(4) A Regional Council or District Council, as the case may be, may with the previous approval of the Governor make rules regulating:

(a) The constitution of village council and courts and the powers to be exercised by them under this paragraph;
(b) The procedure to be followed by village councils or courts in the trial of suits and cases under sub-paragraph (1) of this paragraph;

(c) The procedure to be followed by the Regional or District Council or any court constituted by such Council in appeals and other proceedings under sub-paragraph (2) of this paragraph;
(d) The enforcement of decisions and orders of such Councils and courts.
(e) All other ancillary matters for the carrying out of the provisions of sub-paragraphs (I) and (2) of this paragraph.

5. Conferment of Powers under Code of Civil Procedure, 1908, and Code of Criminal Procedure, 1898, on the Regional and District Council and on certain Courts and Officers for the Trial of Certain Suits, Cases and Offences

(1) The Governor may, for the trial of suits or cases arising out of any law in force in any autonomous district or region being a law specified in that behalf by the Governor, or for the trial of offences punishable with death, transportation for life, or imprisonment for a term of not less than five years under the Indian Penal Code or under any other law for the time being applicable to such district or region, confer on the District Council or the Regional Council having authority over such district or region or, on courts constituted by such District Council or on any officer appointed in that behalf by the Governor, such powers under the Code of Civil Procedure, 1908, or, as the case may be, the Code of Criminal Procedure, 1898, as he deems appropriate, and thereupon the said Council, court or officer shall try the suits, cases or offences in exercise of the powers so conferred.

(2) The Governor may withdraw or modify any of the powers conferred on a District Council, Regional Council, court or officer under sub-paragraph (1) of this paragraph.

(3) Save as expressly provided in the paragraph Code of Civil Procedure, 1908, and the Code of Criminal Procedure, 1898, shall not apply to the trial of any suits, cases, or offences in an autonomous district or in any autonomous region to which the provisions of this paragraph apply.

6. Powers of the district council to establish primary schools, etc.: The District Council for an autonomous district may establish, construct, or manage primary schools, dispensaries, markets, cattle pounds, ferries, fisheries, roads and waterways in the district and in particular, may prescribe the language and the manner in which primary education shall be imparted in the primary schools in the district.

7. District and Regional Funds: (1) There shall be constituted for such autonomous district, a District Fund and for each autonomous region, a Regional Fund to which shall be credited all moneys received respectively by the District Councils for that district and the Regional Council for that region in the course of the administration of such District or region as the case may be, in accordance with the provisions of this Constitution.

2. Subject to the approval of the Governor, rules may be made by the District Council and by the Regional Council for the management of the District Fund or, as the case may be, the Regional Fund, and the rules so made may prescribe the procedure to be followed in respect of payment of money into the said Fund, the withdrawal of moneys there from, the custody of moneys therein and any other matter connected with or ancillary to the matters aforesaid,

8. Powers to Assess and Collect Land Revenue and to Impose Taxes: (1) The Regional Council for an autonomous region in respect of all lands within such region and the District Council for an autonomous district in respect of all lands within the district except those which are in the areas under the authority of Regional Council, if any, within the district, shall have the power to assess and collect revenue in respect of such lands in accordance with the principles for the time being followed by the Government or Assam in assessing lands for the purpose of land revenue in the State of Assam generally,

(2) The Regional Council for an autonomous region in respect of areas within such region and the District Council for an autonomous district in respect of all areas in the district except those which are under the authority of Regional Councils, if any, within the district, shall have power to levy and collect taxes on lands and buildings, and tolls on persons resident within such areas.

(3) The District Council for an autonomous district shall have the power to levy and collect all or any of the following taxes within such district, that is to say:

(a) Taxes on professions, trades, calling and employments;
(b) Taxes on animals, vehicles and boats;
(c) Taxes on the entry of goods into a market for sale therein and tolls on passengers and goods carried in ferries; and
(d) Taxes for the maintenance of schools, dispensaries or roads

(4) A Regional Council or District Council, as the case may be, may make regulation to provide for the levy and collection of any of the taxes specified in sub-paragraphs (2) and (3) of this paragraph.

9. Licences or Leases for the Purposes of Prospecting for, or Extraction of Minerals: (1) Such share of the royalties accruing each year from licences or leases for the purpose of prospecting for, or the extraction of minerals granted by the Government of Assam in respect of any area within an autonomous district as may be agreed upon between the Government of Assam and the District Councils of such district shall be made over to that District Council.

(2) If any dispute arises as to the share of such royalties to be made over to a District Council, it shall be referred to the Governor for determination and the amount determined by the Governor in his discretion shall be deemed to be the amount payable under sub-paragraph (1) of this paragraph to the District Council and the decision of the Governor shall be final.

10. Power of District Council to Make Regulations for the Control of Money Lending and Trading by Non-Tribals: (1) The District Council of an autonomous district may make regulations for the regulation and control of money-lending or trading within the district by persons other than Scheduled Tribes resident in the district.

(2) In particular and without prejudice to the generality of the foregoing power, such regulations may:

(a) Prescribe that no one except the holder of a licence issued in that behalf shall carry on the business of money lending;
(b) Prescribe the maximum rate of interest, which may be charged or recovered by a moneylender;
(c) Provide for the maintenance of accounts by moneylenders and for the inspection of such accounts by officers appointed in that behalf of the District Councils;
(d) Prescribe that no person who is not a member of the Scheduled tribes resident in the district shall carry on wholesale or retail business in any commodity except under a licence issued in that behalf by the District Council:

Provided that no regulations may be made under this paragraph unless they are passed by a majority of not less than three-fourths of the total membership on the District Council;

Provided further that it shall not be competent under any such regulations to refuse the grant of a licence to a money-lender or a trader who has been carrying on business within the district since before the time of the making of such regulations.

3. All regulations made under this paragraph shall be submitted forthwith to the Governor and, until assented to by him shall have no effect.

11. Publication of Laws, Rules and Regulations Made under the Schedule: All laws, rules and regulations made under this Schedule by a District Council or a Regional council shall be published forthwith in the Official Gazette of the State and shall on such publication have the force of law.

12. Application of Acts of Parliament and of the Legislature of the State to Autonomous District and Autonomous Regions: (1) Notwithstanding any thing in the Constitution:

(a) No Act of the Legislature of the state in respect of any of the matters specified in Paragraph 3 of this Schedule as matters with respect to which a District Council or a Regional Council may make laws, and no Act of the Legislature of the State prohibiting or restricting the consumption of any non-distilled alcoholic liquor shall apply to any autonomous district or autonomous region unless in either case the District Council for such district or having jurisdiction over such region by public notification so directs, and the District Council in giving such direction with respect to any Act may direct that the Act shall in its application to such district or region or any part thereof have effect subject to such exceptions or modifications as it thinks fit;

(b) The Governor may, by public notification direct that any Act of Parliament or of the Legislature of the State to which the provisions of clause (a) of this sub-paragraph do not apply shall not apply to an autonomous district or an autonomous region, or shall apply to such district or region or any part thereof subject to such exceptions or modifications as he may specify in the notification.

(2) Any direction given under sub paragraph (1) of this paragraph may be given so as to have retrospective effect.

13. Estimated Receipts and Expenditure Pertaining to Autonomous District to be Shown Separately in the Annual Financial Statement: The estimated receipts and expenditure pertaining to an autonomous district, which are to be credited to or is to before the District Council for discussion and then after such discussion be shown separately in the annual financial statement of the State to be laid before the Legislature of the State under article 202.

14. Appointment of Commission to Inquire into and Report on the Administration of Autonomous Districts and Autonomous Regions: (1) The Governor may at any time appoint a Commission to examine and report on any matter specified by him relating to the administration of the autonomous districts and autonomous regions in the State, including matters specified in clauses (c), (d), (e) and (f) of Sub-paragraph J of Paragraph 1 of this Schedule, or may appoint a Commission to inquire into and report from time to time on the administration of autonomous districts and autonomous regions in the State generally and in particular on:

(a) The provision of educational and medical facilities and communications in such districts and regions;
(b) The need for any new or special legislation in respect of such districts and regions; and
(c) The administration of the laws, rules and regulations made by the District and Regional Councils; and define the procedure to be followed by such Commission.

(2) The report of every such Commission with the recommendations of the Governor with respect there to shall be laid before the Legislature of the State by the Minister concerned together with an explanatory memorandum regarding the action proposed to be taken thereon by the Government of Assam.

(3) In allocating the business of the Government of the State among his Ministers the Governor may place one of his Ministers specially in charge of the welfare of the autonomous districts and autonomous regions in the State.

15. Annulment or Suspension of Acts and Resolutions of District and Regional Councils: (1) If at any time the Governor is satisfied that an act or resolution of a District or a Regional Council is likely to endanger the safety of India he may annul or suspend such act or resolution and take such steps as he may consider necessary (including the suspension of the Council and the assumption to himself of all or any of the powers vested in or exercisable by the Council) to prevent the commission or continuance of such act, or the giving or effect to such resolution.

(2) Any order made by the Governor under sub-paragraph (1) of this paragraph together with the reasons therefore shall be laid before the Legislature of the State as soon as possible and the order shall, unless revoked by the Legislature of the State continue in force for a period of twelve months from the date on which it was so made.

Provided that if and so often as a resolution approving the continuance in passed by the Legislature of the State, the order shall unless cancelled by the Governor continue in force for a further period of twelve months from the date on which under this paragraph it would otherwise have ceased to operate.

16. Dissolution of a District or a Regional Council: The Governor may on the recommendation of a Commission appointed under paragraph 14 of this Schedule by public notification order the dissolution of a District or a Regional Council and:

(a) Direct that a fresh general election shall be held immediately for the reconstitution of the Council or
(b) Subject to the previous approval of the Legislature of the State

assume...or place the administration of such area under the Commission appointed under the said paragraph or any other body considered suitable by him for a period not exceeding twelve months.

Provided that when an order under clause (a) of this paragraph has been made, the Governor may take the action referred to in clause (b) of this paragraph with regard to the administration of the area in question pending the reconstitution of the Council on fresh general election.

Provided further that no action shall be taken under clause (b) of this paragraph without giving the District or the Regional Council, as the case may be an opportunity of placing its views before the Legislature of the State.

17. Exclusion of Areas from Autonomous Districts in Forming Constituencies in Such Districts: For the purposes of elections to the Legislative Assembly of Assam the Governor may by order declare that any area within an autonomous district shall as form part of any constituency to fill a seat or seats in the Assembly reserved for any such district but shall form part of a constituency to fill a seat or seats in the Assembly not so reserved to be specified in the order.

18. Application of the Provisions of this Schedule to Areas Specified in Part B of the Table Appended to Paragraph 20: (1) The Governor may:

(a) Subject to the previous approval of the president, by public notification apply all or any of the foregoing provisions of this Schedule to any tribal area specified in Part B of the table appended to paragraph 20 of this Schedule or any part of such area and thereupon such area or part shall be administered in accordance with such provisions, and

(b) With like approval, by public notification, exclude from the said table any tribal area specified in Part B of that table or any part of such area.

(2) Until a notification is issued under sub-paragraph (1) of this paragraph in respect of any tribal area specified in Part B of the said table or any part of such area the administration of such area or part thereof as the case may be, shall be carried on by the President through the Governor of Assam as his agent and the provisions of (article 240) shall apply thereto as if such area or part thereof were in (Union Territory specified in that article).

(3) In the discharge of his functions under sub-paragraph (2) of this paragraph of the agent of the President the Governor shall act in his discretion.

19. Transitional Provisions: (1) As soon as possible after the commencement of this Constitution the Governor shall take steps for the constitution of a District Council for each autonomous district in the State under this Schedule and, until a District Council is so constituted for an autonomous district, the administration of such, district shall be vested in the Governor and the following provisions shall apply to the administration of the areas within such district instead of the foregoing provisions of the Schedule, namely:

(a) No Act of Parliament or of the Legislature of the State shall apply to any such area unless the Governor by public notification so directs that the Governor in giving such a direction with respect to any Act may direct that the Act shall, in its application to the area or to any specified part thereof have effect subject to such exceptions or modifications as he thinks fit.

(b) The Governor may make regulation for the peace and good government of any such area and any regulations so made may repeal or amend any Act of Parliament or of the Legislature of the State or any existing law which is for the time being applicable to such area.

(2) Any direction given by the Governor under clause (a) of Sub-paragraph (1) of this paragraph may be given so as to have retrospective effect.

(3) All regulations made under clause (b) of Sub-paragraph (1) of this paragraph shall be submitted forthwith to the President and until assented to by him, shall have no effect.

20. Tribal Areas: (1) The Areas specified in Parts A and B of the table below shall be the tribal areas within the State of Assam.

(2) The United Khasi-Jaintia Hills District shall comprise the territories which before the commencement of this Constitution were known as the Khasi States and the Khasi and Jaintia Hills District, excluding any areas for the time being comprised within the cantonment and municipality of Shillong, but including so much of the area comprised within the municipality of Shillong, as formed part of the Khasi State of Mylliem:

Provided that for the purposes of Clauses (e) and (f) of Sub-paragraph (1) of Paragraph 3, Paragraph 4, Paragraph 5, Paragraph 6, Sub-paragraph (2), Clauses (a), (b) and (d) of Sub-paragraph 4 of Paragraph 8 and Clause (d) of Sub-paragraph 2 of Paragraph 10 of this Schedule, no part of the area comprised within the municipality of Shillong shall be deemed to be within the District.

1. [(2A) The Mizo District shall comprise the area which at the commencement of this Constitution was known as the Lushai Hills District.]

2. [(2B) The Naga Hills-Tuensang Area shall comprise the area which at the commencement of this Constitution were known as the Naga Hills District and the Naga Tribal Area.]

(3) Any reference in the table below to any district [other than the United Khasi-Jaintia Hills District (and the Mizo District)] or administrative area (other than the Naga Hills-Tuensang Area) shall be construed as a reference to that district or area of the commencement of this Constitution.

Provided that the tribal areas specified in Part B of the table below shall not include any such areas in the plains as may, with the approval of the President, be notified by the Governor of Assam in that behalf.

TABLE

PART A

1. The United Khasi-Jaintia Hills District.
2. The Garo Hills District.
3. The Mizo District.
4. * * * *
5. The North Cachar Hills.
6. The Mikir Hills.

PART B

1. North East Frontier Tract including Balipara Frontier Tract, Tirap Frontier Tract, Abor Hills District and Misimi Hills District.
2. The Naga Hills-Tuensang Area.

21. Amendment of the Schedule: (1) Parliament may from time to time by law amend by way of addition, variation or repeal any of the provisions of this Schedule and, when the Schedule is so amended, any reference to this Schedule in this Constitution shall be construed as a reference to such Schedule as to amended.

(2) No such law as is mentioned in Sub paragraph (1) of this paragraph shall be deemed to be all amendment of this constitution for the purposes of article 368.

The Armed Forces (Special Powers) Act

[*Act 28 of 11 September 1958, provides special powers to the Armed Forces in certain disturbed areas of the country*]

An Act to enable certain special powers to be conferred upon members of the armed forces in disturbed areas in the State of [Arunachal Pradesh, Assam, Manipur, Meghalaya, Mizoram, Nagaland and Tripura][1] .

Be it enacted by Parliament in the Ninth Year of the Republic of India as follows:

1. Short Title and Extent: (1) This Act may be called[2] [The Armed Forces (Special Powers) Act, 1958].

[3][(2) It extends to the whole of the State of [Arunachal Pradesh, Assam, Manipur, Meghalaya, Mizoram, Nagaland and Tripura]4 .

2. Definitions: In this Act, unless the context otherwise requires:

(a) "Armed forces" means the Military forces and the air forces operating as land forces, and includes any other armed forces of the Union so operating;

(b) "Disturbed area," means an area which is for the time being declared by notification under section 3, to be a disturbed area;

(c) All other words and expressions used herein, but not defined and defined in the Air Force Act, 1950 (45 of 1950), or the Army Act, 1950 (46 of 1950) shall have meanings respectively assigned to them in those Acts.

3. Power to Declare Areas to be Disturbed Areas: If, in relation to any State or Union territory of which the Act extends, the Governor of that State or the Administrator of that Union territory or the Central Government, in either case, if of the opinion that the whole or any part of such State or Union territory, as the case may be, is in such a disturbed or dangerous condition that the use of armed forces in aid of the civil powers in necessary, the Governor of that State or the Administrator of that Union territory or the Central Government, as the case may be, may, by notification in the Official Gazette, declare the whole or such part of such State or Union territory to be a disturbed area.

4. Special Power of the Armed Forces: Any commissioned officer, warrant officer, non commissioned officer or any other person of equivalent rank in the armed forces may, in a disturbed area:

(a) If he is of opinion that it is necessary so to do for the maintenance of Public order, after giving such due warning as he may consider necessary, fire upon or otherwise use force, even to the causing of death, against any person who is acting in contravention of any law or order for the time being in force in the disturbed area prohibiting the assembly of five or more persons or the carrying of weapons or of things capable of being used as weapons or of fire-arms, ammunition or explosive substances;

(b) If he is of opinion that it is necessary so to do, destroy any arms dump, prepared or fortified position or shelter from which armed attacks are made or are likely to be made or are attempted to be made, or any structure used as a training camp for armed volunteers or utilised as a hide-out by armed gangs or absconders wanted for any offence;

(c) Arrest, without warrant, any person who has committed a cognisable offence or against whom a reasonable suspicion exists that he has committed or is about to commit a cognisable offence and may use such force as may be necessary to effect the arrest;

(d) Enter and search without warrant any premises to make any such arrest as aforesaid or to recover any person believed to be wrongfully restrained or confined or any property reasonably suspected to be stolen property or any arms, ammunition or explosive substances believed to be unlawfully kept in such premises and may for that Purpose use such force as may be necessary.

5. Arrested Persons to be made Over to the Police: Any person arrested and taken into custody under this Act shall be made over to the officer-in-charge of the nearest police station with the least possible delay, together with a report of the circumstances occasioning the arrest.

6. Protection to Persons Acting under Act: No persecution, suit or other legal proceeding shall be instituted, except with the previous sanction of the Central Government, against any person in respect of anything done or purported to be done in exercise of the powers conferred by this Act.

7. Repeal and Saving: Repealed by Amending and Repealing Act, 1960 (58 of 1960), First Schedule, sec. 2 (26-12-1960).

ENDNOTES

1. Subs. by Act 69 of 1986, sec. 43, for "Assam, Manipur, Meghalaya, Mizoram, Nagaland and Tripura and the Union Territory of Arunachal Pradesh" (wef. 20-2-1987).

2. Subs. by Act 7 of 1972, sec. 3, for "the Armed Forces (Assam and Manipur) Special Powers Act, 1958" (wef. 5-4-1972).
3. Subs. By Act 7 of 1972, sec. 4 (wef. 5-4-1972).
4. Subs. By Act 69 of 1986, sec. 43, for "Assam, Manipur, Meghalaya, Mizoram, Nagaland and Tripura and the Union territory of Arunachal Pradesh" (wef. 20-2-1987).

Naga Peoples' Convention and Government of India Agreement

[*Under a 16-point agreement, statehood was accorded to Nagaland on 28 July 1960 and was brought under the aegis of Ministry of External Affairs. The 16-points pertain to various legislative, administrative and financial provisions*]

The points placed by the delegates of the Naga Peoples Convention before the Prime Minister on July 26, 1960, as finally recast by the Delegation in the light of discussions on 27th and 28th July 1960 with the Foreign Secretary.

1. The Name: The territories that were heretofore known as the Naga Hills Tuensang Area under the Naga Hills-Tuensang Area Act, 1957, shall form a State within the Indian Union and be hereafter known as Nagaland.

2. The Ministry in Charge: The Nagaland shall be under the Ministry of External Affairs of the Government of India.

3. The Governor of Nagaland: (1) The President of India shall appoint a Governor for Nagaland and he will be vested with the executive powers of the Government of Nagaland. He will have his headquarters in Nagaland.

(2) His administrative secretariat will be headed by a Chief Secretary stationed at the Headquarters with other Secretariat staff as necessary.

(3) The Governor shall have special responsibility, regard to law and order during transitional period for so long as the law and order situation continues to remain disturbed on account of hostile activities. In exercising this special responsibility, the Governor shall, after consultation with the Ministry, act in his individual judgement. This special responsibility of the Governor will cease when normalcy returns.

4. Council of Ministers: (1) There shall be a Council of Ministers with a chief Minister at the head to assist and advise the Governor in the exercise of his functions.

(2) The Council of Ministers shall be responsible to the Naga Legislative Assembly.

5. The Legislature: There shall be constituted a Legislative Assembly consisting of elected and nominated members as may be deemed necessary representing different Tribes. Further a duly constituted body of Experts may be formed to examine and determine the principles of representation on democratic basis.

6. Representation in the Parliament: Two elected members shall represent Nagaland in the Union Parliament, that is to say, one for the Lok Sabha and the other for the Rajya Sabha.

7. Acts of Parliament: No Act or Law passed by the Union Parliament affecting the following provisions shall have legal force in the Nagaland unless specifically applied to it by a majority vote of the Nagaland Legislative Assembly:

(1) The Religious or Social Practices of the Nagas.

(2) Naga Customary Laws and Procedure.

(3) Civil and Criminal Justice so far as these concern decisions according to Naga Customary Law.
The existing laws relating to administration of civil and criminal justice as provided in the Rules for the Administration of Justice and Police in the Naga Hills District shall continue to be in force.

(4) The ownership and transfer of land and its resources.

8. Local Self-Government: Each tribe shall have the following units of rule making and administrative local bodies to deal with matters concerning the respective tribes and areas:

(1) The Village Council;

(2) The Range Council; and

(3) The Tribal Council.

The Councils will also deal with disputes and cases involving breaches of customary laws and usages.

9. Administration of Justice:

(a) The existing system of administration of civil and criminal justice shall continue.

(b) Appellate Courts:

(1) The District Court-cum-Sessions Court (for each district), High Court and Supreme Court of India.

(2) The Naga Tribunal for the whole of the Nagaland in respect of cases decided according to Customary Law.

10. Administration of Tuensang District: (1) The Governor shall carry on the administration of the Tuensang District for a period of the10 (ten) years until such time when the tribes in the Tuensang District are capable of shouldering more responsibility of the advance system of administration. The commencement of the ten-year period of Administration will start simultaneously with the enforcement of detailed workings of the constitution in other parts of the Nagaland.

(2) Provided further that Regional Council shall be formed for Tuensang District by elected representatives from all the tribes in Tuensang District, and the Governor may nominate representatives to the Regional Council as well. The Deputy Commissioner will be the ex-officio Chairman of the Council. The Regional Council will elect members to the Naga Legislative Assembly to represent Tuensang District.

(3) Provided further that on the advice of the Regional Council, steps will be taken to start various Councils and Courts, in those areas where the people feel themselves capable of establishing such institutions.

(4) Provided further that no Act or Law passed by the Naga Legislative Assembly shall be applicable to Tuensang District unless specifically recommend by the Regional Council.

(5) Provided further that the Regional council shall supervise and guide the working of the various Councils and Tribal Courts within Tuensang District and wherever necessary depute the local officers to act as Chairman thereof.

(6) Provided further that Councils of such areas inhabited by a mixed population or which have not as yet decided to which specific Tribal Council to be affiliated to shall be directly under the Regional Council for the time being. And at the end of ten years the situation will be reviewed and if the people so desired the period will be further extended.

11. Financial Assistance from the Government of India: To supplement the revenues of the Nagaland, there will be need for the Government of India to payout of the Consolidated Fund of India.

(1) A lump sum each year for the development programme in the Nagaland, and

(2) A grant-in-aid towards meeting the cost of administration.

Proposals for the above grants shall be prepared and submitted by the Government of Nagaland to the Government of India for their approval. The Governor will have general responsibility for ensuring that the funds made available by the Government of India are expended for the purposes for which they have been approved.

12. Consolidation of Forest Areas: The delegation wished the following to be placed on record:

> *"The Naga delegation discussed the question of the inclusion of the Reserve Forests and of contiguous areas inhabited by the Nagas. They were referred to the provisions in Articles 3 and 4 of the Constitution, prescribing the procedure for the transfer of areas from one State to another."*

13. Consolidation of Contiguous Naga Areas: The delegation wished the following to be placed on record:

> *"The Naga leaders expressed the view that other Nagas inhabiting contiguous areas should be enabled to join the new State. It was pointed out to them on behalf of the Government of India that Articles 3 and 4 of the Constitution provided for increasing the area of any State, but that it was not possible for the Government of India to make any commitment in this regard at this stage."*

14. Formation of Separate Naga Regiment: In order that the Naga people can fulfil their desire of playing a full role in the defence forces of India, the question of raising a separate Naga Regiment should be duly examined for action.

15. Transitional Period:

(a) On reaching the political settlement with the Government of India, the Government of India will prepare a Bill for such amendment of the Constitution, as may be necessary, in order to implement the decision. The draft Bill, before presentation to Parliament, will be shown to the delegates of the NPC.

(b) There shall be constituted an Interim Body with elected representatives from every tribe, to assist and advise the Governor in the Administration of the Nagaland during the transitional period. The tenure of office of the members of the Interim Body will be 3 (three) years subject to re-election.

16. Inner Line Regulation: Rules embodied in the Bengal Eastern Frontier Regulation, 1873, shall remain in force in the Nagaland.

Assam Official Language Act

[*The Assam Official Language Act, 1960, received the assent of the Governor of Assam on 17 December 1960 and was published in the Official Gazette on 19 December 1960. The Act introduced Assamese as the official language of Assam, raising protest among a sizeable population and leadership of the non-Assamese speaking people in the state. Relevant provisions of the Act and the deliberations relating to it are reproduced below*]

Section 3

Without prejudice to the provisions of Article 346 of the Constitution of India, and subject as hereinafter provided, Assamese shall be used for all or any of the official purposes of the State of Assam:

Provided that the English language, so long as the use thereof is permissible under Article 343 of the Constitution of India, and thereafter Hindi in place of English, shall also be used for such official purposes of the Secretariat and the offices of the Heads of Departments of the State Government and in such manner as may be prescribed:

Provided further that:

(a) All Ordinances promulgated under Article 213 of the Constitution of India;
(b) All Acts passed by the State legislature;
(c) All Bills to be introduced or Amendments thereto to be moved in the State legislature; and
(d) All Orders, Regulations, Rules and By-Laws issued by the State Government under the Constitution of India or any law made by Parliament or the Legislature of the state; shall be published in the Official Gazette in the Assamese language.

Section 4

Notwithstanding anything in Section 3, only languages which are in use immediately before the commencement of this Act shall continue to be used for administrative and other official purposes up to and including the level of the Autonomous Region or the Autonomous District, as the case may be, until the Regional Councillor or the District Council in respect of the Autonomous Region or Autonomous District as the case may be, by a majority of not less than two-thirds of the members present and voting decide in favour of adoption of any other language for any of the administrative or official purposes within that region or district.

Section 5

Notwithstanding anything in Section 3, the Bengali language shall be used for administrative and other official purposes up to and including the district level in the district of Cachar until the Mohkuma Parishads and Municipal Boards of the district, in a joint meeting by a majority of not less than two-thirds of the members present and voting, decide in favour of adoption of the official language for use in the district for the aforesaid purposes.

Section 6

Notwithstanding anything in Section 3, any examination held by the Assam Public Service Commission, which immediately before the commencement of this Act used to be conducted in the English language shall continue to be so conducted till such time as the use thereof is permissible under Clause (2) of Article 343 of the Constitution of India;

Provided that a candidate shall have the right to choose the language in use in the State of Assam, which was the medium of his university examination.

Section 7

Subject to the provision of this Act, the State Government may by notification issued from time to time, direct the use of the language as may be specified in the notification and in such parts of the State of Assam as may be specified therein:

Provided that:

(a) The right of the various linguistic groups in respect of the medium of instruction in educational institutions as laid down in the Constitution of India shall not be affected;

(b) The State shall not, in granting aid to educational and cultural institutions, discriminate against any such institutions on grounds of language;

(c) The rights to appointments in the Assam Public Services and to contracts and other avocations shall be maintained without discrimination on the grounds of language; and

(d) In regard to noting in the offices in the region or district, if any member of the staff is unable to note in any of the district languages, the use of English shall be permitted by the Heads of Departments so long as the use thereof is permissible under Article 343 of the Constitution of India.

Section 8

The State Government shall have the power to make rules for carrying out the purposes of this Act.

[The above act was to have come into force in all parts of Assam within five years of its receiving the Governor of Assam's assent, that is before 19 December, 1965]

The Assam Official Language (Amendment) Act, 1961 amended Section 5 of the 1960 Assam Official Language Act. As amended, Section 6 read:

Without prejudice to the provisions contained in Section the Bengali language shall be used for administrative and other official purposes up to and including the district level in the district of Cachar.

The Assam Official Language Act, 1960, was further amended in 1964. As amended, it extended the period within which it was to come into force throughout Assam to ten years from the original five years, that is, by 19 December 1970.

The first proviso to Section 3 of the principal Act (of 1960) was also amended to read:

Provided that the English language, so long as the use thereof is permissible for the official purposes of the Union under any law made by Parliament in this behalf, and thereafter Hindi in place of English shall also be used for such official purposes of the Secretariat and the offices of the Heads of Departments of the State Government and in such manner as may be prescribed.

Section 8 of the 1960 Act was also amended by the addition of sub-section (2). The sub-section read:

Every rule made under this section shall be laid, as soon as may be after it is made, before the Assam Legislative Assembly while it is in session for a total period of fourteen days which may be comprised in one session or in two successive sessions, and if, before the expiry of the session in which it was so laid or the sessions immediately following the Assam Legislative Assembly agree in making any modification in the rule or the Assam Legislative Assembly agree that the rule should not be made, the rule shall thereafter have effect only in such modified form or be of no effect, as the case may be; so, however, that any such modification or annulment shall be without prejudice to the validity of anything previously done under that rule.

Discussion held by the Home Minister with Hill Leaders of Assam May 18, 1961.

Participants:

Hill Leaders

1. Capt. Williamson Sangma

2. Shri S.D.D. Nichols Roy
3. Shri T. Cajee
4. Shri Raidangingti
5. Shri P.C. Langthasa
6. Ch. Saprawnga
7. Shri Hoover Hynniewta

Officials of Home Ministry

- Shri B.N. Jha, Secretary
- Shri V. Viswanathan, Special Secretary
- Shri Hari Sharma, Additional Secretary
- Shri P.N. Kaul, Deputy Secretary
- Shri Harmander Singh, Deputy Secretary
- Ministry of External Affairs

Capt. Sangma stated that the proposal made by the Prime Minister, although satisfactory from the point of view of the development of the hill areas, did not solve the language problem, which was of vital importance to the people of the area. The Assam Government were going ahead with the implementation of the Assam Official Language Act which would lead to the domination of the hill people by the people of the plains. With the enforcement of the Language Act, it would become obligatory for the Hill people to learn Assamese in order to get into State Services and also to be able to work in the Secretariat.

Home Minister observed that the situation was not peculiar to Assam and that it would be advantageous if the Hill people learnt the regional language. It would be the duty of the Assam Government to see that those who do not know Assamese language are not put to a disadvantage.

Capt. Sangma stated that in Garo Hills District, the Assam Government had been opening new schools with the medium of instructions as Assamese. The schools run by the tribal people are not being given grants-in-aid, after the passing of the Assam Official Language Bill. What the Assamese wanted was that no other language should flourish in Assam except the Assamese language.

Captain Sangma further stated that the present policy of the State Government was that all other communities in Assam should be assimilated with the Assamese. In support of his contention, he referred to the late Home Minister's Language formula, which was evolved after consultation with the parties concerned and considered as the best solution of the complicated language problem in the State, but was completely disregarded by the Chaliha Government. If this formula was firm it should not have been abandoned merely because Captain Sangma resigned from the

Cabinet. He added that even though the Bengali and Assamese languages were akin to each other, the bitterness still existed between the two communities on account of the last July disturbances in Assam.

Home Secretary pointed out that the IAS officers allotted to various States had to learn the regional languages.

Captain Sangma stated that so far the hill people in Assam were concerned they were confronted with a peculiar problem. In some other States people had to learn two languages; in Punjab-Hindi and Punjabi; but in case of hill people, they would be called upon to learn three languages, *viz.*, their own mother language Assamese and Hindi or English. The hill people would never accept the domination by the Assamese. In support of his contention, he referred to the order issued by the Assam Government, relating to the procurement of agricultural land. Under that order, land was allotted to those persons who were indigenous residents of Assam The Cachar people had made a protest against the issue of this order, but the Hill people were not affected by this order because they were protected under the provision of the Sixth Schedule to the Constitution.

Shri Nichols Roy then referred to the proposal made by the Prime Minister on the 17 May 1961, for "Scottish pattern" autonomy for the hill region in Assam. He stated that the hill people would be prepared to consider the proposals of the Prime Minister and examine them in detail in case an assurance was given that the language difficulties would be solved.

In reply, Home Minister stated that the Scottish model autonomy for the hill region would provide fuller opportunities for the development of hill areas which should be more important from the point of view of the hill people The Government of India are anxious that the backward areas should get adequate opportunities in the matter of development and should be on the level of other areas which are better developed. By giving such opportunities, their legitimate grievances would be mitigated to a large extent.

Shri Nichols Roy stated that at present in the Assam Secretariat, 12-1/2 per cent employees were from the bill region, who did not know Assamese language at all. The younger people of the tribal region will also be compelled to learn Assamese language.

It was urged that in Assam only 50 per cent of the people spoke Assamese language as mother tongue. In view of this, there was no justification for introducing Assamese as the official language. It was stated that the hill people were handicapped both in regard to State Services, and Central Services, as they did not get opportunities of getting into those services at all because of the language difficulties.

The Assam Government had been following a policy of not giving grants-in-aid to tribal schools. The State Government had been opening schools with Assamese language as the medium of instruction. It is clear; therefore, that the State Government's policy was to impose Assamese on the non-Assamese-speaking people. This was precisely the reason why a demand for a separate State had been made by the Hill Leaders.

Home Minister made a suggestion that to facilitate learning of Assamese by the hill people, it would be advantageous if a college where Assamese language would be taught was established. He casually remarked that in respect of Uttar Pradesh where Hindi is the official language, he had made a suggestion that a college should be opened where the Hindi students could acquire adequate knowledge of English, enabling them to compete in the competitive examinations along with the English knowing students.

Home Minister also stated that Government of India's policy is to develop the national language along with the regional languages. In course of time, the difficulties that were being experienced should disappear.

Shri Nichols Roy raised the question of terms of reference of the proposed Commission. He stated that the Commission should be added to go into the language problem and should propose amendments to the Official Language Act.

Home Minister stated that the Prime Minister had made it clear at the meeting on the preceding day that the proposed Commission would not recommend any amendments to the Assam Official Language Act but it would look into the difficulties which the hill people might experience in respect of language outside the District administration.

Shri Nichols Roy suggested that the Commission might also be required to go into the merits of the proposal for the separation of the hill areas. Home Minister emphasised that it should be everybody's endeavour to work for integration and not to think in terms of separation or direct action. The objective should be to find out ways and means for a settlement.

Speech by Dr. S. Radhakrishnan, President of India

[*Dr. S. Radhakrishnan's speech on the occasion of the inauguration of the state of Nagaland on 1 December 1963 is provided below. The speech is an important example of not only the philosophical foresight and prowess of the former President, but is also indicative of the all-embracing arc which characterises India's vision of a federal republic*]

Friends,

I have great pleasure in inaugurating the new State of Nagaland. It takes an honoured place today as the Sixteenth State of the Indian Union. Indian society has always been a multi-lingual, multi-racial and multi-religious one, having a variety of racial and ethnic groups

Kirata huna'ndhra pulinda pukkasha
Abhira kanka yavanah khasadayah

Though diverse in origin, all these different communities were united by a common purpose. In accord with the traditional outlook of our country, ever since the achievement of Independence, attempts have been made, as your Chief Minister has just said, to see a separate Naga State within the Indian Union. These attempts to secure to you the fullest freedom to manage your own affairs have culminated in the creation of Nagaland State.

The Constitution (Thirteenth Amendment) Act, 1962, setting up the new State of Nagaland, provides that no Act of Parliament in respect of:

Religious or social practices of the Nagas,

Naga customary law and procedure,

Administration of civil and criminal justice involving decisions according to the Naga customary law, and

Ownership and transfer of land and its resources shall apply to the new state unless the Legislative Assembly of Nagaland by a resolution so decides. This way, the Constitution respects your distinctive identity.

The Fundamental Rights enshrined in our Constitution, such as equality before law, prohibition of discrimination on grounds of religion, race, caste, sex or place of birth, equality of opportunity in matters of public employment, freedom of conscience and free profession, practice and propagation of religion will apply to the people of Nagaland.

The rule of law and government by the consent of the governed are essence of democracy. Government must be the custodian of the general welfare of its people and not of any special interest. The Government must capture the hearts and minds of the people. The administrators must exercise the human, the healing touch in their relations with the people and should not deprive the Naga of their innocent joys, their songs and dances, their feasts and festivals which are not repugnant to our moral sense.

The special powers vested in the Governor to maintain law and order will cease to apply in the absence of any internal unrest. It is my profound hope that the people of Nagaland will whole-heartedly work under the Constitution and help to build up a prosperous and progressive State.

You have not only the qualities of loyalty, valour and discipline but also the habits of industry, an innate sense of beauty and artistic skill. Your women occupy prominent position in the Tribal Councils, etc. You have also proved your ability as civil administrators in more recent times.

The resources of Nagaland, limited as they are, will have to be developed to the fullest extent and yet there may be need for Central assistance for purposes of development and administration. I am sure this assistance will be available for the Naga people in full measure. Considerable progress has already been made in agriculture, education, health services, communications, etc., but the pace of development will have to be speeded up. I have no doubt that whatever money is provided by the Centre will be spend for the welfare of the people of Nagaland. I do hope that the Naga people will take the fullest advantage of the fresh opportunities afforded to them and share in the building up of prosperity and progress in the country. We are still at the beginning of a new era and much hard work lies ahead. But nothing can stem the tide of progress of India if 450 million people are determined to achieve it by hard work, discipline and determination.

May I also express the hope that, now that the wishes of the Nagas have been fully met, normal conditions will rapidly return to the State, and those who are still unreconciled will come forward to participate in the development of Nagaland. The highest position in the country is open to every Naga: in the Parliament, in the Central Cabinet and in the various services, military and civil.

Understanding and friendship help to build a society where hatred and violence tend to disrupt it. Let us avoid the latter and adopt the former. On this auspicious day I make an appeal to all the Naga people: let all past rancour and misunderstanding be forgotten and let a new chapter of progress, prosperity and goodwill be written on the page which opens today. I once again say that a bright future awaits the brave people of Nagaland.

Text of the Peace Mission's Proposals

[*In 1964, a Peace Mission was constituted for Nagaland. Headed by the then Chief Minister of Assam, B.P. Chaliha, the other two members of the Mission were J.P. Narayan and Revd. Michael Scott, the mission was the first ever Confidence Building Measure on Nagaland, and one that achieved some notable successes*]

It has been a matter of considerable satisfaction to the Peace Mission, as to all other in Nagaland and in the rest of India, that since firing ceased on 6th September, 1964, for the first time in ten years people in Nagaland are experiencing what normalcy is. The Peace Mission feels that it is the normal obligation of everyone in Nagaland and more so, of the Peace Mission, in whom so much confidence and faith have been reposed, to see what this peace becomes everlasting in Nagaland. It is in pursuance of this that the Peace Mission is addressing this communication to both the parties.

2. But first it should be placed on record to the honour of both parties that have been in conflict that the attempt to find peace and agreement to a cease-fire was adventurous step which issued from their deep desire to find an honourable way to terminate such a bitter, wasteful and protracted conflict.

3. The marked difference in the atmosphere that prevails in Nagaland today as compared with that prevailing prior to the cessation of operation will probably be only realised by those who have lived or worked in Nagaland where there was fear as soon as darkness began and a sense of insecurity resulting from the ever present possibility of sudden violence. Today, the people are returning to their normal occupations. Families are being re-united, the biggest harvest for many years has been gathered and there is a feeling of hope in Nagaland which makes every delegate engaged in the peace talks only too conscious of the heavy burden of decision on those who have to take it, the life and happiness of so many being dependant on the decisions that are taken. In all this, it is fair to pay tribute not only to the Government of India for their humanity and imagination, but also to the leaders of the Baptist Church for whom this initiative was the result of much thought and powerful consideration of the good of both India and Nagaland.

4. The Nagaland Peace Talks, which started on 23rd of September, 1964, have now come to a stage where the NFG Delegation have placed their demands for consideration by the Government of India. This was in response to the statement of the leader of the Government of India delegation at Chedema on November 14th, wherein the Government of India also stated their position and understanding of the problem, as they saw it.

5. The Nagaland Federal Delegation have claimed that the Nagas had never been conquered by the Indian Army or ruled by an Indian Government, although their territory had been forcibly annexed by the British Army and the British Government about a century ago. Nevertheless, their right of self-determination, they claim, belonged to them separately as a people from the Sovereign Independent State of India, and they are now demanding recognition of this independence, which as they say, India herself demanded and heroically struggled for under the historic slogan of Swaraj.

6. The Government of India's position on the other hand, is that Nagaland formed an integral part of India before 1947 and that with the Transfer of Power to India by the British Parliament; Nagaland became part of India in the same way as all other States in India. At the same time the Government of India claim that they have already accepted the need for granting the fullest autonomy to Nagaland by constituting the State of Nagaland. So as to ensure the fullest development of the Nagas and to guarantee their separate ethnic and cultural entity and to ensure their traditional right and their resources accordingly, the Nagas are not ruled by any alien power but are ruling themselves.

7. The Peace Mission notes that a section of the Naga people accepted the status of Statehood thus conferred upon Nagaland as being in their best interest. Another section did not consider that it satisfied the aims and objectives they had been fighting for. Thus, there are these two divergent positions of the Government of India and the NFG confronting each other.

8. Though the two positions appear to be far apart, the Peace Mission believes that, with goodwill and understanding on both sides, a solution acceptable to both are be found.

9. As earlier stated, the Peace Mission reiterates that it is under an inescapable moral obligation to ensure maintenance of peace and settlement of all outstanding problems through peaceful means. The Peace Mission believes that there is no human problem that cannot be solved by peaceful means. The Peace Mission further believes that the Governments concerned and the people concerned share and subscribe to this view.

10. While the Peace Mission fully agrees and endorses the principle that all subject peoples have the right to self-determination and that no group of people have the right to self-determination and that no group of people is competent to rule over another, it also has to invite the attention of the Nagaland Federal Government to certain historical processes that had taken place to give birth to the Union of India and to the emergence of the great concepts and ideals underlying the Union Constitution.

11. The British had concurred at several stages and in diverse manner, various parts of the Indian sub-continent, comprising different ethnic groups, political systems and religious beliefs. However, under the aegis of the Indian National Congress and since 1920, under the leadership of Mahatma Gandhi, these various different peoples, representing diverse linguistic, cultural, ethnic and religious elements came together against foreign colonial rule and developed a consciousness of nationhood. Unfortunately, this common struggle against foreign imperialism that had welded these diverse people in the Indian Subcontinent into one nation did not somehow have an appreciable impact on the Nagas. This was, no doubt, due to the policy of isolation and exclusion, so deftly practiced by British rulers, who believed in creating pockets contrary to each other and hoping to rule in perpetuity by dividing the peoples. In any case, this great national movement of unification which freed India including Nagaland from the yoke of foreign rule did not bring within its embracing sweep the Naga population to the same extent as it did the other parts of the sub-continent. Thus, in 1947 when all the diverse people of India who had been brought under British rule, voluntarily agreed to form the Union of India and to share in the common endeavour to ensure that in great Union the ideals of Fraternity, Liberty, Justice and Equality, as enshrined in the Constitution are fully achieved, for the common benefit of all the same response and sense of participation was not noticeable in the Naga areas.

12. The Peace Mission, in the circumstances appreciates and understands the desire of the Nagas for self-determination and their urge to preserve their integrity. The Peace Mission also appreciates the courage and tenacity, displayed by the Naga people in their endeavour to achieve this goal. The objectives which they have placed before themselves in their memorandum "Naga Peace Declaration" dated the 17th December, 1964, and addressed to the Peace Mission namely their desire to find peace, their resolve to maintain their integrity and to resist entanglement in war, are all extremely laudable and should commend themselves to all peace loving people. It is however to be noted that this Declaration, in itself does not resolve the political issue. Therefore, some appropriate meeting point has to be found, where the aims and ideals of the NFG can

be achieved, at the same time, making it possible for the Government of India to accept these within the framework of the political settlement to be mutually agreed upon.

13. The Peace Mission in the pursuit of a settlement through peaceful means, to which the Government of India as well as the NFG equally subscribe, would like both the Government of India and the NFG to consider seriously whether such a meeting point could not be reached. On the other hand, the NFG could on their own volition decide to be a participant in the Union of India and mutually settle the terms and conditions for that purpose. On the other hand, the Government of India could consider to what extent the pattern and structure of the relationship between the Nagaland and the Government of India should be adopted and recast, so as to satisfy the political aspirations of all sections of Naga opinion and to make it possible for the ideals of peace as expressed in the Naga Peace Declaration to be substantially realized.

14. The Peace Mission would like, in all earnestness to impress, upon both sides that the approach, herein suggested, is not only the fairest but the only practical one in the given circumstances; and it fervently hopes that it will commend itself to the Government of India as well as to the Nagaland Federal Government.

15. The Peace Mission reiterates that the peace now obtaining the Nagaland should be made everlasting. With that object in view, the Peace Mission offered certain suggestions, whereupon both the parties had unequivocally affirmed and declared that they would renounce war and violence as a means for political settlement. This declaration of renunciation of war and use of armed force, it is earnestly emphasized, must not be deviated from by any means. The Peace Mission's proposal following this bilateral declaration of renunciation of war, to deposit all underground arms in safe custody and to withdraw all Indian Security forces from law and order duties could not unfortunately, be implemented.

16. Nevertheless, the Peace Mission would earnestly desire that, in faithful pursuance of the Declaration of renunciation of use of armed forces, both parties take concrete steps to remove all frictions. There have been numerous complaints and counter-complaints from both. The Peace Mission would suggest that the NFG require all arms issued to its forces to be concentrated at one or several places, in their armouries and under their custody so that there can be no basis for any future complaint of their forces parading with arms or extorting money or supplies under threat. They should also seriously ask themselves whether further recruiting and movement out of Nagaland towards Pakistan does not create an impression that these are only acts preparatory towards resumption of hostilities and if so, they should take remedial measure by putting a stop to such

recruitment and movement. The Government of India should ensure that its security forces and the civil administration do continue to abide strictly with the terms of the agreement, both in spirit and letter.

17. The Peace Mission makes a fervent appeal for consideration of the suggestions, contained in this paper and for all action that is possible for the maintenance of peace.

Bimala Prasad Chaliha Jai Prakash Narayan Michael Scott

Dated: 20.12.1964

The Unlawful Activities (Prevention) Act

[The Act was passed in 1967]

CHAPTER I
PRELIMINARY

1. (1) Short Title and Extent: This Act may be called the Unlawful Activities (Prevention) Act, 1967.

[1]*[(2) It extends to the whole of India provided that it shall come into force in the State of Jammu and Kashmir on such date as the Central Government may, by notification in the Official Gazette, appoint.]

2. Definitions: In this Act, unless the context otherwise requires,

(a) "Association" means any combination or body of individuals;

(b) "Cession of a part of the territory of India" includes admission of the claim of any foreign country to any such part;

(c) "Prescribed" means prescribed by rules made under this Act;

(d) "Secession of a part of the territory of India from the Union" includes the assertion of any claim to determine whether such part will remain a part of the territory of India;

(e) "Tribunal" means the Tribunal constituted under section 5;

(f) "Unlawful activity", in relation to an individual or association, means any action taken by such individual or association (whether by committing an act or by words, either spoken or written, or by signs or by visible representation or otherwise),

(i) Which is intended, or supports any claim, to bring about, on any ground whatsoever, the cession of a part of the territory of India or the secession of a part of the territory of India from the Union, or which incites any individual or group of individuals to bring about such cession or secession;

(ii) Which disclaims, questions, disrupts or is intended to disrupt the sovereignty and territorial integrity of India;

[1]*[(g) "Unlawful association" means any association

(i) Which has for its object any unlawful activity, or which encourages or aids persons to undertake any unlawful activity, or of which the members undertake such activity; or (ii) which has for its object any activity which is punishable under section 153A or section 153B of the Indian Penal Code

(45 of 1860), or which encourages or aids persons to undertake any such activity, or of which the members undertake any such activity: Provided that nothing contained in sub-clause (ii) shall apply to the State of Jammu and Kashmir.]

[2]*[2A. Construction of reference to laws not in force in Jammu and Kashmir. Any reference in this Act to a law, which is not in force in the "State of Jammu and Kashmir shall, in relation to that State, be construed as a reference to the corresponding law, if any, in force in that State.]

CHAPTER II
UNLAWFUL ASSOCIATIONS

3. Declaration of an Association as Unlawful: (1) If the Central Government is of opinion that any association is, or has become, an unlawful association, it may, by notification in the Official Gazette, declare such association to be unlawful.

(2) Every such notification shall specify the grounds on which it is issued and such other particulars as the Central Government may consider necessary: Provided that nothing in this sub-section shall require the Central Government to disclose any fact which it considers to be against the public interest to disclose.

(3) No such notification shall have effect until the Tribunal has, by an order made under section 4, confirmed the declaration made therein and the order is published in the Official Gazette: Provided that if the Central Government is of opinion that circumstances exist which render it necessary for that Government to declare an association to be unlawful with immediate effect, it may, 765 for reasons to be stated in writing, direct that the notification shall, subject to any order that may be made under section 4, have effect from the date of its publication in the Official Gazette.

(4) Every such notification shall, in addition to its publication in the Official Gazette, be published in not less than one daily newspaper having circulation in the State in which the principal office, if any, of the association affected is situated, and shall also be served on such association in such manner as the Central Government may think fit and all or any of the following modes may be followed in effecting such service, namely: (a) by affixing a copy of the notification to some conspicuous part of the office, if any, of the association; or (b) by serving a copy of the notification, where possible, on the principal office-bearers, if any, of the association; or (c) by proclaiming by beat of drum or by means of loudspeakers, the contents of the notification in the area in which the activities of the association are ordinarily carried on; or (d) in such other manner as may be prescribed.

4. Reference to Tribunal: (1) Where any association has been declared unlawful by a notification issued under sub-section (1) of section 3, the Central Government shall, within thirty days from the date of the publication of the notification under the said sub-section, refer the notification to the Tribunal for the purpose of adjudicating whether or not there is sufficient cause for declaring the association unlawful. (2) On receipt of a reference under sub-section (1), the Tribunal shall call upon the association affected by notice in writing to show cause, within thirty days from the date of the service of such notice, why the association should not be declared unlawful. (3) After considering the cause, if any, shown by the association or the office-bearers or members thereof, the-Tribunal shall hold an inquiry in the manner specified in section 9 and after calling for such further information as it may consider necessary from the Central Government or from any office-bearer or member of the association, it shall decide whether or not there is sufficient cause for declaring the association to be unlawful and make, as expeditiously as possible and in any case within a period of six months from the date of the issue of the notification under sub-section (1) of section 3, such order as it may deem fit either confirming the declaration made in notification or canceling the same. 766 (4) The order of the Tribunal made under sub-section (3) shall be published in the Official Gazette.

5. Tribunal: (1) The Central Government may, by notification in the Official Gazette, constitute, as and when necessary, a tribunal to be known as the "Unlawful Activities (Prevention) Tribunal" consisting of one person, to be appointed by the Central Government: Provided that no person shall be so appointed unless he is a Judge of a High Court. (2) If, for any reason, a vacancy (other than a temporary absence) occurs in the office of the presiding officer of the Tribunal, then, the Central Government shall appoint another person in accordance with the provisions of this section to fill the vacancy and the proceedings may be continued before the Tribunal from the stage at which the vacancy is filled. (3) The Central Government shall make available to the Tribunal such staff as may be necessary for the discharge of its functions under this Act. (4) All expenses incurred in connection with the Tribunal shall be defrayed out of the Consolidated Fund of India. (5) Subject to the provisions of section 9, the Tribunal shall have power to regulate its own procedure in all matters arising out of the discharge of its functions including the place or places at which it will hold its sittings. (6) The Tribunal shall, for the purpose of making an inquiry under this Act, have the same powers as are vested in a civil court under the Code of Civil Procedure, 1908 (5 of 1908), while trying a suit, in respect of the following matters, namely: (a) the summoning and enforcing the attendance of any witness and examining him on oath; (b) the discovery and production of any document or other material object producible as evidence; (c) the reception of evidence on affidavits; (d) the requisitioning of any public record from any court or office; (e) the issuing of any commission for the examination of witnesses. (7) Any proceeding before the Tribunal shall be deemed to be a judicial proceeding within the meaning of sections 193 and 228 of 767 the Indian Penal Code (45 of 1860) the Code of Criminal Procedure, 1898 (5 of 1898).

6. Period of Operation and Cancellation of Notification: (1) Subject to the provisions of sub-section (2), a notification issued under section 3 shall, if the declaration made therein is confirmed by the Tribunal by an order made under section 4, remain in force for a period of two years from the date on which the notification becomes effective.

(2) Notwithstanding anything contained in sub-section (1), the Central Government may, either on its own motion or on the application of any person aggrieved, at any time, cancel the notification issued under section 3, whether or not the declaration made therein has been confirmed by the Tribunal.

7. Power to Prohibit the Use of Funds of an Unlawful Association: (1) Where an association has been declared unlawful by a notification issued under section 3 which has become effective under sub-section (3) of that section and the Central Government is satisfied, after such inquiry as it may think fit, that any person has custody of any moneys, securities or credits which are being used or are intended to be used for the purpose of the unlawful association, the Central Government may, by order in writing, prohibit such person from paying, delivering, transferring or otherwise dealing in any manner whatsoever with such moneys, securities or credits or with any other moneys, securities or credits which may come into his custody after the making of the order, save in accordance with the written orders of the Central Government and a copy of such order shall be served upon the person so prohibited in the manner specified in sub-section (3).

(2) The Central Government may endorse a copy of the prohibitory order made under sub-section (1) for investigation to any gazetted officer of the Government it may select, and such copy shall be a warrant whereunder such officer may enter in or upon any premises of the person to whom the order is directed, examine the books of such person, search for moneys, securities or credits, and make inquiries from such person or any officer, agent or servant of such person, touching the origin of any dealings in any moneys, securities or credits which the investigating officer may suspect are being used or are intended to be used for the purpose of the unlawful association.

(3) A copy of an order made under this section shall be served in the manner provided in the Code of Criminal Procedure, 1898 (5 of 1898), for 768 the service of a summons, or, where the person to be served is a corporation, company, bank or other association, it shall be served on any secretary, director or other officer or person concerned with the management thereof, or by leaving it or sending it by post addressed to the corporation, company, bank or other association at its registered office, or where there is no registered office, at the place where it carries on business.

(4) Any person aggrieved by a prohibitory order made under sub-section (1) may, within fifteen days from the date of the service of such order, make an application to the Court of the District Judge within the local limits of whose jurisdiction such person voluntarily resides or carries on business or personally works for gain, to establish that the moneys, securities or credits in respect of which the prohibitory order has been made are not being used or are not intended to be used for the purpose of the unlawful association and the Court of the District Judge shall decide the question.

(5) Except so far as is necessary for the purposes of any proceedings under this section, no information obtained in the course of any investigation made under sub-section (2) shall be divulged by any gazetted officer of the Government, without the consent of the Central Government.

(6) In this section, "security" includes a document whereby any person acknowledges that he is under a legal liability to pay money, or whereunder any person obtains a legal right to the payment of money.

8. Power to Notify Places for the Purpose of an Unlawful Association: (1) Where an association has been declared unlawful by a notification issued under section 3, which has become effective under sub-section (3) of that section, the Central Government may, by notification in the Official Gazette, notify any place, which in its opinion is used for the purpose of such unlawful association.

Explanation: For the purposes of this sub-section, "place" includes a house or building, or part thereof, or a tent or vessel.

(2) On the issue of a notification under sub-section (1), the District Magistrate within the local limits of whose jurisdiction such notified place is situate or any officer authorised by him in writing in this behalf shall make a list of all movable properties (other than wearing-apparel, cooking vessels, beds and beddings, tools of artisans, implements of husbandry, cattle, grain and foodstuffs and such other articles as he considers to be of a trivial nature) found in the notified place in the presence of two respectable witnesses.

(3) If, in the opinion of the District Magistrate, any articles specified in the list are or may be used for the purpose of the unlawful association he may make an order prohibiting any person from using the articles save in accordance with the written orders of the District Magistrate.

(4) The District Magistrate may thereupon make an order that no person who at the date of the notification was not a resident in the notified place shall, without the permission of the District Magistrate, enter, or be on or in, the notified place: Provided that nothing in this sub-section shall apply to any near relative of any person who was a resident in the notified place at the date of the notification.

(5) Where in pursuance of sub-section (4), any person is granted permission to enter, or to be on or in, the notified place, that person shall, while acting under such permission, comply with such orders for regulating his conduct as may be given by the District Magistrate.

(6) Any police officer, not below the rank of a sub-inspector, or any other person authorised in this behalf by the Central Government may search any person entering, or seeking to enter, or being on or in, the notified place and may detain any such person for the purpose of searching him: Provided that no female shall be searched in pursuance of this sub-section except by a female.

(7) If any person is in the notified place in contravention of an order made under sub-section (4), then, without prejudice to any other proceedings, which may be taken against him, he may be removed therefrom by any officer or by any other person authorised in this behalf by the Central Government.

(8) Any person aggrieved by a notification issued in respect of a place under sub-section (1) or by an order made under sub-section (3) or sub-section (4) may, within thirty days from the date of the notification or order, as the case may be, make an application to the Court of the District Judge within the local limits of whose jurisdiction such notified place is situate—(a) for declaration that the place has not been used for the purpose of the unlawful association; or (b) for setting aside the order made under sub-section (3) or sub-section (4), 770 and on receipt of the application the Court of the District Judge shall, after giving the parties an opportunity of being heard, decide the question.

9. Procedure to be Followed in the Disposal of Applications under This Act: Subject to any rules that may be made under this Act, the procedure to be followed by the Tribunal in holding any inquiry under sub-section (3) of section 4 or by a Court of the District Judge in disposing of any application under sub-section (4) of section 7 or sub-section (8) of section 8 shall, so far as may be, be the procedure laid down in the Code of Civil Procedure, 1908 (5 of 1908), for the investigation of claims and the decision of the Tribunal or the Court of the District Judge, as the case may be, shall be final.

CHAPTER III
OFFENCES AND PENALTIES

10. Penalty for being Members of an Unlawful Association: Whoever is and continues to be a member of an association declared unlawful by a notification issued under section 3 which has become effective under sub-section (3) of that section, or takes part in meetings of any such unlawful association, or contributes to, or receives or solicits any contribution for the purpose of, any such un-lawful association, or in any way assists the operations of any such unlawful association, shall be punishable with imprisonment for a term which may extend to two years, and shall also be liable to fine.

11. Penalty for Dealing with Funds of an Unlawful Association: If any person on whom a prohibitory order has been served under sub-section (1) of section 7 in respect of any moneys, securities or credits pays, delivers, transfers or otherwise deals in any manner whatsoever with the same in contravention of the prohibitory order, he shall be punishable with imprisonment for a term which may extend to three years, or with fine, or with both, and notwithstanding anything contained in the Code of Criminal Procedure, 1898 (5 of 1898), the court trying such contravention may also impose on the person convicted an additional fine to recover from him the amount of the moneys or credits or the market value of the securities in respect of which the prohibitory order has been contravened or such part thereof as the court may deem fit.

12. Penalty for Contravention of an Order Made in Respect of Notified Place

(1) Whoever uses any article in contravention of a prohibitory order in respect thereof made under sub-section (3) of section 8 771 shall be punishable with imprisonment for a term which may extend to one year, and shall also be liable to fine.

(2) Whoever knowingly and willfully is in, or effects or attempts to effect entry into, a notified place in contravention of an order made under sub-section (4) of section 8 shall be punishable with imprisonment for a term which may extend to one year, and shall also be liable to fine.

13. Punishment for Unlawful Activities: (1) Whoever

(a) Takes part in or commits, or

(b) Advocates abets, advises or incites the commission of, any unlawful activity, shall be punishable with imprisonment for a term which may extend to seven years, and shall also be liable to fine.

(2) Whoever, in any way, assists any unlawful activity of any association, declared unlawful under section 3, after the notification by which it has been so declared has become effective under sub-section

(3) of that section, shall be punishable with imprisonment for a term which may extend to five years, or with fine, or with both. (3) Nothing in this section shall apply to any treaty, agreement or convention entered into between the Government of India and the Government of any other country or to any negotiations therefor carried on by any person authorised in this behalf by the Government of India.

14. Offences to be Cognizable: Notwithstanding anything contained in the Code of Criminal Procedure, 1898 (5 of 1898), an offence punishable under this Act shall be cognizable.

CHAPTER IV
MISCELLANEOUS

15. Continuance of Association: An association shall not be deemed to have ceased to exist by reason only of any formal act of its dissolution or change of name but shall be deemed to continue so long as any actual combination for the purposes of such association continues between any members thereof.

ENDNOTES

1. Subs. by Act 24 of 1969, s. 2, for sub-section (2). The Act comes into force in the State of Jammu and Kashmir on 1.9.1969, vide Notifn. No. G.S.R. 2098, dated 30.8.1969, Gazette of India, Exty., Part II, Sec. 3(i), page 615.
2. Subs. by Act 31 of 1972, s. 4, for cl. (g).
3. Ins. by Act 24 of 1969, s. 3.

North Eastern Areas (Reorganisation) Act

[*A Bill to provide for the establishment of the States of Manipur and Tripura and to provide for the formation of the State of Meghalaya and the Union Territories of Mizoram and Arunachal Pradesh by reorganisation of the existing State of Assam was passed on 12 December 1971*]

Be it enacted by Parliament in the Twenty-second Year of (the Republic of India) as follows:

PART I
PRELIMINARY

Short Title

1. This Act may be called the North-Eastern Area (Reorganisation) Act, 1971.

Definitions

2. In this Act, unless the context otherwise requires:

(a) "Administrator" means the administrator of a Union Territory appointed by the President under article 239 of the Constitution;
(b) "Appointed day" means the day which the Central Government may, by notification in the Official Gazettes appoint;
(c) "Article" means an article of the Constitution;
(d) "Common High Court" means the Gauhati High Court (the high Court of Assam, Nagaland, Meghalaya, Manipur and Tripura) referred to in clause (b) of sub-section (1) of section 28;
(e) "Election Commission" means the Election Commission appointed by the President under article324.
(f) "Existing State of Assam" means the State of Assam as existing immediately before the appointed day;
(g) "Law" includes any enactment, ordinance, regulation, order, byelaws, rule, scheme, notification or other instrument having, immediately before the appointed day, the force of law in the whole or any part of the existing State of Assam or the autonomous State of Meghalaya or the Union territory of Union territory of Manipur or the Tripura, as the case may be;
(h) "Sitting member", in relation to either House of Parliament or

the Legislative Assembly of the existing State of Assam, means a person who immediately before the appointed day, is a member of that House or that Assembly;

(i) "Successor State", in relation to the existing State of Assam, or means the State of Assam or Meghalaya, and includes also the Union in relation to the Union territory of Mizoram;

(j) "Treasury" includes a sub-treasury.

PART II

ESTABLISHMENT OF THE STATE OF MANIPUR

Establishment of the State of Manipur and Tripura and Formation of the State of Meghalaya and of the Union Territories of Mizoram and Arunachal Pradesh

3. On and from the appointed day there shall be established a new State, to be known as the State of Manipur, comprising the territories which immediately before that day were comprised in the Union territory of Manipur.

Establishment of the State of Tripura

4. On and from the appointed day there shall be established a new State, to be known as the State of Tripura, comprising the territories which immediately before that day were comprised in the Union territory of Tripura.

Formation of the State of Meghalaya

5. On and from the appointed day there shall be formed a new State, to be known as the State of Meghalaya comprising:

(a) The territories which immediately before that day were comprised in the autonomous State of Meghalaya formed under section 3 of the Assam Reorganization (Meghalaya) Act, 1969; and

(b) So much of the territories comprised within the cantonment and municipality of Shillong as did not form part of that autonomous State.

And thereupon the said territories shall cease to form part of the existing State of Assam.

Formation of the Union Territory of Mizoram

6. On and from the appointed day there shall be formed a new Union territory, to be known as the Union territory of Mizoram, comprising the territories which immediately before that day were comprised in the Mizo District in the existing State of Assam and thereupon the said territories shall cease to form part of the existing State of Assam.

Formation of the Union Territory of Arunachal Pradesh

7. On and from the appointed day there shall be formed a new Union territory, to be known as the Union territory of Arunachal Pradesh, comprising the territories which immediately before that day were comprised in the tribal areas specified in Part B of the table appended to paragraph 20 of the Sixth Schedule to the Constitution (but excluding the areas covered by notification No. TAD/R/35/50/10J, dated the 23rd February 1951 issued by the Governor of Assam under the proviso to sub-paragraph (3 of the said paragraph 20) and known as the North East Frontier Agency and thereupon the; said territories shall cease to form part of the existing State of Assam.

Territories of the State of Assam

8. On and from the appointed day the State of Assam shall comprise the territories of the existing State of Assam other than those specified in sections 5, 6 and 7.

Amendment of First Schedule to the Constitution

9. On and from the appointed day, in the First Schedule to the Constitution:

(a) Under the heading "I THE STATES":

  (i) In the paragraph relating to the territories of the State of Assam, the following shall be added at the end, namely: And the territories specified in sections 5, 6 and 7 of the North-Eastern Areas (Reorganisation) Act, 1971;

  (ii) After entry 18, the following entries shall be inserted, namely:

19. Manipur

The territory which immediately before the commencement of this Constitution was being administered as if it were a Chief Commissioner's Province under the name of Manipur.

20. Tripura

The territory which immediately before the commencement of this Constitution was being administered as if it were a Chief Commissioner's Province under the name of Tripura.

21. Meghalaya

The territories specified in section 5 of the North-Eastern Areas (Reorganisation) Act, 1971.

(b) Under the beading "II THE UNION TERRITORIES":

  (i) Entries 2 and 3 shall be omitted and entries 4 to 9 shall be re-numbered as entries 2 to 7 respectively;

(ii) After entry 7 as so re-numbered the following entries shall be inserted, namely:

8. Mizoram

The territories specified in section 6 of the North Eastern, Areas (Reorganisation Act.1971.

9. Arunachal Pradesh

The territories specified in section 7 of the North-Eastern Areas (Reorganisation) Act, 1971.

Text of the White Paper Issued by the Government of Nagaland

[*The Government of Nagaland, on 31 August 1972, prepared a White Paper on the question of insurgency in the state*]

1. Political Magnanimity of the Government of India: As it was the express desire and wish of the Naga people to have a separate State within the Indian Union, the Government of India under the leadership of Pandit Jawaharlal Nehru granted to the Nagas the highest political status. In spite of this, there remained a section of the Nagas unreconciled and continued to disturb peace in Nagaland. Therefore, the Government of India out of its political magnanimity gave an opportunity to the underground Nagas to lay down arms and bring concrete proposals at a round table to discuss and resolve the Naga problem.

A Peace Mission was constituted for this purpose and to give effect to it a period of suspension of operations was ushered in.

The State Government did everything possible to enable the underground leaders to move freely in and outside the State to discuss among themselves resulting in the six-round of talks with the Government spent to the tune of Rs. 9 lakh.

They were given full opportunity to settle the Naga political problem, but they did not reside from their original stand of independence and sovereignty and the political talks thus ended in deadlock.

When it became clear that there could be no way out to resolve the political question, the Peace Mission suggested a. formula whereby "the Nagas should of their own volition decide to participate in the Indian Union while the Government of India could consider the pattern and relationship between the Nagas and the Government of India that would by and large meet the aspirations of all sections of Naga opinion." The State Government, the Church leaders and public of Nagaland fully supported the proposal and asked the underground leaders to consider it seriously, but they discarded the mandate of the people.

2. N.N.C. and Federal Responsible: The terms of agreement for the stoppage of operations in Nagaland were signed by the Peace Mission and the Underground. This was welcomed by the Governor and his acceptance was conveyed to the Peace Mission. From the very beginning, however, the Federal group started violating the terms of the stoppage of operations. During the period of stoppage of operations they sent two groups to communist China to get military training and to bring sophisticated modern arms to wage a war and kill more people in Nagaland.

The peace period which was ushered in with great effort and difficulty was aimed at to create goodwill and understanding among the people and to enable the Naga leaders to settle the Naga political question in a peaceful way. However, the peace period, which was, would have been source of peace, progress and peaceful settlement of the Naga problem has been sadly turned into a curse for the Nagas by the so-called Federal underground leaders.

In August 1967, Mr. A.Z. Phizo and his host advisor Rev Michael Scott went to New York with a view to table the Naga case in the UNO. They discovered that there was no way whatsoever but to settle the problem with Delhi. This being the case, it was incumbent on Phizo to refer back to his associates in Nagaland the next course open to them, but instead, he was at his wits end and acted like a dictator and asked his associates to turn to communist China to receive military training and to wage a war on the soil of Nagaland. The peoples' mandate was that a settlement must be acceptable to both Government of India and the Nagas, but they ignored the mandate and became warmongers, thus bringing more confusion and uncertainties and making the chances of a settlement more difficult.

The Government of India, the State Government and the people of Nagaland have waited eight long years with great patience for the underground leaders to settle the Naga problem but they did everything that would make restoration of peace and settlement of the political question rather impossible. The so-called NNC and the Federal groups are determined to secede Nagaland from the Union of India, and to wage a war which are unlawful under the law of the country.

The Government of India and the Government of Nagaland have been left, therefore, with no option but to remove the impediment of obedience to the law for ensuring full protection to the peace loving and law-abiding citizens of Nagaland. That is why the Government have declared the so-called N.N.C., the Federal Government and the Federal Army as unlawful associations under the Unlawful Activities (Prevention) Act, No. 37 of 1967.

3. N.N.C., Federal Government and Federal Army are Unlawful: The Governor of Nagaland in a special broadcast over All India Radio, Kohima, on the 31st August, 1972 announced the momentous decisions unanimously taken by the Government of India, the Governor and the State Government of Nagaland towards normalisation of the State and for the establishment of permanent peace as given under:

(i) Discontinuance of the practice of extending from month to month the order for the Suspension of Operations in Nagaland from 1st September 1972.

(ii) To declare all bodies which have as their aim the secession of Nagaland from India as unlawful association. Thus, with the notification issued by the Central Government on the 31st August 1972, the Naga National Council, Naga Federal Government and Naga Federal Army are now unlawful associations within the meaning of Unlawful Activities (Prevention) Act, No. 37 of 1967.

(iii) Known members and known over ground supporters of these unlawful associations who continue by word or deed to support secessionist activities would be dealt with under the said Act.

(iv) According to the customary usage, Nagas have age-long tradition to revere and value Oath Taking as something sacred and totally binding forever. Our members of the Nagaland Legislature have taken their oath in the name of God to bear not only true faith and allegiance to the Constitution of India but also to uphold the sovereignty and integrity of India. Collaboration with the underground by some of our MLAs will be tantamount to betrayal of the Oath taken which is highly deplorable from the traditional and customary Naga point of view. Therefore, they are reminded that as elected members of the Nagaland legislative Assembly they have both moral obligation and Constitutional responsibility in this regard and to prove their unquestionable loyalty and wholehearted devotion to the Constitution and the sovereignty and integrity of India.

These decisions are intended to only ensure that the peace-loving and law-abiding citizens of Nagaland are spared from the continued depredations and harassment caused to them by some Section of an armed group, whose aim is nothing but to plunge the State into bloodshed.

The Naga public, the State Government and the Government of India have waited with patience for too long a period with a ray of hope and belief that this armed group will eschew cult of violence and come forward with some concrete proposal or suggestion to iron out their differences. But they belied all such hopes of persuasion and reasonableness. Instead, they have continued the tempo of violence and disorder in its various forms.

Is it not, therefore, the primary duty and moral responsibility of a Government established by law to ensure protection to life and property of its people and to thwart such hooliganism and vandalism?

4. Cooperation: The State Government would like to assure the people of Nagaland that these decisions will in no way affect their normal avocation in life, but are only intended to redouble the efforts of the State Government to ensure their own safety and progress.

The Government appeals to those Nagas who have taken recourse to the misguided way of life to immediately renounce the use of force, declare themselves over ground and join in the efforts to bring lasting peace to the State of Nagaland for stability, progress and prosperity.

With the enforcement of the Unlawful Activities {Prevention} Act, 1967, in Nagaland it is now incumbent on the part of the villagers to totally refuse any refugee to the underground in their villagers. It should also be the responsibility of the villagers to ensure in their own interest that they do not harbour any anti-State and criminal activities such as intimidation and threats, extortion of money and rations, kidnapping and recruitment, sack and slaughter by the underground. The Government will do its utmost to ensure that adequate protection by the police is provided to safeguard the interests of the villagers.

The Government sincerely appeals to all our Naga brothers and sisters to totally dissociate themselves from such unlawful associations and desist from the practice of giving succour to the nefarious activities of the underground. We also seek the unstinted cooperation and support of the people of Nagaland to all wings of the State Government in its genuine and sincere efforts to establish lasting peace on which alone hinges the development and prosperity of our State.

Peace cannot be maintained without obedience to law. The obstacles in the way of enforcement of the law to ensure full protection to the Jaw-abiding and peaceful citizens of Nagaland have been removed by the Government in the hope that the people will also readily support with their matching contribution in ending the present turmoil in Nagaland.

5. Stand of the State Government and UNO: The State Government would like to reassure the people of Nagaland that the discontinuance of the stoppage of operations does not mean at all that hostilities are going to be resumed. On the contrary, it means that the Government is taking a giant step towards the establishment or peace in Nagaland.

All the law abiding and peace-loving citizens in the villages and towns will be protected by the civil authorities with the help of Police Force as in any other State in our Country.

The Army will act only when called for in aid of Civil power and it will not operate in the villages.

It is the intention of the Government of Nagaland to apply Unlawful Activities (Prevention) Act, 1967. With understanding and compassion. Those who have previously fore-sworn secession but who now decide to give up this unrealistic idea has nothing to fear under this law. All those who wish to live a peaceful and settled life will be given protection and rehabilitation.

The State Government and the Nagaland Nationalist organisation are pledged to support any concrete proposal or suggestions, whether economic, social or political coming from any quarter or political party in Nagaland which are aimed at the welfare and betterment of the Naga people.

Nagaland Accord: The Shillong Agreement

[*An Accord was signed between the Governor of Assam, L.P. Singh and the representatives of Nagaland's underground organisations on 11 November 1975 whereby certain issues, including the "acceptance of the constitution of India" and "deposition of arms" etc were discussed and agreed upon*]

The following representatives of the underground organisations met the Governor of Nagaland, Shri L.P. Singh representing the Government of India, at Shillong on 10th and 11th November 1975.

- Shri. I. Temjenba
- Shri. S. Dahru
- Shri Veenyiyl Rhakhu
- Shri. Z. Ramyo
- Shri M. Assa
- Shri Kevi Yallay

There was a series of four discussions. Some of the discussions were held with the Governor alone; at other, the Governor was assisted by the two Advisors for Nagaland, Shri M. Ramunny, and Shri. H. Zopianga, and Shri M.L. Kampani, Joint Secretary in the Ministry of Home Affairs. All the five members of the Liaison Committee, namely Rev. Longri Ao, Dr. M. Aram, Shri. L. Lungalang, Shri Kenneth Kerhuo, and Shri Lungshim Shaiza, participated in the discussions.

The following were the outcome of the discussions:

The representatives of the underground organisations conveyed their decision, of their own volition, to accept, without condition, the Constitution of India.

It was agreed that the arms, now underground, would be brought out and deposited at appointed places. Details for giving effect of this agreement will be worked out between them and representatives of the Government, the security forces, and members of the Liaison Committee.

It was agreed that the representatives of the underground organisations should have reasonable time to formulate other issues for discussion for final settlement.

Dated Shillong, 11 November 1975

Sd/-
(I. Temjenba)

Sd/-
(S. Dahru)

Sd/-
(Z. Ramyo)

Sd/-
(M. Assa)

Sd/-
(Kevi Yallay)

On behalf of the Representative of the Underground organisations.

Sd/-
(L.P. Singh)
On behalf of the Government of India

Supplementary Agreement of January 5, 1976

Implementation of Clause II of the Shillong Accord of November 11, 1975.

It was decided that the collection of arms, initially at collection centres, would commence as early as possible, and will be completed by 25th January 1976. Initial places of collection to be decided through discussion between Commissioner, representatives of underground organisations and the members of the Liaison Committee.

Once all arms are collected, these will be handed over to Peace Council team at the respective places of collection.

Peace Council team will arrange to transport the arms from collection centres to Chedema peace camp and arrange guards, etc., for safe custody of arms.

Similar arrangement at agreed place/places will be made in Manipur with the concurrence of the Manipur Government.

The underground may stay at peace camps to be established at suitable places, and their maintenance will be arranged only by the Peace Council. Any voluntary contribution from any source will be made to the Peace Council who will utilize the fund according to necessity.

Sd/-
(L.P. Singh)
Governor

Sd/-
(Biseto Medom Keyho)

Sd/-
(Pukrove Nakru)

Sd/-
(Z. Ramyo)

Sd/-
(I. Temjenba)

Place: Shillong, Dated January 5, 1976

Disturbed Areas (Special Courts) Act

[*An Act to provide for the speedy trial of certain offences in certain areas came into force in 1976. The Act also provided for the setting up of Special Courts*]

1. Short Title, Extent and Commencement: (1) This Act may be called the Disturbed Areas (Special Courts) Act, 1976.

(2) It extends to the whole of India except the State of Jammu and Kashmir.

(3) It shall come into force on such date as the Central Government may, by notification in the Official Gazette, appoint and different dates may be appointed for different States or for different parts thereof.

2. Definitions: In this Act, unless the context otherwise requires,

(a) "Code" means the Code of Criminal Procedure, 1973; (2 of 1974)

(b) "Disturbed area" means an area declared as a disturbed area under section 3;

(c) "Period of disturbance" in relation to a disturbed area, means the period during which it is to be a disturbed area for the purposes of section 3;

(d) "Scheduled offence" means an offence specified in the Schedule being an offence forming part or arising out of, or connected with, any such disturbance as is referred to in section 3;

(e) "Special Court" means a Special Court constituted under section 4;

(f) Words and expressions used but not defined in this Act, and defined in the Code shall have the meanings respectively assigned to them in the Code.

3. Declaration of an Area as Disturbed Area: (1) Where a State Government is satisfied that

(i) There was, or (ii) there is, in any area within a State extensive disturbance of the public peace and tranquillity, by reason of differences or disputes between members of different religious, racial, language or regional groups or castes or 4. 15-8-1976: Vide Notification S.O. 549(E), Dtd. 13-8-1976. Communities, it may, by notification in the Official Gazette, declare such area to be a disturbed area.

(2) A notification issued under sub-section (1) in respect of any area shall specify the period during which the area shall, for the purposes of this section, be a disturbed area and where the State Government is satisfied that there was such disturbance of public peace and tranquillity as is referred to in sub-section (1) in that area from any date prior to the issue of such notification, the period specified in the notification may commence from that date: Provided that (a) no period commencing from a date earlier than three months before the date of publication of the notification shall be specified therein; and (b) so much of the period specified in such notification as is subsequent to the date of publication of the notification shall not, in the first instance, exceed three months but the State Government may amend such notification to extend such period from time to time by any period not exceeding three months at any one time if in the opinion of the State Government there continues to be in such area such disturbance of public peace and tranquillity as is referred to in sub-section (1): Provided further that where the State Government is satisfied that there is no longer such disturbance of public peace and tranquillity as is referred to in sub-section (1) in such area, it shall amend the notification issued under that sub-section in respect of that area to limit the period specified therein (whether originally or by amendment under the preceding proviso) accordingly.

4. Constitution of Special Courts: (1) The State Government may, for the purpose of providing speedy trial of scheduled offences committed in disturbed areas, by notification in the Official Gazette, constitute as many Special Courts as may be necessary in or in relation to such disturbed area or areas as may be specified in the notification.

(2) A Special Court shall consist of a single judge who shall be appointed by the High Court upon a request made by the State Government.

Explanation: In this sub-section, the word "appoint" shall have the meaning given to it in the Explanation to section 9 of the Code.

(3) A person shall not be qualified for appointment as a judge of a Special Court unless— (a) he is qualified for appointment as a judge of a High Court, or (b) he has, for a period of not less than one year, been a Sessions Judge or an Additional Sessions Judge.

(4) Notwithstanding anything contained in sub-section (3), a person shall not be eligible for being appointed as, and for being, a Judge of a Special Court in any State after he has attained the age at which Sessions Judges in that State have to retire from service.

5. Jurisdiction of Special Courts: (1) Notwithstanding anything contained in the Code or any other law, a scheduled offence committed in any disturbed area at any time during the period during which it is a disturbed area shall be triable, whether during or after such period, only by the Special Court constituted in or in relation to the disturbed area in which the offence has been committed.

(2) When trying any scheduled offence, a Special Court may also try any offence other than the scheduled offence with which the accused may, under the Code, be charged at the same trial if the offence is connected with the scheduled offence.

6. Procedure and Powers of Special Courts: (1) Every scheduled offence shall be cognisable.

(2) A Special Court may take cognisance of any scheduled offence (a) where under the Code such offence is an offence triable exclusively by a Court of Session, upon its being committed to it under section 209 of the Code as if the Special Court were a Court of Session; (b) in any other case, upon a police report of the facts together with a certificate from the public prosecutor to the effect that the offence is triable exclusively by the Special Court.

(3) Where a scheduled offence is an offence triable exclusively by a Court of Session under the Code, a Special Court shall have all the powers of a Court of Session and shall try such offence as if it were a Court of Session, so far as may be in accordance with the procedure prescribed in the Code for trial before a Court of Session.

(4) Where a scheduled offence is an offence which is punishable with imprisonment for a term exceeding three years but which, according to the provisions of the Code, is not an offence triable exclusively by a Court of Session, a Special Court may on taking cognisance of the offences perform the functions of a Magistrate under section 207 of the Code and thereafter try such offence so far as may be in accordance with the procedure prescribed in the Code for trial before a Court of Session as if the Special Court were a Court of Session and the case had been committed to it for trial under the provisions of the Code.

(5) Where a scheduled offence is punishable with imprisonment for a term not exceeding three years or with fine or with both, a Special Court may, notwithstanding anything contained in sub-section (1) of section 260 or section 262 of the Code, try the offence in a summary way in accordance with the procedure prescribed in the Code and the provisions of sections 263 to 265 of the Code, shall so far as may be, apply to such trial: Provided that when, in the course of a summary trial under this sub-section, it appears to the Special Court that the nature of the case is such that it is-undesirable to try it summarily, the Special Court shall recall any witnesses who may have been examined and proceed to rehear the case in the manner provided by the provisions of the Code for the trial of such offence and the said provisions shall apply to and in relation to a Special Court as they apply to and in relation to a Magistrate: Provided further that in the case of any

conviction in a summary trial under this section, it shall be lawful for a Special Court to pass a sentence of imprisonment for a term not exceeding two years.

(6) A Special Court may, with a view to obtaining the evidence of any person suspected to have been directly or indirectly concerned in, or privy to, an offence, tender a pardon to such person on condition of his making a full and true disclosure of the whole circumstances within his knowledge relating to the offence and to every other person concerned whether as principal or abettor in the commission thereof and any pardon so tendered shall, for the purposes of section 308 of the Code, be deemed to have been tendered under section 307 thereof.

7. Power to Transfer Cases to Regular Courts: Where, after taking cognisance of any offence, a Special Court is of opinion that the offence is not a scheduled offence, it shall, notwithstanding that it has no jurisdiction to try the case, transfer the case for trial, to any court having jurisdiction under the Code and the court to which the case is transferred may proceed with the case as if it had taken cognisance of the offence.

8. Appeal and Revision: The High Court may exercise, so far as they may be applicable, all the powers conferred by Chapters XXIX and XXX of the Code on a High Court, as if a Special Court is a Court of Session trying cases within the local limits of the jurisdiction of the High Court.

9. Overriding Effect of Act: (1) The provisions of this Act shall have effect notwithstanding anything contained in the Code or any other law, but save as expressly provided in this Act, the provisions of the Code shall, in so far as they are not inconsistent with the provisions of this Act apply to the proceedings before a Special Court; and for the purposes of the said provisions of the Code, the Special Court shall be deemed to be a Court of Session and the person conducting a prosecution before a Special Court shall be deemed to be a public prosecutor.

(2) In particular and without prejudice to the generality of the provisions contained in sub-section (1), the provisions of sections 326 and 475 of the Code shall, so far as may be, apply to the proceedings before a Special Court, and for this purpose references in those provisions to a Magistrate shall be construed as references to the Special Court.

10. Savings: (1) Nothing in this Act shall affect the jurisdiction exercisable by, or the procedure applicable to, any court or other authority under any law relating to the naval, military or air forces or any other armed forces of the Union.

(2) For the removal of doubts, it is hereby declared that for the purposes of any such law as is referred to in sub-section (1), a Special Court shall be deemed to be a court of ordinary criminal Justice.

THE SCHEDULE
[See Section 2(D)]

1. Offences under the following provisions of the Indian Panel Code: (45 of 1860)
   - Section 120B;
   - Sections 143 to 145, 147, 148, 151 to 155, 157, 158 and 160;
   - Sections 182, 183, 186 to 190;
   - Sections 193 to 195, 199, 201 to 203, 211 to 214, 216, 216A and 225
   - Sections 295 to 298;
   - Sections 302, 303, 304, 307, 308, 323 to 335, 341 to 348, 352 to 358, 363 to 369 and 376;
   - Sections 379, 380, 382, 384 to 387, 392 to 399, 402, 411, 412, 426, 427, 431, 435, 436, 440, 447 to 462;
   - Sections 504 to 506 and 509.
2. Offences under the following provisions of the Arms Act, 1959: (54 of 1959)
   - Sections 25 to 30.
3. Offences under the following provisions of the Indian Explosives Act, 1884: (—of 1884)
   - Sections 6(3) and 8(2).

The National Security Act

[*Enacted on 27 December 1980, the National Security Act, provides for preventive detention of persons in certain cases*]

1. Act Objective: An Act to provide for preventive detention in certain cases and for matters connected therewith. BE it enacted by Parliament in the Thirty-first Year of the Republic of India as follows:

2. Definitions: In this Act, unless the context otherwise requires,

(a) "Appropriate Government" means, as respects a detention order made by the Central Government or a person detained under such order, the Central Government, and as respects a detention order made by a State Government or by an officer subordinate to a State Government or as respects a person detained under such order, the State Government;

(b) "Detention order" means an order made under section 3;

(c) "Foreigner" has the same meaning as in the Foreigners Act, 1946 (31 of 1946);

(d) "Person" includes a foreigner;

(e) "State Government", in relation to a Union territory, means the administrator thereof.

3. Power to Make Orders Detaining Certain Persons: (1) The Central Government or the State Government may,

(a) If satisfied with respect to any person that with a view to preventing him from acting in any manner prejudicial to the defence of India, the relations of India with foreign powers, or the security of India, or

(b) If satisfied with respect to any foreigner that with a view to regulating his continued presence in India or with a view to making arrangements for his expulsion from India, it is necessary so to do, make an order directing that such person be detained.

(2) The Central Government or the State Government may, if satisfied with respect to any person that with a view to preventing him from acting in any manner prejudicial to the security of the State or from acting in any manner prejudicial to the maintenance of Public order or from acting in any manner prejudicial to the maintenance of supplies and services essential to the community it is necessary so to do, make an order directing that such person be detained.

Explanation: For the purposes of this sub-section, "acting in any manner prejudicial to the maintenance of supplies and services essential to the community" does not include "acting in any manner prejudicial to the maintenance of supplies of commodities essential to the community" as defined in the Explanation to sub-section (1) of section 3 of the Prevention of Black-marketing and Maintenance of Supplies of Essential Commodities Act, 1980 (7 of 1980), and accordingly, no order of detention shall be made under this Act on any ground on which an order of detention may be made under that Act.

(3) If, having regard to the circumstances prevailing or likely to prevail in any area within the local limits of the jurisdiction of a District Magistrate or a Commissioner of Police, the State Government is satisfied that it is necessary so to do, it may, by order in writing, direct, that during such period as may be specified in the order, such District Magistrate or Commissioner of Police may also, if satisfied as provided in sub-section (2), exercise the powers conferred by the said sub-section: Provided that the period specified in an order made by the State Government under this sub-section shall not, in the first instance, exceed three months, but the State Government may, if satisfied as aforesaid that it is necessary so to do, amend such order to extend such period from time to time by any period not exceeding three months at any one time.

(4) When any order is made under this section by an officer mentioned in sub-section (3), he shall forthwith report the fact to the State Government to which he is subordinate together with the grounds on which the order has been made and such other particulars as, in his opinion, have a bearing on the matter, and no such order shall remain in force for more than twelve days after the making thereof unless, in the meantime, it has been approved by the State Government: Provided that where under section 8 the grounds of detention are communicated by the officer making the order after five days but not later than ten days from the date of detention, this sub-section shall apply subject to the modification that, for the words "twelve days", the words "fifteen days" shall be substituted.

(5) When any order is made or approved by the State Government under this section, the State Government shall, within seven days, report the fact to the Central Government together with the grounds on which the order has been made and such other particulars as, in the opinion of the State Government, have a bearing on the necessity for the order.

4. Execution of Detention Orders: A detention order may be executed at any place in India in the manner provided for the execution of warrants of arrest under the Code of Criminal Procedure, 1973 (2 of 1974).

5. Power to Regulate Place and Conditions of Detention: Every person in respect of whom a detention order has been made shall be liable

(a) To be detained in such place and under such conditions,

(b) Including conditions as to maintenance, discipline and punishment for breaches of discipline, as the appropriate Government may, by general or special order, specify; and

(c) To be removed from one place of detention to another place of detention, whether within the same State or in another State, by order of the appropriate Government: Provided that no order shall be made by a State Government under clause

(d) For the removal of a person from one State to another State except with the consent of the Government of that other State.

6. Detention Orders not to be Invalid or Inoperative on Certain Grounds: No detention order shall be invalid or inoperative merely by reason

(a) That the person to be detained thereunder is outside the limits of the territorial jurisdiction of the Government or officer making the order, or

(b) That the place of detention of such person is outside the said limits.

7. Powers in Relation to Absconding Persons: (1) If the Central Government or the State Government or an officer mentioned in sub-section (3) of section 3, as the case may be, has reason to believe that a person in respect of whom a detention order has been made has absconded or is concealing himself so that the order cannot be executed, that Government or officer may (a) make a report in writing of the fact to a Metropolitan Magistrate or a Judicial Magistrate of the first class having jurisdiction in the place where the said person ordinarily resides; (b) by order notified in the Official Gazette direct the said person to appear before such officer, at such place and within such period as may be specified in the order.

(2) Upon the making of a report against any person under clause (a) of sub-section (1), the provisions of sections 82, 83, 84 and 85 of the Code of Criminal Procedure, 1973 (2 of 1974), shall apply in respect of such person and his property as if the detention order made against him were a warrant issued by the Magistrate.

(3) If any person fails to comply with an order issued under clause (b) of sub-section (1), he shall, unless he proves that it was not possible for him to comply therewith and that he had, within the period specified in the order, informed the officer mentioned in the order of the reason which rendered compliance therewith impossible and of his whereabouts, be

punishable with imprisonment for a term which may extend to one year, or with fine, or with both.

(4) Notwithstanding anything contained in the Code of Criminal Procedure, 1973 (2 of 1974), every offence under sub-section (3) shall be cognizable.

8. Grounds of Order of Detention to be Disclosed to Persons Affected by the Order: (1) When a person is detained in pursuance of a detention order, the authority making the order shall, as soon as may be, but ordinarily not later than five days and in exceptional circumstances and for reasons to be recorded in writing, not later than ten days from the date of detention, communicate to him the grounds on which the order has been made and shall afford him the earliest opportunity of making a representation against the order to the appropriate Government.

(2) Nothing in sub-section (1) shall require the authority to disclose facts, which it considers to be against the public interest to disclose.

9. Constitution of Advisory Boards: (1) The Central Government and each State Government shall, whenever necessary, constitute one or more Advisory Boards for the purposes of this Act.

(2) Every such Board shall consist of three persons who are, or have been, or are qualified to be appointed as, Judges of a High Court, and such persons shall be appointed by the appropriate Government.

(3) The appropriate Government shall appoint one of the members of the Advisory Board who is, or has been, a Judge of a High Court to be its Chairman, and in the case of a Union territory, the appointment to the Advisory Board of any person who is a Judge of the High Court of a State shall be with the previous approval of the State Government concerned.

10. Reference to Advisory Boards: Save as otherwise expressly provided in this Act, in every case where a detention order has been made under this Act, the appropriate Government shall, within three weeks from the date of detention of a person under the order, place before the Advisory Board constituted by it under section 9, the grounds on which the order has been made and the representation, if any, made by the person affected by the order, and in case where the order has been made by an officer mentioned in sub-section (3) of section 3, also the report by such officer under sub-section (4) of that section.

11. Procedure of Advisory Boards: (1) The Advisory Board shall, after considering the materials placed before it and, after calling for such further information as it may deem necessary from the appropriate Government or from any person called for the purpose through the appropriate Government or from the person concerned, and if, in any particular case, it considers it essential so to do or if the person concerned desires to be heard, after hearing him in person, submit its report to the appropriate Government within seven weeks from the date of detention of the person concerned.

(2) The report of the Advisory Board shall specify in a separate part thereof the opinion of the Advisory Board as to whether or not there is sufficient cause for the detention of the person concerned.

(3) When there is a difference of opinion among the members forming the Advisory Board, the opinion of the majority of such members shall be deemed to be the opinion of the Board.

(4) Nothing in this section shall entitle any person against whom a detention order has been made to appear by any legal practitioner in any matter connected with the reference to the Advisory Board; and the proceedings of the Advisory Board and its report, excepting that part of the report in which the opinion of the Advisory Board is specified, shall be confidential.

12. Action upon the Report of the Advisory Board: (1) In any case where the Advisory Board has reported that there is, in its opinion, sufficient cause for the detention of a person, the appropriate Government may confirm the detention order and continue the detention of the person concerned for such period as it thinks fit.

(2) In any case where the Advisory Board has reported that there is, in its opinion, no sufficient cause for the detention of a person, the appropriate Government shall revoke the detention order and cause the person concerned to be released forthwith.

13. Maximum Period of Detention: The maximum period for which any person may be detained in pursuance of any detention order which has been confirmed under section 12 shall be twelve months from the date of detention: Provided that nothing contained in this section shall affect the power of the appropriate Government to revoke or modify the detention order at any earlier time.

14. Revocation of Detention Orders: (1) Without prejudice to the provisions of section 21 of the General Clauses Act, 1897 (10 of 1897), a detention order may, at any time, be revoked or modified, (a) notwithstanding that the order has been made by an officer mentioned in sub-section (3) of section 3, by the State Government to which that officer is subordinate or by the Central Government; (b) notwithstanding that the order has been made by a State Government, by the Central Government.

15. Temporary Release of Persons Detained: (1) The appropriate Government may, at any time, direct that any person detained in pursuance of a detention order may be released for any specified period either without conditions or upon such conditions specified in the direction as that person accepts, and may, at any time, cancel his release.

(2) In directing the release of any person under sub-section (1), the appropriate Government may require him to enter into a bond with or without sureties for the due observance of the conditions specified in the direction.

(3) Any person released under sub-section (1) shall surrender himself at the time and place, and to the authority, specified in the order directing his release or canceling his release, as the case may be.

(4) If any person fails without sufficient cause to surrender himself in the manner specified in sub-section (3), he shall be punishable with imprisonment for a term, which may extend to two years, or with fine, or with both.

(5) If any person released under sub-section (1) fails to fulfill any of the conditions imposed upon him under the said sub-section or in the bond entered into by him, the bond shall be declared to be forfeited and any person bound thereby shall be liable to pay the penalty thereof.

16. Protection of Action Taken in Good Faith: No suit or other legal proceeding shall lie against the Central Government or a State Government, and no suit, prosecution or other legal proceeding shall lie against any person, for anything in good faith done or intended to be done in pursuance of this Act.

17. Act not to have Effect with Respect to Detentions under State Laws: (1) Nothing in this Act shall apply or have any effect with respect to orders of detention, made under any State law, which are in force immediately before the commencement of the National Security Ordinance, 1980 (11 of 1980), and accordingly every person in respect of whom an order of detention made under any State law is in force immediately before such commencement, shall be governed with respect to such detention by the provisions of such State law or where the State law under which such order of detention is made is an Ordinance (hereinafter referred to as the State Ordinance) promulgated by the Governor of that State and the State Ordinance has been replaced (i) before such commencement, by an enactment passed by the Legislature of that State, by such enactment; or (ii) after such commencement, by an enactment which is passed by the Legislature of that State and the application of which is confined to orders of detention made before such commencement under the State Ordinance, by such enactment, as if this Act had not been enacted.

(2) Nothing in this section shall be deemed to bar the making under section 3, of a detention order against any person referred to in sub-section (1) after the detention order in force in respect of him as aforesaid immediately before the commencement of the National Security Ordinance, 1980 (11 of 1980), ceases to have effect for any reason whatsoever.

Explanation: For the purposes of this section, "State law" means any law providing for preventive detention on all or any of the grounds on which an order of detention may be made under sub-section (2) of section 3 and in force in any State immediately before the commencement of the said Ordinance.

18. Repeal and Saving: (1) The National Security Ordinance, 1980 (11 of 1980), is hereby repealed.

(2) Notwithstanding such repeal, anything done or any action taken under the said Ordinance shall be deemed to have been done or taken under the corresponding provisions of this Act, as if this Act had come into force on the 23rd day of September, 1980, and, in particular, any reference made under section 10 of the said Ordinance and pending before any Advisory Board immediately before the date on which this Act receives the assent of the President may continue to be dealt with by that Board after that date as if such Board had been constituted under section 9 of this Act.

ENDNOTE

1. Ins. by Act 60 of 1984, s. 2 (wef. 21-6-1984).

Policing in the North-East

[*In May 1981 the Seventh Report of the National Police Commission prepared a shaping document "Policing in the North East", which sought to go into various aspects of policing in the North East and suggest far reaching recommendations for a more efficient system of police administration and for the control of insurgency in the geo-strategically located region*]

The North East has been in a state of turmoil for some years now. Some of the recent incidents of violence, in Tripura, where the number of persons killed were one of the highest in any riot in recent years. Manipur, Meghalaya, Assam, Mizoram and on Assam-Nagaland border, show how inflammable the situation is. They are posing a serious threat to the security and stability not only of this region but of the entire country. The police set-up, which has been expanded in most of these States only recently, and that too in an ad hoc manner, has miserably failed to cope up with the situation. The problems of policing in the North East are far too complex and varied. They require a highly professional, well-organised and trained police force, which is at the same time aware and responsive to the needs of the tribals, to deal with them. An ad hoc approach in dealing with this highly complicated and explosive situation will not do. The whole country is already paying very high price for this situation and if not effectively dealt with, many have to pay a much higher price, even endangering the stability and security of the country.

The region comprises of 7 States, popularly known as the 7 sisters: Assam, Meghalaya, Nagaland, Manipur, Tripura, Mizoram and Arunachal Pradesh. It has a population of over 20 million and covers an area of about 2.55 lakh square kilometers—almost 8 per cent of the total area of the country. Mostly hilly, it is one of the most picturesque parts of the country. Railways have hardly penetrated the region, and even though many new roads have been constructed, the communications are still very spare and difficult. The remote areas in the interior are still completely isolated; one sometimes wonders whether the march of history has passed them by. The region is situated on the very sensitive borders of our country. The long international borders stretch along China, Tibet, Bhutan, Burma and Bangladesh. It is connected with the rest of the country by a narrow strip of land—17 miles broad—near the "Doars" in West Bengal. The traumatic experience of the 1962 war with China has left its imprint on the minds of the people. There is a climate of insecurity. The realisation dawned on them of the first time, how tenuous these geographical links were with the rest of the country.

Historical Perspective

From the beginning of the British rule, the North East was treated as a non-regulated area. Any legal enactments made for the rest of the country could not automatically be enforced in these areas, except when they were specifically adopted for them. The administrative system as it developed in this region was quite different from that in the rest of the country. Most of the administration was left by the British to the tribal chiefs. A number of armed outposts were later set up, not with the intention of administering the tribals, but only to keep a watch over them. There was no regular policing. The British had a great deal of difficulty in dealing with the tribals residing in the hilly areas of the North-East and they deliberately kept certain areas as "excluded areas" from the rest of the country with two fold objectives:

1. To keep the area as a buffer region between India and the neighbouring countries; and
2. To protect them from exploitation by the plainsmen.

The influence of the missionaries in the late 19th and the early 20th century has given the traditional tribal culture a veneer of western culture. The tribals, particularly the educated sections, have increasingly taken to the western dress, music and dancing. Moreover, the script of the tribal language is mostly English and a large section of the tribal population is Christian.

The Lushai Hills, now known as Mizoram, Naga Hills, Khasi, Jaintia and Garo Hills were partially administered, while NEFA, now known as Arunachal Pradesh was totally "excluded". NEFA was administered through a political officer on the basis of a single line administration. It was only in 1950 that the whole region was integrated into the State of Assam. After 1950 the tribal district of Assam were entitled to a differential administration in accordance with the provisions of the Article 244(2) read with the Sixth Schedule of the Indian Constitution. Autonomous district councils were set up to administer the tribal areas. Nagaland State was constituted in 1962. The States of Manipur, Tripura, Meghalaya, Mizoram and Arunachal Pradesh were constituted under the North Eastern Areas Act in 1972, it was hoped that by giving a political identity to the different people in this region it would be easier to tackle the area's problems. However, even the grant of Statehood has not led to easing of tensions in the region. On the other, few tensions in the shape of inter-State border disputes, friction between the tribals and the non-tribals, intra-tribal rivalries, linguistic clashes etc. have emerged and have been creating serious problems of law and order. Because of the prolonged isolation of this area from the rest of the country, a feeling of separation has grown. Living in isolation they have got used to living freely with minimum or no government control. They tend to resent any kind of discipline from any authority. Local grievances and aspirations have further encouraged separatist tendencies. As neglected people the fear of being exploited by the migrants from the plains and absorbed into the neighbouring States haunts them. This fear has led to eruption of violence quite frequently. There are extremist elements among the tribals in these areas, who will not be satisfied with anything short of complete separation from India. These extremist elements, it is suspected, are receiving support from some foreign countries, which are interested for their own reasons in destabilising this strategic region. There are reports that the Mizo National Front has its headquarters in the Chittagong Hill Tracts of Bangladesh and has been receiving arms and ammunition and training facilities from various countries, particularly China. Some of the Naga rebel leaders are living in England; while quite a few are marking time in the neighbouring areas of north Burma for an opportunity to resume terrorist activities. Meiteis in Manipur are known to have developed pro-China links. Meiteis are Vaishnavs and have strong cultural links with Hinduism, but are now openly hostile to India, even to Hinduism. The younger elements are claiming that they are culturally and ethnically closer to China and not to India. The possibility of a linkup between the extremist elements in the North East can no longer be ruled out. Investigation of some of the incidents by Mizo hostiles in Tripura and the bordering areas of Mizoram has pointed to such a link.

The fact that the tribals have suddenly emerged from an era of isolation and extreme economic backwardness of the region are two of the major causes of this hostility. The Central Government has been spending huge funds to force the pace of development in this region, but the benefits of the economic activity have unfortunately gone only to a small section of the people. The contractors, the bureaucrats and the politicians have cornered most of the development benefits. The problems of the tribals in the interior areas have not been solved and they continue to suffer, even though the per capita public expenditure in this region is the highest in India. The backlog of neglect of centuries has to be wiped out and this huge task cannot be accomplished in a short time. The spread of education has not been an unmixed blessing. There is a danger that the increase in the educated unemployed will outstrip the economic growth. The educated unemployed are easy prey to the propaganda of the extremist elements. The corruption and inefficiency of the administrative machinery has further created a sense of abhorrence of the outsiders in the minds of the people. The hated foreigner is known as Vai in Mizoram, Mayang in Manipur, Teppremyic in Nagaland and Dakhar in Meghalaya. There is no doubt that the solution to the problem of backwardness of the area lies in its development and not in isolation, but the hatred of the "foreigner" has become an emotional obsession with the people and any influx, even of engineers, administrators etc., who are so very necessary for the development work is looked upon with suspicion. The economic backwardness of the region, poor communications and remoteness of the area are responsible for this isolation, which has become emotional as well as physical. Unfortunately, pursuit of unimaginative policies, instead of integrating them with the rest of the country has only succeeded in further alienating them. There is complete separation between the tribals and the non-tribals living in these areas. In there anxiety to integrate these areas with the rest of the country, the policy makers did not quite appreciate the historical background and the tribal social structure, before deciding to introduce the central law and system of administration in this region. The demand of separation has taken the shape of insurgency in Nagaland and Mizoram. The situation in Manipur is also causing anxiety. It is very sensitive region from the international point of view. The Super Powers and major powers like China have a direct interest in this region. It is easy to exploit the anti-Indian sentiments in this region. India is vulnerable here and can be hit at a very low cost. The fear of infiltration of foreigners has become a very major problem. Because of the tremendous pressure of population in Bangladesh a large number of people have been migrating to the neighbouring tribal areas for the last few years. The situation in Tripura, where the local tribal population has become a minority in their own land has created fears, which are now altogether baseless, in the minds of the tribals that unless something radical is done they will also be overwhelmed by the migrants. The pressure of population from the plain areas to the hills in this region itself has added another dimension to the problem.

The tribals have become aware of their rights and are not prepared to be mute spectators of the exploitation of their resources and their own exploitation by others. Literacy among some tribes, particularly in Mizoram is very high. As mentioned earlier the tremendous increase in the educated unemployed makes their areas a fertile ground for hostile propaganda. The local economy is still very backward and cannot bear the administrative superstructure, which is almost entirely financed by the funds provided by the Central Government. Widespread corruption in the administrative machinery, a problem we have dealt with separately later in this chapter, has eroded the credibility of the Administration. There is still no industry and agriculture is still by and large based on the practice of "jhooming", a system of shifting cultivation. Economic development of this region both in the field of industry and agriculture will have to take place in a big way. They are a proud people and conscious of their own sense of identity. The tribal culture has its own social value system and nothing should be done to upset it. They do not suffer from a sense of personal insecurity because the tribe takes the responsibility for maintaining all its members. It may sound strange but even after many years a tribal, when he comes back to his own village, can walk into any house and expect to be given shelter and food, even if the householders are total strangers to him. They are not servile and the tribal society does not suffer from elitism. The driver of a Chief Minister can still sit in the drawing room on the same sofa with the Chief Minister and have tea with him. They are not greedy and acquisitive and have a very healthy attitude towards life. The figures of the tribal population are given below:

State/UT	*Total Population (in Lakh)*	*Scheduled Tribe Population (in Lakh)*	*Percentage of Tribal Total Population of the State*
Assam	146.25	16.07	10.98
Manipur	10.73	3.34	31.13
Meghalaya	10.12	8.14	80.43
Nagaland	5.16	4.58	88.76
Tripura	15.56	4.51	28.98
Arunachal Pradesh	4.68	3.69	78.85
Mizoram	3.32	3.13	94.28

The tribals used to consider themselves as free people during the British rule, but shortsighted policies allowed an unfortunate impression to grow, no doubt aided and abetted by mischievous propaganda, that they have been subjugated to after the exploitation and departure of the British. The policy makers in Delhi rightly decided that the solution of the border problem lay in bringing the area into the mainstream of the country's life by properly administering it, and extending to it the benefits of development economy, but unfortunately they did not quite appreciate the historical perspective and the tribal social structure and temper their effort to these vital factors. The tribal was not used to too much government control and it was a mistake to force our administrative system on them. The situation was further aggravated by the fact that the senior and middle level bureaucrats and the police officers that were sent to these areas were total misfits. These being remote and inaccessible areas there was a natural reluctance on the part of good officers to be posted to these areas with the result that the bulk of the officers sent to these areas were rejects and misfits. They were the people who were primarily responsible for the image of the "ugly Indian." We have separately discussed the problems of personnel and given some suggestions.

In Meghalaya, Nagaland and Arunachal Pradesh the tribal village is for all practical purposes an autonomous unit and the authority of the village Council has been recognised and maintained. The Council performs the duties of the police. Inter-tribal rivalries, spread of education, and political pressures have, to some extent eroded the credibility of the village Councils, but they still wield considerable influence. The tribal system is still the most suitable system in the area of policing and for satisfying the tribals' social needs. No effort should be made to interfere with this system on the plea that the modern system of policing as in the rest of the country is necessary. In the interior tribal areas the customary tribals institutions should be allowed and encouraged to continue to administer the area. Police interference should be minimum and should depend on the gravity of the offence. In the urbanised areas, which are connected by roads or railway a more formal police structure will require to be established, so that it can deal with the problems of crime and criminals more effectively. While laying broad principles for policing in this region, it would be convenient to divide the area into three divisions:

1. Border areas,
2. Urbanised centres which are connected by roads or railways, and
3. Interior tribal areas, where the communications are very difficult and life is still very insulated.

Police presence should be concentrated in the border areas and other important areas from the law and order point of view. In Assam and the plains areas of Tripura the modern pattern of policing as prevailing in the rest of the country can be extended. In the urbanised areas like Aizawl and Kohima and other areas which have been linked with railway or roads should have the infrastructure of modern policing to cope with the increasing number of crimes and criminals, but it should take seriously into account the tribal laws, customs and institutions. Thus policing in these areas will have to be a judicious mixture of the tribal system and the modern system. The interior tribal areas should be left to be policed entirely by the traditional tribal institutions. As regards policing of the border areas we have discussed the subject separately in the later part of this chapter. The underlying principle for the North East should be minimum policing; no interference in the tribal laws, customs and institutions; policing on the basis of the gravity of offence and the sensitivity of areas i.e. border areas and areas having mixed population of different tribes and non-tribals.

The tribal criminal justice system of pre-litigation settlement is more responsive to social needs and no attempt should be made to change it under the garb of introducing the modern police system. Our criminal justice system in the rest of the country is becoming more and more ritualistic and the poor are finding it increasingly difficult to get any justice from it. The victim has hardly got any place in the scheme of things. Why should such an outdated criminal justice system be extended to the tribal areas, where their own system is much more effective, sophisticated, cheap and speedy? Under Article 13(3) (a) of the Constitution the definition of "law" includes customs or usage having the force of law. The Regional Councils and the District Council constituted under para 2 of the Sixth Scheduled have been vested with powers to make laws under the provisions of the Sixth Schedule. Various rules have been framed for the administration of criminal justice. The provisions of the Cr. P.C. have not been automatically extended to these areas. The State Government has been empowered to extend any of the provisions of the Cr. P.C. to such areas or parts thereof as may be notified by the State Government. There is no separation between the executive and the judiciary and it is our considered opinion that this arrangement should continue, till socio-economic changes justify any modification. There is need for effectively and speedily dealing with the extremist elements.

The Tribal Councils should continue to deal with the types of criminal offences they are dealing with at present. Whilst efforts should be made to remove some of the anomalies in the functioning of the tribal councils, in our opinion it is not necessary to codify the traditional laws. In Nagaland such efforts have only created confusion. We appreciate that the tribal criminal justice system will come under pressure with the increased tempo of the economic and political activities. Moreover, political interference in the impartial functioning of the tribal Councils is already affecting their credibility. No doubt certain modifications of the system will have to be introduced with the passage of time, but it needs to be emphasised that these tribal Councils are discharging a very valuable and important function and any reform made in the law and the police administration should try to strengthen this machinery and not weaken it. We have recommended in our report a system of Gram Nyayalayas. In the urbanised areas penetrated by railway and roads a similar system can be introduced. This model could also be followed in those areas where the traditional tribal and village Councils are finding it difficult to deal effectively with the increasing number of disputes between the tribals and non-tribals. The object is to provide cheap justice to the people with simple procedures on the principles of natural justice without any exploitation by the lawyers.

The problem of crime in the tribal areas is still not very serious. These areas are so far relatively free from crime, though with the increased contacts with the outside world the number of crimes and criminals is bound to go up. In dealing with crime and criminals in the area the main problem of the police is that it is spread thinly over a very large area. The police officers have to travel for days on foot before they can even reach a scene of crime. Even serious cases like murder are hardly investigated. Because of the distance involved the reporting of the cases is delayed and the subsequent response of the police is also poor. Even though there is no sustained investigation crime does not pose a serious problem. In the tribal areas it is not very difficult to identify the accused even without the help of the police. Moreover, once an accused is caught it does not require much pressure or persuasion to made his confess his crime. They are much more truthful and hence readily confess their guilt. The absence of lawyers of course, is one of the most important factors for this state of affairs. In places like Imphal and Kohima the number of lawyers has considerably increased and the situation is undergoing a change, but still in most of the tribal areas ordinary crime is, at present, not posing a very serious problem. In the interior places where it may not be necessary to open new police stations, it would suffice if a police party visits these areas periodically. The police in the headquarters should maintain close touch with the village Councils. Because of very difficult communications the information system is not very efficient and the feedback is relatively poor. This is incidentally one more reason in our opinion, for being very careful before introducing any changes in these areas.

Police Stations

We cannot fix any criteria for the establishment of a new police station. The factors such as population, areas, crime will have to be taken into consideration but the approach will have to be flexible. In areas where mixed population given rise to disputes between tribals and non-tribals and between different tribals, new police stations/police posts should be opened to inculcate a sense of security. The condition of the buildings of the police stations in this region is uniformly very poor and this needs to be attended to urgently. Proper buildings are also necessary from the security point of view, because of the activities of hostile elements. There should be proper security arrangements for the protection of the police stations. The system of maintenance of records in the police stations should be simplified, taking into consideration the capacity of an average tribal police officer. Only the essential records with simple procedures should be maintained. Similarly, the investigation procedures should be simplified. There is no point in extending the already out of date Assam Police Manual to these areas. A new Police Manual taking into consideration the special requirements of the region should be drafted expeditiously so that the force can start functioning on the right lines.

Insurgency

Insurgency is the most serious problem in Mizoram, Nagaland, bordering areas of Tripura and Manipur. In recent years the problem has also spread to plains of Manipur. In Manipur the activities of extremists among the Meiteis have introduced a new dimension of urban terrorism to the problem. The security forces, including the army and the paramilitary forces, are present in large numbers to deal with the activities of the insurgents. The problem in the long run, however, has to be tackled by the police. The main difficulty in dealing with the activities of the insurgents is their identification. The methods sometimes followed, which may be effective temporarily, have led to avoidable bitterness. The practice of surrounding village lining up all the male members, then searching the village has caused a lot of harassment to innocent people. While it is true that no insurgency activity can flourish without the support of the people, it must also be appreciated that any action, which further alienates the local population, will only help the insurgents. Ultimately the problem will have to be tackled by isolating the extremist elements and winning over the local population. The lesson learnt both in Mizoram and Nagaland tell us that effective police action can be very successful. The capacity of the police to absorb casualties is relatively low but it can play important complementary role to the army and para-military forces in tackling the situation. The army should, however, as far as possible, not be passed for day-to-day policing. Such a role is not the function of the armed forces and by using them for such purposes we can only succeed in belittling these forces, our ultimate forces in the eye of the people. This is not fair to our gallant armed forces. The present situation in Manipur, particularly in the valley where the army has almost taken over fully the subordinate role of the police in dealing with the activities of the Meitei extremists, is largely due to the failure of the police itself. This is due in no small measure because of its own weaknesses, particularly because of the wrong personnel policies, and the political and bureaucratic interference in its day-to-day functioning. The police must be organised on proper lines and it must be allowed to play its legitimate role. In addition we recommend the following measures to deal more effectively with the problem of insurgency:

1. The police should concentrate more on the border area and those areas, which are known for providing shelter to the extremists. There is no point in spreading the police too thin over a large area. Best use should be made of the available resources.
2. The police should be given modern arms and ammunition, instead of the antiquated.303 rifles. The insurgents are armed with modern automatic weapons.
3. Identity cards should be issued to all male members of the population over 16 years of age. The identity cards should carry an attested photograph of the person concerned. These should be renewed at regular intervals.
4. There should be strict control on the sale and stock of explosive material. The places where explosives are stocked should be provided with adequate security.
5. There should be very stringent control on the possession of arms and ammunition. There are large numbers of unlicensed arms in the area and every effort should be made to capture them.
6. One important aspect, which is not given the importance, it deserves, is public relations. This is a big mistake. The insurgents depend for their survival on the support they receive from the local population. The extremist elements through false propaganda try to create a feeling of hostility against the security forces. The police and the security forces operating in the area should have a separate public relations department. It should be the responsibility of this department to counter any propaganda bringing the police and the security forces into disrepute by readily and truthfully giving to the media the correct facts of incidents and situation. Positive steps should be taken to win over the confidence of the people.
7. Murder of any government official or looting of any public property should be severely and promptly dealt with. Misplaced sympathy or any delay in taking firm action can do a lot of damage in lowering the morale of the public, police and the security forces.

Intelligence Set up

The success or failure of operations against the insurgents will depend largely on how successfully the extremist elements can be identified. This in turn will depend on how promptly and correctly the intelligence agencies are able to collect information about them. At present this responsibility is being shared by many intelligence agencies. The Intelligence Bureau, the Army Intelligence, the Border Security Force, the RAW, the SSB, in addition to the local intelligence set up have all been operating in this region. It has been brought to our notice that due to lack of coordination, at times these agencies have been functioning at cross purpose, instead of working towards a common objective i.e. identification and capture of the hostile elements. Rivalries among junior functionaries of these agencies have been hampering the operations against the insurgents. There are reports that at times even the sources of one agency are exposed and threatened by the other. We were informed that in one insurgency torn Union Territory the source of one of the agencies escorted by their intelligence officers was forcibly kidnapped along with the officers by the officers of another agency. This situation is exploited by the hostile elements. There have also been cases where clever sources have taken more than one agency for a ride. It is absolutely essential that the work of all these agencies and its members should be constituted at the level of the Lt. Governor in the Union Territories and at the level of Governor in the States. A coordination committee with the representatives of all the agencies as its members should be constituted by the Governor or Lt. Governor. This Committee should meet as frequently as possible and at least once a month to take stock of the current situation, compare notes and plan new strategy. All information should be conveyed directly to the Lt. Governor or the Governor for appropriate action or instructions instead of routing it through their own headquarters, as is the practice at present. Any delay in passing information renders it sometimes absolutely useless, because by the time the information filters down to the operational level, the extremists have already managed to slip away or move away from that area.

Personnel Policy

Wrong choice of personnel posted to these areas is one single most important cause of the administration into disgrace. The posts in the North East are considered as punishment posts and officers with bad record, who have to be got rid of, are usually sent there. These officers, from the day they join their place of posting in the North-East, are disgruntled and take little or no interest in their work. Some of them have taken to heavy drinking and other bad habits unbecoming of an officer. How can such officers be expected to instill confidence in the mind of the people? Quite a few of them have no knowledge either of their area or of the people. The fact that more discretion has to be allowed to the officers at the operational level in these areas and because of the importance of the police problems it is imperative that only the best officers of the highest calibre are posted to this region. To attract the best available talent it is no use appealing to their patriotism alone. The posts will have to be made much more attractive so that suitable and talented officers with vision and enthusiasm volunteer for them. The present additional allowances and other facilities provided to them are most inadequate. These will have to be improved. Posting in these areas should be a plus point in an officer's career. In some recent cases the government has not cared to look after the officers on return from a successful tenure in the North East. Some of them on return found themselves without any job for months together and had to cool their heels till they could be adjusted into some insignificant post. This has proved as a great deterrent to officers posted to these areas and has also denigrated the prestige of the posts in the North East. Consequently it has become a problem to find suitable willing officers for these posts. Those posted to these areas make all types of excuses and pull every possible string to get out of these postings. Some of the posts remain unfilled for months and years because one after the other the officers posted manage to get their posting orders cancelled. A more imaginative personnel policy is the basis of a sound administrative system. Even in countries like the Soviet Union officers posted to Siberia and other difficult regions are paid much higher allowances and perks as compared to similar posts in the Moscow-Leningrad-Kiev region, which is the most developed area in USSR. We strongly recommend that the following steps should be taken to make these posts attractive:

1. Generous additional allowances should be sanctioned for all posts in the North East. This should be at least 50 per cent of the basic pay available to the officer in his own cadre.
2. One free passage for the officers and their families should be given once a year for travelling to their home State and back.
3. If in spite of general allowances/perks senior officers in the same grade show unwillingness to go, comparatively junior officers can be sent on rank promotion. To avoid any malpractices the refusal of senior officers must be in writing.
4. A scale of suitable allowances should be fixed for hostel subsidy up to a maximum of 2 children.

We further recommend that similarly the tribal officers from the region should be encouraged for posting outside the region. The present rules are such that tribal officers when posted outside the tribal area suffer loss in their emoluments and other facilities. They not only have to pay income tax when posted in the plain areas, but also loss some allowances which they are entitled to when posted in the tribal areas. This is an anomaly and a disincentive, which should be removed. The tribal officers should, when posted outside the tribal areas, continue to enjoy the same emoluments and facilities as they are entitled to when posted to the tribal region.

Recruitment

In recent years there has been a big increase in the strength of the police, but the recruitment at various levels of the police force has been done in a very haphazard manner. This has not helped in improving the efficiency of the police. There are complaints of nepotism and corruption. Because of the small population the evil of nepotism is much more widespread in these areas. Rules should be framed for recruitment at all levels and there should be no departure from the norms laid down in the rules. To make it a homogenous force, as far as possible, persons from all tribes and sections in the area should be recruited. We have separately dealt with the subject of armed police later in this chapter.

Because of the rapid expansion little or no thought has been given to the promotional policy. While in some cases the promotions have been very rapid, in other cases after the first few years there is complete blockade, with the result that considerable frustration has been caused. Executive and political interference in the internal administration of the police department, which is on a much larger scale in these areas than in the rest of the country, has further affected its moral and efficiency. In Manipur the interference in the police administration has gone to such an extent that the Inspector General cannot promote even an Assistance Sub-Inspector without the consent of the State Government. The State Government is interfering in a big way in the postings and transfers of the officers at the lower and middle ranks. It is, therefore, not surprising that the morale of the police in Manipur is one of the lowest in the whole of the country. The job of policing recently had to be handed over to the army and this has its own chain of undesirable consequences as discussed earlier. Things have come to such a pas that even in Imphal the army had to be called in to deal with the law and order situation.

Lack of supervision at various levels is another cause for inefficiency and indiscipline in the police force of this region. Poor means of communications no doubt make touring of the interior areas somewhat difficult but it should be possible for officers to do much more touring than they have been doing with the available means of communication. At present helicopters are being used exclusively for the VIPs and by the army. There should be closer cooperation between the police administration and the army and the air force, so that full use is made of the available helicopters, which frequently go empty. The police should be allowed to share this facility without adversely affecting the needs of the army. The present instructions restricting the use of the empty seats only to the army officers should be revised to include the police officers as well.

Training

Another important cause of the police failures is poor training of its personnel. The training facilities are most inadequate. In most of the States and the Union Territories after the initial training, which is mostly done outside the region, hardly any other training is given. Recently, the North East Council has started a police training school at Barapani near Shillong. In our view it would be desirable to increase the training facilities at Barapani and it should be possible for this centre to cater to the needs of all the Union Territories and the States in this region except Assam, which can have its own training institution. In addition, all the State and the Union Territories should have their own training institutions to run pre-promotional and refresher courses. Anti-insurgency measures should form an important part of the training syllabus.

Armed Police

In addition to the local armed police, the army and the paramilitary forces are deployed in large numbers in these areas. The para-military forces, though under the operational control of the local police chiefs are not under their disciplinary control, with the result that they have no commitment to the task and are not result oriented. On the other hand the local police tries to pass the buck on to the para-military force and they, especially the Central Reserve Police Force, have become very unpopular in this region. Unless these forces can be motivated to show initiative and drive in dealing with the hostile elements it would not be possible to deal with the insurgents and other complicated problems of law and order. The Border Security Force, the Central Reserve Police Force and the Assam Rifles have tremendous potential. There was a time when the Assam Rifles were the backbone of the law and order machinery in this area. This momentum due to lack of coordination and commitment has been lost over the years. Most of the para-military battalions, it is complained only prepare for the visits of their own senior officers, who live hundreds and sometimes thousands of miles away and come to visit their battalions once a year and that too during fair weather. They have absolutely no interest in the performance and the results achieved by these battalions. Most of the para-military forces outposts have literally become static outposts; they are not running patrols or collecting intelligence to capture the insurgents, arms and ammunition. The local police chief, in our opinion, must have operational and disciplinary control over these forces. There should be close coordination between them, the local police, the army and the intelligence agencies.

To ensure that local pressures do not adversely affect the efficiency, moral and discipline of these forces, we recommend that Article 371A(i)(b) which enables the Governor of Nagaland to have special responsibility for the maintenance of law and order should be extended to any other State when the problem of insurgency raises its head. It should be possible for the Governor or the Lt. Governor to use this personal judgment in discharging this responsibility. He should no doubt, consult the Council of Ministers before making his decision, but the Council of Ministers should not be able to question his judgment.

At present quite a few battalions of para-military forces have been deployed in this region more or less on a permanent basis for the last many years. For obvious reasons this is not a very satisfactory arrangement. This task will have to be taken over in due course as the situation improves by the regional armed police. We recommend that instead of recruiting the armed battalions for each State or Union Territory a North-Eastern Rifles or Armed Police should be constituted for the entire region on the Central Reserve Police Force pattern. Recruitment to these armed battalions should be done from all the 7 States and Union Territories. This should be a composite force for the entire region they should be rotated under orders of the Governor of the North East, or the Ministry of Home Affairs if it is later decided to have more than one Governor in the North East, every three years. These battalions when posted in a State should be completely under the operational and disciplinary control of the local Inspector General. The present battalions of the Assam Rifles and the State Armed Police will have to be reorganised to convert them into the North Eastern Rifles or the Armed Police, whichever nomenclature is preferred. Border areas and infiltration policing the local stretch of borders along the international boundary is a major problem in this region. There are reports that some of the neighbouring countries, not very friendly to us, are supporting the extremists. The explosion of population in Bangladesh is spilling over into the neighbouring States of Assam, Tripura, Meghalaya and Mizoram. In Tripura the tribals have become a minority in their own land. This fear is haunting the Assamese and people of other States in the region. Mischievous elements, with direct or indirect support of some foreign powers are exploiting this fear to create conditions of destabilisation by fanning separatist demands.

At present the borders are being policed by the Border Security Force, the Army and the Assam Rifles. In the interest of more effective policing and better coordination, we recommend that the entire border should be policed by the Border Security Force. The army will, of course, have to continue its supportive role. The distance between the existing border outposts is far too long and needs to be reduced to improve their effectiveness. Many more border outposts will have to be set up within reasonable distance of each other depending on the terrain and other factors, such as road links etc. The difficult terrain makes it very difficult to check the movement of the insurgents. The border police has to play an important role in fighting insurgency. All the forces deployed at the border should be trained in the anti-insurgency measures. Policing in the North East cannot be done in watertight compartments. We would emphasise once again the need for very close coordination between all the agencies operating in the area. In the task of dealing with the infiltrators coordination between the Border Security Force, the police and the civil administration assumes special importance. The problem of infiltration has to be dealt with firmly and with all the resources at our command. The problem of Chakma infiltrators from Chittagong Hill Tracts in Bangladesh into Mizoram needs to be dealt with immediately before it gets out of hand. This problem is further complicated by the fact that the Chakmas are fighting their own battle as "Shanti Bahini" against the Bangladesh Government.

Smuggling is another problem, which has already assumed serious proportions in Manipur. There are complaints of connivance by the police and at the political level. A vested interest has developed among the police, the politician and the extremist elements. In some border areas the insurgents are reported to be organising smuggling to finance their underground activities. The border police has an important role to play in tackling the evil, which is adversely affecting the morale, and functioning of the police and the civil administration. But it will not be possible to tackle this problem without close cooperation between all concerned including the border police.

Anti-corruption

One of the main reasons for the widespread corruption is that the administration intra-structure is too weak to control effectively the huge expenditure being incurred on the developmental activities and in running the security operations. In the absence of social sanction against corrupt methods, which are helping the hostile elements, there is no other alternative except to strengthen the anti-corruption machinery. There is need for reorganising and strengthening both the State anti-corruption branches and the zonal office of the Central Bureau of Investigation. The anti-corruption branch should not be used for dumping the unwanted, corrupt and the inefficient police officers. Only experienced investigating officers with unimpeachable reputation of integrity should be posted to the anti-corruption branch. Special judges to try these cases expeditiously should be appointed within the State, instead of sending them for trial outside the State, as is the practice in some of the States. The audit machinery should also be strengthened. Accountant General's office is located at Guwahati. This arrangement has not been functioning very effectively. Without proper supervision their teams of officials, which go on tours to these States and Union Territories from Guwahati, are very perfunctory in work and there is hardly any follow up of the defects found during the audit. In the absence of the audit reports investigation of the anti-corruption cases are sometimes held up for years.

Jails

The conditions of the jails in the North East are uniformly deplorable. They are mostly housed in makeshift temporary buildings without proper security arrangements. There have been a number of attempts, quite a few of them successful, at jail breaking. All the hard work that goes into the arrest of an extremist comes to naught, when the jails are so crowded that all types of prisoners are put together in these temporary structures. The dangerous criminals are getting mixed up with the ordinary criminals. The security arrangements need to be tightened. Some of the jails are being used to propagate the extremist philosophy and have become sources of recruitment for the insurgents. Proper jail buildings should be constructed without any further delay.

The problem of policing in the North East is very complex. The police, which is still a young force in this region, should be organised on the right lines. It need not blindly imitate the police set up as it exists in the rest of the country. The social, cultural, economic and political structure in which the police has to function is so very different in this region. While tackling the many sensitive law and order problems, the administration should not interfere unduly with the traditional tribal customs, laws and institutions. The tribal sense of identity should not be threatened under the garb of introducing a modern system of policing. On the other hand efforts should be made to strengthen some of the tribal institutions like: ***Gaon Burras*** and village Councils, so that they can play a more useful role even in the future.

At the same time such an infrastructure should be built in the police which would be able to cope with the problems of crime and criminals in the area as they increase more and more with the increased tempo of the economic and political activities. A comprehensive new police manual taking into consideration the special features of those areas should be drafted for the North East.

The Illegal Migrants (Determination by Tribunals) Act

[*Enacted on 25 December 1983, the IM (DT) Act provided for the establishment of Tribunals for the determination of illegal migrants in order to enable the deportation of such migrants. The Act was enacted in the backdrop of large-scale illegal influx into India from across the borders of the eastern and north-eastern regions of the country. It was also enacted with a view to protect the indigenous minority population of India, who were purportedly harassed during the detection and deportation of illegal migrants. The Act which was applicable only in Assam was struck down by the Supreme Court of India on 12 July 2005 as "ultra vires", with the Honourable Court stating in its landmark judgment that, "A deep analysis of the IM (DT) Act and the Rules made thereunder would reveal that they have been purposely so enacted or made so as to give shelter or protection to illegal migrants who came to Assam from Bangladesh on or after 25th March, 1971 rather than to identify and deport them"*]

ACT OBJECTIVE

An Act to provide for the establishment of Tribunals for the determination, in a fair manner, of the question whether a person is an illegal migrant to enable the Central Government to expel illegal migrants from India and for matters connected therewith or incidental thereto. Whereas a good number of the foreigners who migrated into India across the borders of the eastern and north-eastern regions of the country on and after the 25th day of March, 1971, have, by taking advantage of the circumstances of such migration and their ethnic similarities and other connections with the people of India and without having in their possession any lawful authority so to do, illegally remained in India; and whereas the continuance of such foreigners in India is detrimental to the interests of the public of India; and whereas on account of the number of such foreigners and the manner in which such foreigners have clandestinely been trying to pass off as citizens of India and all other relevant circumstances, it is necessary for the protection of the citizens of India to make special provisions for the detection of such foreigners in Assam and also in any other part of India in which such foreigners may be found to have remained illegally; Be it enacted by Parliament in the Thirty-fourth Year of the Republic of India as follows:

CHAPTER I
PRELIMINARY

1. Short Title, Extent and Commencement—(1) This Act may be called the Illegal Migrants (Determination by Tribunals) Act, 1983. (2) It extends to the whole of India. (3) It shall be deemed to have come into force in the State of Assam on the 15th day of October, 1983 and in any other State on such date as the Central Government may, by notification in the Official Gazette, appoint and different dates may be appointed for different States and references in this Act to the commencement of this Act shall be 322 construed in relation to any State as references to the date of commencement of this Act in such State.

2. Application—Nothing in this Act shall apply to or in relation to (a) any person who was in any State and who had been expelled from that State or India before the commencement of this Act in that State or in relation to whose expulsion from such State or India any order made before such commencement under any other law is in force; (b) any person detected as a foreigner at the time of his entry across any border of India; (c) any foreigner who, having entered into India under a valid passport or travel document, continued to remain therein after the expiry of the period for which he was authorised to remain in India under such passport or travel document.

3. Definitions and Construction of References—(1) In this Act, unless the context otherwise requires, (a) "Appellate Tribunal" means an Appellate Tribunal established by the Central Government under sub-section (1) of section 15; (b) "foreigner" has the same meaning as in the Foreigners Act, 1946; (31 of 1946.) (c) "illegal migrant" means a person in respect of whom each of the following conditions is satisfied, namely:(i) he has entered into India on or after the 25th day of March, 1971, (ii) he is a foreigner, (iii) he has entered into India without being in possession of a valid passport or other travel document or any other lawful authority in that behalf; (d) "notification" means a notification published in the Official Gazette; (e) "prescribed" means prescribed by rules made under this Act; (f) "Tribunal" means a Tribunal established by the Central Government under sub-section (1) of section 5. (2) Any reference in this Act to any law, which is not in force in any area, shall, in relation to that area, be construed as a reference to the corresponding law, if any, in force in that area.

4. Overriding effect of the Act—(1) The provisions of this Act or of any rule or order made thereunder shall have effect notwithstanding anything contained in the Passport (Entry into India) Act, 1920 (34 of

1920.) or the Foreigners Act, 1946 (31 of 1946.) or the Immigrants (Expulsion from Assam) Act, 1950 (10 of 1950.) or the Passports Act, 1967 (15 of 1967.) or any rule or order made under any of the said Acts and in force for the time being. (2) In particular and without prejudice to the generality of the provisions of sub-section (1), nothing in the proviso to section 2 of the Immigrants (Expulsion from Assam) Act, 1950 (10 of 1950.) shall apply to or in relation to an illegal migrant as defined in clause (c) of sub-section (1) of section 3.

CHAPTER II
ESTABLISHMENT OF TRIBUNALS

5. Establishment of Illegal Migrants (Determination) Tribunals—(1) The Central Government may, by notification, establish, for the purposes of this Act, as many Illegal Migrants (Determination) Tribunals as it may deem necessary and specify the principal place of sitting of, and the territorial limits within which, each such Tribunal shall exercise its jurisdiction. (2) No person shall be appointed as a member of any such Tribunal unless he is or has been a District Judge or an Additional District Judge in any State. (3) Each Tribunal shall consist of two members. (4) On the establishment of a Tribunal, the Central Government shall appoint one of the members thereof as the Chairman of such Tribunal. (5) Each Tribunal shall sit in its principal place of sitting and in such other place or places as its Chairman may, from time to time, appoint.

6. Filling of Vacancies—If, for any reason, any vacancy occurs in the office of the Chairman or the member of a Tribunal, the Central Government may fill the vacancy by appointing any person who fulfils the qualifications specified in sub-section (2) of section 5, as the Chairman, or, as the case may be, member of such Tribunal.

7. Staff of the Tribunals—The Central Government shall make available to every Tribunal such staff as may be necessary for the discharge of its functions under this Act.

8. References or Applications to Tribunals—(1) If any question arises as to whether any person is or is not an illegal migrant, the Central Government may, whether such question has arisen on a representation made by such person against any order under the Foreigners Act, 1946 (31 of 1946.) requiring him not to remain in India or to any other effect or has arisen in any other manner whatsoever, refer such question to a Tribunal for decision. (2) Any person may make an application to the Tribunal, for its decision, as to whether the person whose name and other particulars are given in the application, is or is not an illegal migrant: (3) "Provided that no such application shall be entertained by the Tribunal unless the person in relation to whom the application is made is found, or resides, within the jurisdiction of the same police station wherein the applicant has his place of residence.";

(3) Every application made under sub-section (2) shall be made in such form and in such manner as may be prescribed and shall be accompanied by affidavits sworn by not less than two persons residing within the jurisdiction of the same police station in which the person referred to in the application is found, or residing, corroborating the averments made in the application, and shall also be accompanied by such fee, being not less than ten and not more than one hundred, rupees, as may be prescribed.

[1]*["(4) Every reference under sub-section (1) shall be made to the Tribunal within the territorial limits of whose jurisdiction the place of residence of the person named in such reference is, at the time of making such reference, situated: Provided that where such person has no place of residence, the reference shall be made to the Tribunal within the territorial limit of whose jurisdiction such person is, at the time of making such reference, found. (5) Every application under sub-section (2) shall be made to the Tribunal within the territorial limits off whose jurisdiction the person named in such application is found or, as the case may be, has his place of residence, at the time of making such application."]

[2]*["8A. Application to the Central Government for reference. (1) Any person may make an application to the Central Government, for decision by a Tribunal, as to whether the person whose name and other particulars are given in the application, is or is not an illegal migrant, and where any such application is received by the Central Government, it may, on the basis of any information in its possession or after making such inquiry as it deems fit, reject the application on the ground that the application is frivolous or vexatious or it does not comply with the requirements of this section or refer such application to a Tribunal for decision. (2) Every application made under sub-section (1) shall be made in such form and in such manner as may be prescribed and shall be accompanied by a declaration by another person residing within the jurisdiction of the same revenue sub-division in which the applicant resides in such form as may be prescribed to the effect that the particulars mentioned in the application are true to his knowledge, information and belief: Provided that no person shall make more than ten such applications or more than ten such declarations. (3) Every reference under sub-section (1) shall be made to the Tribunal within the territorial limits of whose jurisdiction the place of residence of the person named in such reference is, at the time of making such reference, situated: Provided that where such person has no place of residence, the reference shall be made to the Tribunal within the territorial

limits of whose jurisdiction such person is, at the time of making such reference, found."]

9. Powers of the Tribunal—Every Tribunal shall have the same powers as are vested in a civil court under the Code of Civil Procedure, 1908, (5 of 1908.) while trying a suit, in respect of the following matters, namely:(a) summoning and enforcing the attendance of witnesses and examining them on oath; (b) discovery and production of any document; (c) reception of evidence on affidavits;(d) requisitioning of public records from any court or office;(e) issuing of any commission for the examination of witnesses.

10. Procedure with Respect to References under sub-section—(1) of section 8. On receipt of a reference under sub-section (1) of section 8 or sub-section (1) of section 8A the Tribunal shall serve on the person named in such reference, a notice, accompanied by a copy of such reference, calling upon him to make, within a period of thirty days from the date of receipt of such notice, such representation with regard to the averments made in the reference, and to produce such evidence as he may think fit in support of his defence: Provided that if the Tribunal is satisfied that the person aforesaid was prevented by sufficient cause from making his representation and from producing evidence in support of his defence within the said period of thirty days, it may permit him to make his representation and to produce evidence in support of his defence, within such further period, not exceeding thirty days, as it may, by order, specify.

11. Procedure with respect to applications under sub-section (2) of section 8. (1) On receipt of an application under sub-section (2) of section 8, the Tribunal shall issue a notice, accompanied by a copy of the application, to the prescribed authority calling upon it to furnish, after making such inquiry as that authority may deem fit, a report to the Tribunal with regard to the averments made in the application. 1 Subs. by Act 24 of 1988, s. 4. 2 Ins. by s. 5, *ibid.* 3 Subs. b s. 6, *ibid.* 325 (2) If, on a consideration of the report made by the prescribed authority, the Tribunal is satisfied that (a) the person named in the application is not an illegal migrant or that the application is frivolous or vexatious, or has not been made in good faith, the Tribunal shall, after giving the applicant an opportunity to be heard, reject the application; (b) there are reasonable grounds to believe that the person named in the application is an illegal migrant, the Tribunal shall issue a notice accompanied by a copy of the application, to the person named in the application, calling upon him to make, within thirty days from the date of receipt of the notice, such representation with regard to the averments made in the application and to produce such evidence as he may think fit in support of his defence: Provided that if the Tribunal is satisfied that the person aforesaid was prevented by sufficient cause from making his representation and from producing evidence in support of his defence within the said period of thirty days, it may permit him to make his representation and to produce evidence in support of his defence, within such further period, not exceeding thirty days, as it may, by order, specify.

12. Determination of the Question as to Whether a Person is an Illegal Migrant—(1) The Tribunal to which a reference has been made under ["section 8, or section 8A, or to which an application has been made under section 8"] shall after taking such evidence as may be adduced before it may think fit and after hearing such persons as it may deem appropriate, by order, decide the question as to whether the person named in such reference or application, as the case may be, is or is not an illegal migrant: Provided that where for the determination of such question in any case the decision on any issue renders any decision on any other issue or issues unnecessary, the Tribunal may not decide such other issue or issues. 1*["(2) Where the members of the Tribunal differ in their opinion on any point, the Chairman of the Tribunal shall state the point or points on which they differ and make a reference to the President of the Appellate Tribunal which exercises jurisdiction in relation to the Tribunal who shall refer the case for hearing on such point or points by a member of another Tribunal under its jurisdiction and such point or points shall be decided according to the opinion of that member and such decision shall be deemed to be the decision of the Tribunal."] (3) The Tribunal shall send a copy of every order passed by it to the prescribed authority or authorities and to the parties to the reference, or the application, as the case may be. (4) Every order passed under sub-section (1) shall, subject to the decision of the Appellate Tribunal, be final and shall not be called in question in any court.

13. Reference and Application to be Disposed of within Six Months—Every reference made to a Tribunal under ["section 8A or Application made to Tribunal under section 8"] shall be inquired into as expeditiously as possible and every endeavour shall be made to conclude such inquiry within a period of six months from the date of the service, on the person concerned, of a copy of such reference or application. 1 Subs. and ins. by Act 24 of 1988, s. 7. 2 Subs. by s. 8, *ibid.*

14. Appeal—The Central Government, or any person, named in a reference or an application under section 8, or any applicant under sub-section (2) of that section ["or any person named in a reference under section 8"] may, if or he is not satisfied with any order made by a Tribunal under section 12, prefer an appeal to the Appellate Tribunal against such order.

15. Appellate Tribunal—(1) The Central Government may, by notification, establish for each State in which this Act is in force an

Appellate Tribunal to be known as the Illegal Migrants (Determination) Appellate Tribunal for deciding appeals preferred under section 14 against orders made by Tribunals in the State and specify the principal place of sitting of such Appellate Tribunal. (2) No person shall be appointed as a member of an Appellate Tribunal unless he is or has been a Judge of a High Court. (3) An Appellate Tribunal shall consist of as many members, not being less than two and more than six, as the Central Government may think fit. (4) The Central Government shall appoint one of the members of an Appellate Tribunal to be the President thereof. (5) An Appellate Tribunal shall sit in its principal place of sitting or any such other place or places as the President thereof may, from time to time, appoint. (6) The powers and functions of an Appellate Tribunal may be exercised and discharged by benches constituted by the President thereof from amongst the members thereof ["which may either be single member benches or benches consisting of not less than two members"]. (7) The Central Government shall make available to every Appellate Tribunal such staff as may be necessary for the discharge of its functions under this Act. (8) Every memorandum of appeal to an Appellate Tribunal shall be made in such form and in such manner as may be prescribed, and, in the case of an appeal preferred by an applicant under sub-section (2) of section 8, shall also be accompanied by such fee, not being less than twenty-five and more than one hundred rupees, as may be prescribed. (9) Every appeal shall be preferred within thirty days from the date on which the order sought to be appealed against was communicated to the appellant: Provided that the Appellate Tribunal may, if it is satisfied that the appellant was prevented by sufficient cause from preferring the appeal within the said period, admit an appeal after the expiry of the aforesaid period of thirty days. 2*["(10) Every Appellate Tribunal shall have the same powers as are vested in an appellate court under the Code of Civil Procedure, 1908, while hearing an appeal."].

16. Order of the Appellate Tribunal—(1) The Appellate Tribunal may, after giving the parties to the appeal a reasonable opportunity of being heard, pass such orders thereon as it may think fit, confirming, modifying or annulling the order appealed against or may remand the case to the Tribunal which had passed such order with such directions to that Tribunal as the Appellate Tribunal may think fit, for fresh determination after taking additional evidence, if necessary. (2) Where an appeal had been heard by the Appellate Tribunal and the members thereof differ in their opinion on any point, the decision on such point shall, where there is a majority, be according to the opinion of such majority, and where there is no majority and the members are equally divided in their opinion, they shall draw up a statement of the facts of the case and the point or points on which they differ in their opinion and make a reference of the point or points or of the appeal, as the case may be, to the President of such Tribunal, and on receipt of such reference, the President of the Tribunal shall arrange for the hearing of such point or points, or the appeal, by one or more of the members of the Appellate Tribunal, and such point or points, or the appeal, as the case may be, shall be decided according to the opinion of the majority of the members of the Appellate Tribunal, who have heard the appeal, including those who had first heard it. 1*["(3) The Appellate Tribunal shall send a copy of every order passed by it under sub-section (1) to the parties to the appeal, to the Tribunal concerned and to the prescribed authority or authorities."]. (4) Every order passed under sub-section (1), other than an order remanding the case, shall be final and no order passed under that sub-section shall be called in question in any court.

2*["**17. Power of Superintendence by Appellate Tribunals**—(1) Every Appellate Tribunal shall have superintendence over all the Tribunals in the State. (2) Without prejudice to the generality of the foregoing provisions, the Appellate Tribunal may (a) call for returns from any Tribunal; (b) make general rules and specify forms for regulating the practice and proceedings of Tribunals; and (c) specify the forms in which books, entries and accounts shall be kept by the officers of Tribunals."]

CHAPTER III
PROVISIONS APPLICABLE TO ALL TRIBUNALS

18. Procedure—Subject to the provisions of this Act and the rules made thereunder, every Tribunal and every Appellate Tribunal shall have the power to regulate its own procedure in all matters arising out of the exercise of its powers or for the discharge of its functions.

19. Proceeding before Every Tribunal to be Judicial Proceeding for Certain Purposes—Every proceeding before a Tribunal or the Appellate Tribunal shall be deemed to be a judicial proceeding within the meaning of sections 193 and 228, and for the purposes of section 196 of the Indian Penal Code; (45 of 1860.) and every such Tribunal or Appellate Tribunal, as the case may be, shall be deemed to be a civil court for the purposes of section 195 and Chapter XXVI of the Code of Criminal Procedure, 1973. (2 of 1974.)

CHAPTER IV
ENFORCEMENT OF THE ORDERS MADE BY THE TRIBUNALS

20. Expulsion of Illegal Migrant—1*[(1)] Where a person has been determined by a Tribunal, or, as the case may be, by the Appellate Tribunal, to be an illegal migrant, the Central Government shall, by order served on such person, direct such person to remove himself from India within such time and by such route as may be specified in the order and may give such further directions in regard to his removal from India as it may consider necessary or expedient. 1*["(2) Any police officer not below the rank of a Superintendent of Police shall have such powers as may be necessary, including the power to obtain a bond from any person for the due compliance of an order under sub-section (1) and to arrest such person in the event of his failure to furnish such bond to the satisfaction of such police officer."].

CHAPTER V
MISCELLANEOUS

21. Delegation of Powers—The Central Government may, by notification, direct that the powers and duties conferred or imposed on it by this Act, other than the powers conferred by section 28, and the powers conferred by this section, may, subject to such conditions as may be specified in the notification, be exercised or discharged also by (a) any officer subordinate to the Central Government; (b) any State Government or any officer subordinate to that Government. 2*["21A. Power to bind certain persons against whom complaint is made under the Act. Notwithstanding anything contained in any other law for the time being in force, it shall be lawful for a police, if he is satisfied that the circumstances so require and for reasons to be recorded in writing, to direct any person against whom a reference or an application has been made under this Act to enter into a bond with or without sureties for making himself available for the inquiry and observance of such restrictions or conditions as may be specified by such police officer: Provided that if such person fails to enter into such bond he may be arrested and detained in such manner as may be prescribed."]

22. Power to Give Effect to the Orders, etc.—Any authority empowered by or in pursuance of the provisions of this Act to exercise any power, may, in addition to any other action expressly provided for in this Act, take, or cause to be taken, such steps, and use, or cause to be used, such force, as may in its opinion be reasonably necessary for the effective exercise of such power.

23. Bar of Jurisdiction of Civil Courts—Where a Tribunal or Appellate Tribunal has been established for any area for the purpose of determining whether a person is or is not an illegal migrant, no civil court shall have jurisdiction to entertain any question relating to that matter in that area and no injunction or any other order in respect of any action taken by, or before, the Tribunal or Appellate Tribunal in respect of that matter shall be granted or made by any civil court.

24. Transitory Provision—Where in any suit or other legal proceeding pending, whether in a civil court or in any Tribunal established under any other law for the time being in force, immediately before the commencement of this Act, a question arises as to whether a person is or is not an illegal migrant, such court or Tribunal shall, without deciding such question, make an order transferring such suit or other legal proceeding to the Tribunal under this Act within the territorial limits of whose jurisdiction such court or other Tribunal is situated and on such transfer such question shall be dealt with by such Tribunal in accordance with the provisions of this Act.

25. Penalties—Any person who, (a) contravenes or attempts to contravene, or abets the contravention of, any order made under section 20; or (b) fails to comply with any direction given by any such order; or (c) harbours any person who has contravened any order made under section 20 or has failed to comply with any direction given by any such order, 1*["shall be punishable with imprisonment for a term which shall not be less than one year but which may extend to three years and with fine which shall not be less than two thousand rupees: Provided that the court may, for adequate and special reasons to be mentioned in the judgment, impose a sentence of imprisonment for a term of less than one year or a fine of less than two thousand rupees."].

26. Protection of Action Taken in Good Faith—No suit, prosecution or other legal proceeding shall be against any person for anything which is in good faith done or intended to be done under this Act.

27. Power to Remove Difficulties—(1) If any difficulty arises in giving effect to the provisions of this Act, the Central Government may, by order to be published in the Official Gazette, make such provisions, not inconsistent with the provisions of this Act, as appear to it to be necessary or expedient for removing the difficulty: Provided that no such order shall be made after the expiry of a period of two years from the commencement of this Act. (2) Every order made under this section shall, as soon as may be after it is made, be laid before each House of Parliament.

28. Power to Make Rules—(1) The Central Government may, by notification, make rules to carry out the provisions of this Act. (2) In particular and without prejudice to the generality of the foregoing powers, such rules may provide for all or any of the following matters, namely: 1 Subs. by Act 24 of 1988, s. 15. 330 (a) the form and the manner in which an application may be made and the fee which shall accompany such application, as required by sub-section (3) of section 8; 1*["(aa) the form and the manner in which an application, and the form in which a declaration, may be made under sub-section (2) of section 8A;"] 1*["(b) the authority or authorities to be prescribed under section 11, 12 and 16;"]. (c) the form and the manner in which an appeal to the Appellate Tribunal may be preferred and the fee which shall accompany such appeal, as required by sub-section (8) of section 15; 1*["(ca) the manner of arrest and detention under the proviso to section 21A;"] (d) any other matter which is required to be, or may be, prescribed. (3) Every rule made by the Central Government under this Act shall be laid, as soon as may be after it is made, before each House of Parliament, while it is in session, for a total period of thirty days which may be comprised in one session or in two or more successive sessions, and if, before the expiry of the session immediately following the session or the successive sessions aforesaid, both Houses agree in making any modification in the rule or both Houses agree that the rule should not be made, the rule shall thereafter have effect only in such modified form or be of no effect, as the case may be; so, however, that any such modification or annulment shall be without prejudice to the validity of anything previously done under that rule.

29. Repeal and Saving—(1) The Illegal Migrants (Determination by Tribunals) Ordinance, 1983, (8 of 1983.) is hereby repealed. (2) Notwithstanding such repeal, anything done or any action taken under the said Ordinance shall be deemed to have been done or taken under the corresponding provisions of this Act.

ENDNOTES

1. Ins. by Act 24 of 1988, s. 9.
2. Subs. by s. 10, *ibid.*
3. Subs. and Omitted by Act 24 of 1988, s. 11.
4. Subs. by s. 12, *ibid.*
5. Renumbered and ins. by Act 24 of 1988, s. 13.
6. Ins, by s. 14, *ibid.*
7. Ins. and Subs. by Act 24 of 1988, s. 16.

Terrorist Affected Areas (Special Courts) Act

[*This Act was enacted in 1984 for the speedy trial of certain offences in terrorist affected areas*]

1. Objective: An Act to provide for the speedy trial of certain offences in terrorist affected areas and for matters connected therewith. Be it enacted by Parliament in the Thirty-fifth Year of the Republic of India as follows:

2. Definitions: (1) In this Act, unless the context otherwise requires,

(a) "Code" means the Code of Criminal Procedure, 1973 (2 of 1974);

(b) "High Court", in relation to a Special Court, means the High Court within the territorial limits of whose jurisdiction such Special Court is proposed to be, or is, established;

(c) "Judicial zone" means a judicial zone constituted under sub-section (1) of section 3;

(d) "Notification" means a notification published in the Official Gazette;

(e) "Public Prosecutor" means a Public Prosecutor or an Additional Public Prosecutor or a Special Public Prosecutor appointed under section 9 and includes any person acting under the directions of the Public Prosecutor;

(f) "Scheduled offence" means an offence specified in the Schedule being an offence committed in a terrorist affected area;

(g) "Special Court" means a Special Court or an Additional Special Court established under section 4;

(h) "Terrorist" means a person who indulges in wanton killing of persons or in violence or in the disruption of services or means of communications essential to the community or in damaging property with a view to (i) putting the public or any section of the public in fear; or (ii) affecting adversely the harmony between different religious, racial, language or regional groups or castes or communities; or (iii) coercing or overawing the Government established by law; or (iv) endangering the sovereignty and integrity of India;

(i) "Terrorist affected area" means an area declared as a terrorist affected area under section 3;

(j) words and expressions used but not defined in this Act and defined in the Code shall have the meanings respectively assigned to them in the Code.

(2) Any reference in this Act to the Code or any provision thereof shall, in relation to an area in which the Code or such provision is not in force, be construed as a reference to the corresponding law or the relevant provision of the corresponding law, if any, in force in that area.

3. Declaration of Terrorist Affected Area: (1) If the Central Government is of the opinion that offences of the nature specified in the Schedule are being committed in any area by terrorists on such a scale and in such a manner that it is expedient for the purpose of coping with the activities of such terrorists to have recourse to the provisions of this Act, it may, by notification, (a) declare such area to be a terrorist affected area; and (b) constitute such area into a single judicial zone or into as many judicial zones as it may deem fit.

(2) A notification issued under sub-section (1) in respect of an area shall specify the period during which the area shall, for the purposes of this Act, be a terrorist affected area, and where the Central Government is of the opinion that terrorists had been committing in that area, from a date earlier than the date of issue of the notification, offences of the nature specified in the Schedule on such a scale and in such a manner that it is expedient to commence the period specified in the notification from such earlier date, the period specified in the notification may commence from that date: Provided that—(a) no period commencing from a date earlier than six months from the date of publication of the notification shall be specified therein; and (b) so much of the period specified in such notification as is subsequent to the date of publication of the notification shall not, in the first instance, exceed six months, but the Central Government may, by notification, extend such period from time to time by any period not exceeding six months at any one time, if the Central Government, having regard to the activities of terrorists in such area, is of the opinion that it is expedient so to do.

Explanation: For the avoidance of doubts, it is hereby declared that the period specified in a notification issued under this section may commence from a date earlier than the date of commencement of this Act.

4. Establishment of Special Courts: (1) For the purpose of Providing for speedy trial of scheduled offences committed in a judicial zone, the Central Government may establish, by notification, a Special Court in relation to such judicial zone (a) within such judicial zone; or (b) if the Central Government having regard to the exigencies of the situation in such judicial zone considers it expedient so to do, at any place outside such judicial zone but within the State in which such judicial zone is situated.

(2) Notwithstanding anything contained in sub-section (1), if, having regard to the exigencies of the situation prevailing in a State, the State Government is of the opinion that it is expedient to establish in relation to a judicial zone, or in relation to two or more judicial zones, in the State, an Additional Special Court outside the State, for the trial of such scheduled offences committed in the judicial zone or judicial zones, the trial whereof within the State (a) is not likely to be fair or impartial or completed with utmost dispatch; or (b) is not likely to be feasible without occasioning a breach of peace or grave risk to the safety of the accused, the witnesses, the Public Prosecutor and the Judge or any of them; or (c) is not otherwise in the interests of justice, the State Government may request the Central Government to establish in relation to such judicial zone or judicial zones an Additional Special Court outside the State and thereupon the Central Government may, after taking into account the information furnished by the State Government and making such inquiry, if any, as it may deem fit, establish, by notification, such Additional Special Court at such place outside the State as may be specified in the notification.

5. Composition and Apointment of Judges of Special Courts: (1) A Special Court shall be presided over by a judge to be appointed by the Central Government with the concurrence of the Chief Justice of the High Court.

(2) The Central Government may also appoint, with the concurrence of the Chief Justice of the High Court, Additional judges to exercise jurisdiction in a Special Court.

(3) A person shall not be qualified for appointment as a Judge or an Additional judge of a Special Court unless he is immediately before such appointment a Sessions Judge or an Additional Sessions Judge in any State.

(4) For the removal of doubts, it is hereby provided that the attainment by a person, appointed as a Judge or an Additional Judge of a Special Court, of age of superannuation under the rules applicable to him in the Service to which he belongs, shall not affect his continuance as such Judge or Additional Judge.

(5) Where any Additional Judge or Additional Judges is, or are, appointed in a Special Court, the Judge of the Special Court may, from time to time, by general or special order, in writing, provide for the distribution of business of the Special Court among himself and the Additional Judge or Additional Judges and also for the disposal of urgent business in the event of his absence or the absence of any Additional Judge.

6. Place of Sitting: A Special Court may, if it considers it expedient or desirable so to do, sit for any of its proceedings at any place, other than the ordinary place of its sitting, in the State in which it is established:

Provided that if the Public Prosecutor certifies to the Special Court that it is in his opinion necessary for the protection of the accused or any witness or otherwise expedient in the interests of justice that the whole or any part of the trial should be held at some place other than the ordinary place of its sitting, the Special Court may, after hearing the accused, make an order to that effect unless, for reasons to be recorded in writing, the Special Court thinks fit to make any other order.

7. Jurisdiction of Special Court: (1) Notwithstanding anything contained in the Code or in any other law, a scheduled offence committed in a judicial zone in a State at any time during the period during which such judicial zone is, or is part of, a terrorist affected area shall be triable, whether during or after the expiry of such period, only by the Special Court established for such judicial zone in the State: Provided that where the period specified under Sub-section (2) of Section 3 as the period during which an area declared by notification under sub-section (1) of that section to be a terrorist affected area commences from a date earlier than the date on which such notification is issued, then (a) nothing in the foregoing provisions of this sub-section shall apply to a scheduled offence committed in such area in which the whole of the evidence for the prosecution has been taken before the date of issue of such notification; and (b) all other cases involving scheduled offences committed in such area and pending before any court immediately before the date of issue of such notification shall stand transferred to the Special Court having jurisdiction under this section and the Special Court to which such proceedings stand transferred shall proceed with such cases from the stage at which they were pending at that time.

(2) Notwithstanding anything contained in sub-section (1), if in respect of a case involving a scheduled offence committed in any judicial zone in a State, the Central Government, having regard to the provisions of Sub-section (2) of Section 4 and the facts and circumstances of the case and all other relevant factors, is of the opinion that it is expedient that such offence should be tried by the Additional Special Court established in relation to such judicial zone outside the State, the Central Government may make a declaration to that effect: Provided that no such declaration shall be made unless the State Government has forwarded to the Central Government a report in writing containing a request for making of such declaration.

Explanation: Where an Additional Special Court is established in relation to two or more judicial zones, such Additional Special Court shall be deemed, for the purposes of this sub-section, to have been established in relation to each of such judicial zones.

(3) A declaration made under Sub-section (2) shall not be called in question in any court.

(4) Where any declaration is made in respect of any offence committed in a judicial zone in a State, any prosecution in respect of such offence shall be instituted only in the Additional Special Court established in relation to such judicial zone outside the State, and if any prosecution in respect of such offence is pending immediately before such declaration in any other court, the same shall stand transferred to such Additional Special Court and such Additional Special Court shall proceed with such case from the stage at which it was pending at that time.

8. Powers of Special Courts with Respect to Other Offences: (1) When trying any scheduled offence, a Special Court may also try any offence other than the scheduled offence with which the accused may, under the Code, be charged at the same trial if the offence is connected with the scheduled offence.

(2) If, in the course of any trial under this Act, it is found that the accused person has committed any offence, the Special Court may, whether such offence is or is not a scheduled offence, convict such person of such offence and pass any sentence authorised by law for the punishment thereof.

9. Public Prosecutors: (1) For every Special Court, the Central Government shall appoint a person to be the Public Prosecutor and may appoint one or more persons to be the Additional Public Prosecutor or Additional Public Prosecutors: Provided that the Central Government may also appoint for any case or class of cases a Special Public Prosecutor.

(2) A person shall be eligible to be appointed as a Public Prosecutor or an Additional Public Prosecutor or a Special Public Prosecutor under this section only if he has been in practice as an Advocate for not less than seven years or has held any post, for a period of not less than seven years, under the Union or a State, requiring special knowledge of law.

(3) Every person appointed as a Public Prosecutor or an Additional Public Prosecutor or a Special Public Prosecutor under this section shall be deemed to be a Public Prosecutor within the meaning of clause (u) of Section 2 of the Code, and the provisions of the Code shall have effect accordingly.

10. Procedure and Powers of Special Courts: (1) A Special Court may take cognizance of any scheduled offence, without the accused being committed to it for trial, upon receiving a complaint of facts, which constitute such offence, or upon a police report of such facts.

(2) Where a scheduled offence is punishable with imprisonment for a term not exceeding three years or with fine or with both, a Special Court may, notwithstanding anything contained in sub-section (1) of Section 260 or Section 262 of the Code, try the offence in a summary way in accordance with the procedure prescribed in the Code and the provisions of sections 263 to 265 of the Code, shall, so far as may be, apply to such

trial: Provided that when, in the course of a summary trial under this sub-section, it appears to the Special Court that the nature of the case is such that it is undesirable to try it in a summary way, the Special Court shall recall any witnesses who may have been examined and proceed to re-hear the case in the manner provided by the provisions of the Code for the trial of such offence and the said provisions shall apply to and in relation to a Special Court as they apply to and in relation to a Magistrate: Provided further that in the case of any conviction in a summary trial under this section, it shall be lawful for a Special Court to pass a sentence of imprisonment for a term not exceeding two years.

(3) A Special Court may, with a view to obtaining the evidence of any person supposed to have been directly or indirectly concerned in, or privy to, an offence, tender a pardon to such person on condition of his making a full and true disclosure of the whole circumstances within his knowledge relative to the offence and to every other person concerned whether as principal or abettor in the commission thereof, and any pardon so tendered shall, for the purposes of Section 308 of the Code, be deemed to have been tendered under Section 307 thereof.

(4) Subject to the other provisions of this Act, a Special Court shall, for the purpose of trial of any offence, have all the powers of a Court of Session and shall try such offence as if it were a Court of Session so far as may be in accordance with the procedure prescribed in the Code for the trial before a Court of Session.

(5) Subject to the other provisions of this Act, every case before an Additional Special Court shall be dealt with as if such case had been transferred under section 406 of the Code to such Additional Special Court.

11. Power of Supreme Court to Transfer Case: Whenever it is made to appear to the Supreme Court that an order under this section is expedient for the ends of justice, it may direct that any particular case be transferred from one Special Court to another Special Court.

12. Protection of Witnesses: (1) Notwithstanding anything contained in the Code, all proceedings before a Special Court shall be conducted in camera: Provided that where the Public Prosecutor so applies, any proceedings or part thereof may be held in open court.

(2) A Special Court may, on an application made by a witness in any proceedings before it or by the Public Prosecutor in relation to such witness or on its own motion, take such measures as it deems fit for keeping the identity and address of the witness secret.

(3) In particular and without prejudice to the generality of the provisions of Sub-section (2), the measures which a Special Court may take under that sub-section may include (a) the holding of the proceeding at a protected place; (b) the avoiding of the mention of the names and

addresses of the witnesses in its orders or judgments or in any records of the case accessible to public; (c) the issuing of any directions for securing that the identity and addresses of the witnesses are not disclosed.

(4) Any person who contravenes any direction issued under sub-section (2) shall be punishable with imprisonment for a term, which may extend to one year and with fine, which may extend to one thousand rupees.

13. Power to Transfer Cases to Regular Courts: Where after taking cognizance of any offence, a Special Court is of opinion that the offence is not a scheduled offence, it shall, notwithstanding that it has no jurisdiction to try such offence, transfer the case for trial of such offence to any court having jurisdiction under the Code and the court to which the case is transferred may proceed with the trial of the offence as if it has taken cognizance of the offence.

14. Appeal: (1) Notwithstanding anything contained in the Code, an appeal shall lie as a matter of right from any judgment, sentence or order, not being interlocutory order, of a Special Court to the Supreme Court both on facts and on law.

(2) Except as aforesaid, no appeal or revision shall lie to any court from any judgment, sentence or order of a Special Court.

(3) Every appeal under this section shall be preferred within a period of thirty days from the date of the judgment, sentence or order appealed from: Provided that the Supreme Court may entertain an appeal after the expiry of the said period of thirty days if it is satisfied that the appellant had sufficient cause for not preferring the appeal within the period of thirty days.

15. Modified Application of Certain Provisions of the Code: (1) Notwithstanding anything contained in the Code or any other law, every scheduled offence shall be deemed to be a cognizable offence within the meaning of clause (c) of Section 2 of the Code and "cognizable case" as defined in that clause shall be construed accordingly.

(2) Section 167 of the Code shall apply in relation to a case involving a scheduled offence subject to the modifications that—(a) the reference in sub-section (1) thereof to "Judicial Magistrate" shall be construed as a reference to "Judicial Magistrate or Executive Magistrate"; (b) the references in sub-section (2) thereof to "fifteen days", "ninety days" and sixty days", wherever they occur, shall be construed as references to "thirty days", "one year" and "one year", respectively; and (c) Sub-section (2A) thereof shall be deemed to have been omitted.

(3) Sections 366 to 371 and section 392 of the Code shall apply in relation to a case involving a scheduled offence subject to the modifications that the references to "Court of Session" and "High Court", wherever

occurring therein, shall be construed as references to "Special Court" and "Supreme Court", respectively.

(4) Nothing in section 438 of the Code shall apply in relation to any case involving the arrest of any person on an accusation of having committed a scheduled offence in a terrorist affected area.

(5) Notwithstanding anything contained in the Code, no person accused of a scheduled offence shall, if in custody, be released on bail or on his own bond unless (a) the Public Prosecutor has been given an opportunity to oppose the application for such release, and (b) where the Public Prosecutor opposes the application, the court is satisfied that there are reasonable grounds for believing that he is not guilty of such offence and that he is not likely to commit any offence while on bail.

(6) The limitations on granting of bail specified in Sub-section (5) are in addition to the limitations under the Code or any other law for the time being in force on granting of bail. [Ins. by Act 45 of 1985, S.2.]

***15A. Abolition of Certain Special Courts:** Where the area comprising a judicial zone has ceased to be a terrorist affected area and no cases are pending before a Special Court or an Additional Special Court established in relation to such judicial zone, the Central Government may, by notification in the Official Gazette, abolish such Special Court or Additional Special Court.]

16. Overriding Effect of Act: (1) The provisions of this Act shall have effect notwithstanding anything contained in the Code or any other law, but save as expressly provided in this Act, the provisions of the Code shall, in so far as they are not inconsistent with the provisions of this Act, apply to the proceedings before a Special Court; and for the purpose of the said provisions of the Code, the Special Court shall be deemed to be a Court of Session.

(2) In particular and without prejudice to the generality of the provisions contained in Sub-section (1), the provisions of Sections 326 and 475 of the Code shall, as far as may be, apply to the Proceedings before a Special Court, and for this purpose any reference in those provisions to a Magistrate shall be construed as a reference to the Special Court.

17. Delegation: The Central Government may, by notification, delegate, subject to such conditions as may be specified, all or any of the powers exercisable by it under this Act [except the power under Sub-section (2) of Section 4 and the power under Sub-section (2) of Section 7] to the State Government.

18. Power to Make Rules: The Supreme Court may, by notification, make such rules, if any, as it may deem necessary for carrying out the purposes of this Act.

19. Saving: (1) Nothing in this Act shall affect the jurisdiction exercisable by, or the procedure applicable to, any court or other authority under any law relating to the naval, military or air forces or any other armed forces of the Union.

(2) For the removal of doubts, it is hereby declared that for the purposes of any such law as is referred to in Sub-section (1), a Special Court shall be deemed to be a Court of ordinary criminal justice.

Assam Accord
(Memorandum of Settlement)

[*Concluding six years of agitation in Assam over the vexed issue of illegal migration, the Government of India signed a Memorandum of Settlement with the leaders of the AASU and the AAGSP in the wee hours of India's thirty-eighth Independence Day. Signed in the presence of (and at the personal initiative of) the then Prime Minister, Rajiv Gandhi, on 15 August 1985, debate continues about the success of the Accord and the fulfillment of the Accord provisions. Indeed, the Centre have convened a tripartite meeting with the AASU leaders on a number of occasions in order to discuss the Accord. The discussion continues 24 years after the Accord was signed Excerpts are below*

Government have all along been most anxious to find a satisfactory solution to the problem of foreigners in Assam. The All Assam Students Union (AASU) and the All Assam Gana Sangram Parishad (AAGSP) have also expressed their keenness to find such a solution.

The AASU through their Memorandum dated 2nd February 1980 presented to the late Prime Minister Smt. Indira Gandhi, conveyed their profound sense of apprehensions regarding the continuing influx of foreign nationals into Assam and the fear about adverse effects upon the political, social, culture and economic life of the State.

Being fully alive to the genuine apprehensions of the people of Assam, the then prime minister initiated the dialogue with the AASU/AAGSP. Subsequently, talks were held at the prime minister's and home minister's level during the period 1980-83. Several rounds of informal talks were held during 1984. Formal discussions were resumed in March 1985.

Keeping all aspects of the problem including constitutional and legal provisions, international agreements, national commitments and humanitarian considerations, it has been decided to proceed as follows:

Foreigners Issue

5.1 For purposes of detection and deletion of foreigners, 1.1.1966 shall be the base data and year.

5.2 All persons who came to Assam prior to 1.1.1966, including those amongst them whose names appeared on the electoral rolls used in 1967 elections shall be regularised.

5.3 Foreigners who came to Assam after 1.1.1966 (inclusive) and up to 24th March 1971 shall be detected in accordance with the provisions of the Foreigners Act, 1946 and the Foreigners (Tribunals) Order 1964.

5.4 Names of foreigners so detected will be deleted from the electoral rolls in force. Such persons will be required to register themselves before the Registration Officers of the respective districts in accordance with the provisions of the Registration of Foreigners Act, 1939 and the Registration of Foreigners Rules, 1939.

5.5 For this purpose, Government of India will undertake suitable strengthening of the government machinery.

5.6 On the expiry of a period of ten years following the date of detection, the names of all such persons, which have been deleted from the electoral rolls, shall be restored.

5.7 All persons who were expelled earlier, but have since re-entered illegally into Assam shall be expelled.

5.8 Foreigners who came to Assam on or after March 25, 1971 shall continue to be detected, deleted and practical steps shall be taken to expel such foreigners.

5.9 The Government will give due consideration to certain difficulties expressed by the AASU/AAGSP regarding the implementation of the Illegal Migrants (Determination by Tribunals) Act, 1983.

Safeguards and Economic Development

Constitutional, legislative and administrative safeguards, as may be appropriate shall be provided to protect, preserve and promote the culture, social, linguistic identity and heritage of the Assamese people.

The Government take this opportunity to renew their commitment for the speedy all round economic development of Assam, so as to improve the standard of living of the people. Special emphasis will be placed on education and science and technology through establishment of national institutions.

Other Issues

8.1 The Government will arrange for the issue of citizenship certificates in future only by the authorities of the Central Government.

8.2 Specific complaints that may be made by the AASU/AAGSP about irregular issuance of Indian Citizenship Certificates (ICC) will be looked into.

The international border shall be made secure against future infiltration by erection of physical barriers like walls, barbed wire fencing and other obstacles at appropriate places. Patrolling by security forces on land and riverine routes all along the international border shall be adequately intensified. In order to further strengthen the security arrangements, to prevent effectively future infiltration, an adequate number of check posts shall be set up.

9.2 Besides the arrangements mentioned above and keeping in view security considerations, a road all along the international border shall be constructed as to facilitate patrolling by security forces. Land between border and the road would be kept free of human habitation, wherever possible. Riverine patrolling along the international border would be intensified. All effective measures would be adopted to prevent infiltrators crossing or attempting to cross the international border.

It will be ensured that relevant laws for prevention of encroachment of government lands in tribal belts and blocks are strictly enforced and unauthorized encroachers evicted as laid down under such laws.

It will be ensured that the relevant law restricting acquisition of immovable property by foreigners in Assam is strictly enforced. It will be ensured that Birth and Death Registers are duly maintained.

Restoration of Normalcy

The All Assam Student's Union (AASU) and the all Assam Gana Sangram Parishad (AAGSP) call off the agitation assure full co-operation and dedicate themselves towards the development of the country.

The Central and the State Government have agreed to:

- Review with sympathy and withdraw cases of disciplinary action taken against employees in the context of the agitation and to ensure that there is no victimization;
- Frame a scheme for ex-gratia payment to next of kin of those who were killed in the course of the agitation;
- Give sympathetic consideration to proposal for relaxation of upper age limit for employment in public services in Assam, having regard to exceptional situation that prevailed in holding of academic and competitive examinations, etc., in the context of agitation in Assam;
- Undertake review of detention cases, if any, as well as cases against persons charged with criminal offences in connection with the agitation, except those charged with commission of heinous offences;
- Consider withdrawal of the prohibitory orders/notifications in force, if any.

The Ministry of Home Affairs will be the nodal Ministry for the implementation of the above.

Signed/-
(P.K. Mahanta)
President
All Assam Student's Union

Signed/-
(R.D. Pradhan)
Home Secretary
Govt. of India
Signed/-
(B.K. Phukan)
General Secretary
All Assam Students Union

Signed/-
(Smt. P.P. Trivedi)
Chief Secretary
Govt. of Assam

Signed/-
(Biraj Sharma)
Convenor
All Assam Gana Sangram Parishad

In the presence of

Signed/-
(Rajiv Gandhi)
Prime Minister of India

Date: 15 August 1985
Place: New Delhi

Election Commission will be requested to ensure preparation of fair electoral rolls.

Time for submission of claims and objections will be extended by 30 days, subject to this being consistent with the Election rules.

The Election Commission will be requested to send Central Observers.

Signed/-
Home Secretary

Oil refinery will be established in Assam.

Central Government will render full assistance to the State Government in their efforts to re-open:

Ashok Paper Mill
Jute Mills

I.I.T. will be set-up in Assam.

Mizoram Accord
(Memorandum of Settlement)

[A Memorandum of Settlement was signed between Laldenga of the Mizo National Front and the Government of India on 30 June 1986. The settlement, which provided statehood to Mizoram, among a variety of other concessions and benefits, came after protracted and virulent insurgency in the Lushai Hills. The Accord has also been hailed as one of the most successful Accords that has been anvilled by the Government of India]

Preamble

Government of India have all along been making earnest effort to bring about an end to the disturbed condition in Mizoram and to restore peace and harmony.

Toward this end, initiative was taken by the late Prime Minister Smt. Indira Gandhi on the acceptance by Shri Laldenga on behalf of the Mizo National Front (MNF) of the two conditions, namely, cessation of violence by MNF and to hold talks within the framework of the Constitution. A series of discussions were held with Shri Laldenga. Settlement on various issues reached during the course of talks is incorporated in the following paragraphs.

Restoration of Normalcy

With a view to restoring peace and normalcy in Mizoram, the MNF Party, in their part undertake within the agreed time-frame, to bring out all underground personnel of the MNF with their arms, ammunitions, and equipments, to ensure their return to civil life, to abjure violence and generally to help in the process of restoration of normalcy. The modalities of bringing out all underground personnel and the deposit of arms, ammunitions and equipments will be as worked out. The implementation of the foregoing will be under the supervision of the Central Government.

The MNF party will take immediate steps to amend its articles of Association so as to make them conform to the provision of Law.

The Central Government will take steps for the settlement and rehabilitation of underground after considering the scheme proposed in this regard by the Government of Mizoram.

The MNF will not undertake to extend any support to the Tripura National Volunteer (TNV), Peoples' Liberation Army of Manipur (PLA) and any other such group by way of training, supply of arms of providing protection or in any other matters.

Legal Administrative and Other Steps

With a view to satisfying the desires and aspirations of all sections of the people of Mizoram, the Government will initiate measures to confer Statehood on the Union Territory of Mizoram subject to the other stipulation contained in this Memorandum of Settlement.

To give effect to the above, the necessary legislative and administrative measures will be undertaken, including those for the enactment of Bills for the amendment of the Constitution and other laws for the conferment of Statehood as aforesaid, to come into effect on a date to be notified by the Central Government.

The amendment aforesaid shall provide, among other things, for the following:

The territory of Mizoram shall consist of the territory specified in Section 6 of the North Eastern Areas (Reorganization) Act, 1971.

Notwithstanding anything contained in the Constitution, no act of Parliament in respect of (a) Religion or Social practices of the Mizos, (b) Mizo customary Law or procedure, (c) Administration of Civil and Criminal Justice involving decisions according to Mizo customary Law, (d) Ownership and transfer of land, shall apply to the State of Mizoram unless the Legislative Assembly of Mizoram by a resolution so decides.

Provided that nothing in this Clause shall apply to any Central Act in force in Mizoram immediately before the appointed day.

Article 170 Clause (1) shall, in relation to Legislative Assembly of Mizoram, have effect as if for the word *sixty* the word *forty* has been substituted.

Soon after the Bill of Conferment of Statehood becomes law, and when the President is satisfied that normalcy has returned and that conditions are conducive to the holding of free and fair elections, elections to the Legislative Assembly will be initiated.

(a) The Centre will transfer resource to the new Government keeping in view the change in Status from a Union Territory to a State and will include resources to cover the revenue gap for the year.

(b) Central assistance for Plan will be fixed taking note of any residuary gap in resources so as to sustain the approved plan outlay and the pattern of assistance will be as in the case of Special category State.

Border trade in local produced or grown agriculture commodities could be allowed under a scheme to be formulated by the Central Government, subject to international arrangement with neighbouring Countries.

The Innerline Regulation, as now in force in Mizoram, will not be amended or repealed without consulting the State Government.

Other Matters

The rights and privileges of the minorities in Mizoram as envisaged in the constitution shall continue to be preserved and protected and their social and economic advancement shall be ensured.

Steps will be taken by the Government of Mizoram at the earliest to review and codify the existing customs, practices, law or other usages relating to the matters specified in Clauses (a) to (b) of para 4.3 (II) of the memorandum, keeping in view that an individual Mizo may prefer to be governed by Acts of Parliament dealing with such matters and which are of general application.

The question of Unification of Mizo inhabited areas of other States to form one administrative unit was raised by the MNF delegation. It was pointed out to them, on behalf of the Government of India, that Article 3 of the Constitution of India describes the procedure in this regard but that the Government cannot make any commitment in this respect.

It was also pointed out on behalf of the Government that as soon as Mizoram becomes a State:

The Provisions of Part XVII of the Provision of the Constitution will apply and the State will be liberty to adopt any one or more language to be used for all or any of the official purposes of the State.

It is open to the State to move the establishment of the separate University in the State in accordance with the prescribed procedure.

In the light of the Prime Minister's Statement at the Joint Conference of the Chief Justices, Chief Minister and Law Ministers held at New Delhi on 31 August, 1985 Mizoram will be entitled to have a High Court of its own if it so wishes.

(a) It was noted that there is already a scheme in force for payment of ex-gratia amount to heirs/dependants of persons who were killed during disturbances in 1966 and thereafter in the Union Territory of Mizoram. Arrangement will be made to expeditiously disburse payment to those eligible persons who have already applied but who had not been made such payment so far.

It was noted that consequence on verification done by a joint team of officers, the Government of India had already made arrangement for payment of compensation in respect of damage to crop: building destroyed/ damaged during the action in Mizoram, and rented charges of building and land occupied by security force. There may, however, be some claim which were referred and verified by the above team but is not yet settled expeditiously. Arrangement will also be made for payment of pending claim of rented charges or land/building occupied by the security forces.

Sd/-
LALDENGA
On behalf of
Mizo National Front

Sd/-
R.D. PRADHAN
Home Secretary
Government of India

Sd/-
LALKHAMA
Chief Secretary
Government of Mizoram

Date: 30 June 1986
Place: New Delhi

Terrorist and Disruptive Activities (Prevention) Act[1]

[*Amended by Act 43 of 1993*]
[*Enacted on 3 September 1987, and commonly known as TADA, the act was the first and only legislative effort by the Government of India to define and counter terrorist activities. It was formulated in the backdrop of increasing terrorist violence in Punjab, which found pronouncement in other parts of the country too, including New Delhi. The Act, which was criticised on various counts by human rights organisations and political parties, was permitted to lapse in May 1995 though cases initiated while it was in force continue to hold legal validity*]

An Act to make special provisions for the prevention of, and for coping with, terrorist and disruptive activities and for matters connected therewith or incidental thereto.

Be it enacted by Parliament in the Thirty-eighth year of the Republic of India as follows:

CHAPTER I
PRELIMINARY

1. *Short Title, Extent, Application, Commencement, Duration and Savings*: (1) This Act may be called the Terrorist and Disruptive Activities (Prevention) Act, 1987.

(2) It extends to the whole of India, and it applies also,

(a) to citizens of India outside India;
(b) to persons in the service of the Government, wherever they may be; and
(c) to persons on ships and aircraft registered in India, wherever they may be.

(3) Sections 5, 15, 21 and 22 shall come into force at once and the remaining provisions of this Act shall be deemed to have come into force on the 24th day of May 1987.

(4) It shall remain in force for a period of[2] [eight years] from the 24th day of May 1987, but its expiry under the operation of this sub-section shall not affect,

(a) the previous operation of, or anything duly done or suffered under this Act or any rule made thereunder or any order made under any such rule, or

(b) any right, privilege, obligation or liability acquired accrued or incurred under this Act or any rule made thereunder or any order made under any such rule, or

(c) any penalty, forfeiture or punishment incurred in respect of any offence under this Act or any contravention of any rule made under this Act or of any order made under any such rule, or

(d) any investigation, legal proceeding or remedy in respect of any such right, privilege, obligation, liability, penalty, forfeiture or punishment as aforesaid.

and any such investigation, legal proceeding or remedy may be instituted, continued or enforced and any such penalty, forfeiture or punishment may be imposed as if this Act had not expired.

2. Definitions: (1) In this Act, unless the context otherwise requires,

(a) "abet", with its grammatical variations and cognate expressions, includes,—

(i) the communication or association with any person or class of persons who is engaged in assisting in any manner terrorists or disruptionists;

(ii) the passing on, or publication of, without any lawful authority, and information likely to assist the terrorists or disruptionists, and the passing on, or publication of, or distribution of, any document or matter obtained from terrorists or disruptionists;

(iii) the rendering of any assistance, whether financial or otherwise, the terrorists or disruptionists;

(b) "Code" means the Code of Criminal Procedure 1973 (2 of 1974);

(c) "Designated Court" means a Designated Court constituted under Section 9;

(d) "Disruptive activity" has the meaning assigned to it in Section 4, and the expression "disruptionists" shall be construed accordingly;

(e) "High Court" means the High Court of the State in which a judge or an additional judge of a Designated Court was working immediately before his appointment as such judge or additional judge;

(f) "notified area" means such area as the State Government may, by notification in the official Gazette, specify;

(g) "public prosecutor" means a Public Prosecutor or an Additional Public Prosecutor or a Special Public Prosecutor appointed under

Section 13, and includes any person acting under the directions of the Public Prosecutor;

(gg[3]) "property" means property and assets of any description, whether corporeal or incorporeal, movable or immovable, tangible or intangible and deeds and instruments evidencing title to, or interest in, such property or assets, derived or obtained from the terrorist Act and includes proceeds of terrorism;]

(h) "terrorist act" has the meaning assigned to it in sub-section (1) of Section 3, and the expression "terrorist" shall be construed accordingly;

(i) words and expressions used but not defined in this Act and defined in the Code shall have the meaning respectively assigned to them in the Code.

(2) Any reference in this Act to any enactment or any provision thereof shall, in relation to an area in which such enactment or such provision is not in force, be construed as a reference to the corresponding law or the relevant provision of the corresponding law, if any, in force in that area.

CHAPTER II
PUNISHMENTS FOR, AND MEASURES FOR COPING WITH, TERRORIST AND DISRUPTIVE ACTIVITIES

3. Punishment for Terrorist Acts: (1) Whoever with intent to overawe the Government as by law established or to strike terror in the people or any section of the people or to alienate any section of the people or to adversely affect the harmony amongst different sections of the people does any act or thing by using bombs, dynamite or other explosive substances or inflammable substances or lethal weapons or poisons or noxious gases or other chemicals or by any other substances (whether biological or otherwise) of a hazardous nature in such a manner as to cause, or as is likely to cause, death of, or injuries to, any person or persons or loss of, or damage to, or destruction of, property or disruption of any supplies or services essential to the life of the community, or detains any person and threatens to kill or injure such person in order to compel the Government or any other person to do or abstain from doing any act, commits a terrorist act.

(2) Whoever commits a terrorist act, shall,—

(i) if such act has resulted in the death of any person, be punishable with death or imprisonment for life and shall also be liable to fine;

(ii) in any other case, be punishable with imprisonment for a term which shall not be less than five years but which may extend to imprisonment for life and shall also be liable to fine.

(3) Whoever conspires or attempts to commit, or advocates, abets, advises or incites or knowingly facilitates the commission of, a terrorist act or any act preparatory to a terrorist act, shall be punishable with imprisonment for a term which shall not be less than five years but which may extend to imprisonment for life and shall also be liable to fine.

(4) Whoever harbours or conceals, or attempts to harbour or conceal, any terrorist shall be punishable with imprisonment for a term which shall not be less than five years but which may extend to imprisonment for life and shall also be liable to fine.

(5)[4] Any person who is a member of a terrorists gang or a terrorist organisation, which is involved in terrorist acts, shall be punishable with imprisonment for a term which shall not be less than five years but which may extend to imprisonment for life and shall also be liable to fine.

(6) Whoever holds any property derived or obtained from commission of any terrorist act or has been acquired through the terrorist funds shall be punishable with imprisonment for a term which shall not be less than five years but which may extend to imprisonment for life and shall also be liable to fine.]

4. Punishment for Disruptive Activities: (1) Whoever commits or conspires or attempts to commit or abets, advocates, advises, or knowingly facilitates the commission of, any disruptive activity or any act preparatory to a disruptive activity shall be punishable with imprisonment for a term which shall not be less than five years but which may extend to imprisonment for life and shall also be liable to fine.

(2) For the purposes of sub-section (1), "disruptive activity" means any action taken, whether by act or by speech or through any other media or in any other manner whatsoever,

(i) which questions, disrupts or is intended to disrupt, whether directly or indirectly, the sovereignty and territorial integrity of India; or

(ii) which is intended to bring about or supports any claim, whether directly or indirectly, for the cession of any part of India or the secession of any part of India from the Union.

Explanation: For the purposes of this sub-section,

(a) "cession" includes the admission of any claim of any foreign country to any part of India, and

(b) "secession" includes the assertion of any claim to determine whether a part of India will remain within the Union.

(3) Without prejudice to the generality of the provisions of sub-section (2), it is hereby declared that any action taken, whether by act or

by speech or through any other media or in any other manner whatsoever, which—

(a) advocates, advises, suggests or incites; or

(b) predicts, prophesies or pronounces or otherwise expresses, in such manner as to incite, advice, suggest or prompt,

the killing or the destruction of any person bound by oath under the constitution to uphold the sovereignty and integrity of India or any public servant shall be deemed to be a disruptive activity within the meaning of this section.

(4) Whoever harbours or conceals, or attempts to harbour or conceal, any disruptionists shall be punishable with imprisonment for a term which shall not be less than five years but which may be extend to imprisonment for life and shall also be liable to fine.

2. Habeas Corpus

In habeas corpus proceedings if the detention is legal at the time of the disposal of the petition the Court cannot order release of the person detained by issuing a writ of habeas corpus. Therefore, the legality or otherwise of the detention shall also be considered on the date of final disposal of the petition. Bacha Bora v. State of Assam, 1991 Cr LJ 2782 (Gau).

5. Possession of Certain Unauthorised Arms, etc. in Specified Areas: Where any person is in possession of any arms and ammunition specified in Columns 2 and 3 of Category I or Category III (a) of Schedule I to the Arms Rules, 1962, or bombs, dynamite or other explosive substances unauthorisedly in a notified area, he shall, notwithstanding anything contained in any other law for the time being in force, be punishable with imprisonment for a term which shall not be less than five years but which may extend to imprisonment for life and shall also be liable to fine.

6. Enhanced Penalties: (1) If any person with intend to aid any terrorist or disruptionist, contravenes any provision of, or any rule made under the Arms Act, 1959, the Explosives Act, 1884, the Explosives Substances Act, 1908 or the Inflammable Substances Act, 1952, he shall, notwithstanding anything contained in any of the aforesaid Acts or the rules made thereunder, be punishable with imprisonment for a term which shall not be less than five years but which may extend to imprisonment for life and shall also be liable to fine.

(2) For the purposes of this section, any person who attempts to contravene or abets, or attempts to abet, or does any act preparatory to the contravention of any provision of any law, rule or order, shall be deemed to have contravened that provision, and the provision of sub-section (1) shall, in relation to such person, have effect subject to the modification

that the reference to "imprisonment for life" shall be construed as a reference to "imprisonment for ten years".

7. Conferment of Powers: (1) Notwithstanding anything contained the Code or in any other provision of this Act, the Central Government may, if it considers it necessary or expedient so to do,

(a) for the prevention of, and for coping with, any offence under Section 3 or Section 4; or

(b) for any case or class or group of cases under Section 3 or Section 4;

in any State or part thereof, confer, by notification in the official Gazette, on any officer of the Central Government, powers exercisable by a police officer under the Code in such State or part thereof or, as the case may be, for such case or class or group of cases and in particular, the powers of arrest, investigation and prosecution of persons before any Court.

(2) All officers of police and all officers of Government are hereby required and empowered to assist the officer of the Central Government referred to in sub-section (1), in the execution of the provisions of this Act or any rule or order made thereunder.

(3) The provisions of the Code shall, so far as may be and subject to such modifications made in this Act, apply to the exercise of the powers by an officer under sub-section (1).

7-A.[5] **Powers of Investigating Officers:** If an officer investigating an offence committed under this Act has reason to believe that any property in relation to which an investigation is being conducted is a property derived or obtained from the commission of any terrorist act and includes proceeds of terrorism he shall, with the approval of the Superintendent of Police, make an order seizing such property and where it is not practicable to seize such property, he may make an order of attachment directing that such property shall not be transferred or otherwise dealt with except with the prior permission of the officer making such order, or of the Designated Court and a copy of such order shall be served on the persons concerned:

Provided that the investigating officer shall duly inform the Designated Court within forty-eight hours of the attachment of such property and the said Court shall either confirm or revoke the order of attachment so issued.

8. Forfeiture of Property of Certain Persons: (1) Where a person has been convicted to any offence punishable under this Act or any rule made thereunder, the Designated Court may, in addition to awarding any punishment, by order in writing, declare that any property, movable or immovable or both, belonging to the accused and specified in the order, shall stand forfeited to the Government free from all encumbrances.

(2) Where any person is accused of any offence under this Act or any

rule made thereunder, it shall be open to the Designated Court trying him to pass an order that all or any properties, movable or immovable or both belonging to him, shall, during the period of such trial, be attached, and where such trial ends in conviction, the properties so attached shall stand forfeited to Government free from all encumbrances.

(3) (a) If upon a report in writing made by a police officer or an officer referred to in sub-section (1) of Section 7, any Designated Court has reason to believe that any person, who has committed an offence punishable under this Act or any rule made thereunder, has absconded or is concealing himself so that he may not be apprehended, such court may, notwithstanding anything contained in Section 82 of the Code, publish a written proclamation requiring him to appear at a specified place and at a specified time not less than fifteen days but not more than thirty days from the date of publication of such proclamation.

(b) The Designated Court issuing a proclamation under Clause (a) may, at any time, order the attachment of any property, movable or immovable or both, belonging to the proclaimed person, and thereupon the provisions of Sections 83 to 85 of the Code shall apply to such attachment as if such attachment were made under that Code.

(c) If, within six months from the date of the attachment, any person, whose property is, or has been, at the disposal of the Government under sub-section (2) of Section 85 of the code, appears voluntarily or is apprehended and brought before the Designated Court by whose order the property was attached, or the Court to which such Court is subordinate, and proves to the satisfaction of such Court that he did not abscond or conceal himself for the purpose of avoiding apprehension and that he had not received such notice of the proclamation as to enable him to attend within the time specified therein, such property or, if the same has been sold, the net proceeds of the sale and the residue of the property, shall, after satisfying therefrom all costs incurred in consequence of the attachment, be delivered to him.

(4) Where any shares in a company stand forfeited to the Government under this sub-section, then, the company shall, notwithstanding anything contained in the Companies Act, 1956, or the articles of association the company, forthwith register the Government as the transferee of such shares.

CHAPTER III
DESIGNATED COURTS

9. Designated Courts: (1) The Central Government or a State Government may, by notification in the official Gazette, constitute one or more Designated Courts for such area or areas, or for such case or class or group of cases as may be specified in the notification.

(2) Where a notification constituting a Designated Court for any area or areas or for any case or class or group of cases is issued by the Central Government under sub-section (1), and a notification constituting a Designated Court for the same area or areas or for the same case or class or group of cases has also been issued by a State Government under that sub-section, the Designated Court constituted by the Central Government, whether the notification constituting such Court is issued before or after the issue of the notification constituting the Designated Court by the State Government, shall have, and the Designated Court constituted by the State Government shall not have, jurisdiction to try any offence committed in that area or areas or, as the case may be, the case or class or group of cases, and all cases pending before any Designated Court constituted by the State Government shall stand transferred to the Designated Court constituted by the Central Government.

(3) Where any question arises as to the jurisdiction of any Designated Court, it shall be referred to the Central Government whose decision thereon shall be final.

(4) A Designated Court shall be presided over by a Judge to be appointed by the Central Government or, as the case may be, the State Government, with the concurrence of the Chief Justice of the High Court.

(5) The Central Government or, as the case may be, the State Government may also appoint, with the concurrence of the Chief Justice of the High Court additional Judges to exercise jurisdiction in a Designated Court.

(6) A person shall not be qualified for appointment as a Judge or an additional Judge of a Designated Court unless he is, immediately before such appointment a Sessions Judge or an additional Sessions Judge in any State.

(7) For the removal of doubts, it is hereby provided that the attainment by a person appointed a judge or an Additional Judge of a Designated Court of the age of superannuation under the rules applicable to him in the service to which he belongs, shall not affect his continuance as such Judge or Additional Judge.

(8) Where any Additional Judge or Additional Judges is or are appointed in a Designated Court, the Judge of the Designated Court may, from time to time, by general or special order, in writing, provide for the distribution of business of the Designated Court among himself and the additional Judge or Additional Judges and also for the disposal of urgent business in the event of his absence or the absence of any Additional Judge.

10. Place of Sitting: A Designated Court may, on its own motion or on an application made by the Public Prosecutor, and if it considers it expedient or desirable so to do, sit for any of its proceedings at any place, other than its ordinary place of sitting:

Provided that nothing in this section shall be construed to change the place of sitting of a Designated Court constituted by a State Government to any place outside that State.

11. Jurisdiction of Designated Courts: (1) Notwithstanding anything contained in the Code, every offence punishable under any provision of this Act or any rule made thereunder shall be triable only by the Designated Court within whose local jurisdiction it was committed or, as the case may be, by the Designated Court constituted for trying such offence under sub-section (1) of Section 9.

(2) If, having regard to the exigencies of the situation prevailing in a State, the Central Government is of the opinion that,—

(a) the situation prevailing in such State is not conducive to a fair, impartial or speedy trial, or

(b) it is not likely to be feasible without occasioning the breach of peace or grave risk to the safety of the accused, the witnesses, the Public Prosecutor and the Judge of the Designated Court or any of them, or

(c) it is not otherwise in the interests of justice,

It may, with the concurrence of the Chief Justice of India (such occurrence to be obtained on a motion moved in that behalf by the Attorney General), transfer any case pending before a Designated Court in that State to any other Designated Court within that State or in any other State.

(3) Where the whole or any part of the area within the local limits of the jurisdiction of a Designated Court has been declared to be, or forms part of, any area which has been declared to be a disturbed area under any enactment for the time being in force making provision for the suppression of disorder and restoration and maintenance of public order, and the Central Government is of opinion that the situation prevailing in the State is not conducive to fair, impartial or speedy trial within the State, of offences under this Act or the rules made thereunder which such Designated Court is competent to try, the Central Government may, with the concurrence of the Chief Justice of India, specify, by notification in the official Gazette, in relation to such Court (hereafter in this sub-section referred to as the local Court) a Designated Court outside the State (hereinafter in this section referred to as the specified court), and thereupon,

(a) it shall not be competent at any time during the period of operation of such notification, for such local court to exercise any jurisdiction in respect of, or try, any offence under this Act or the rules made thereunder;

(b) the jurisdiction which would have been, but for the issue of such notification, exercisable by such local court in respect of such offences committed during the period of operation of such notification shall be exercisable by the specified court;

(c) all cases relating to such offences pending immediately before the date of issue of such notification before such local court shall stand transferred on that date to the specified court;

(d) all cases taken cognizance of by, or transferred to, the specified court under Clause (b) or Clause (c) shall be dealt with and tried in accordance with this Act (whether during the period of operation of such notification or thereafter) as if such offences had been committed within the local limits of the jurisdiction of the specified court or, as the case may be, transferred for trial to it under sub-section (2).

Explanation 1: A notification under this sub-section in relation to any local court shall cease to operate on the date on which the whole or, as the case may be, the aforementioned part of the area within the local limits of its jurisdiction, ceases to be a disturbed area.

Explanation 2: For the purposes of this section, "Attorney-General" means the Attorney General of India or, in his absence, the Solicitor-General of India or, in the absence of both, one of the Additional Solicitors-General of India.

12. Power of Designated Courts with Respect to Other Offences: (1) When trying any offence, a Designated Court may also try any other offence with which the accused may, under the Code, be charged at the same trial if the offence is connected with such other offence.

(2) If, in the course of any trial under this Act of any offence, it is found that the accused person has committed any other offence under this Act or any rule made thereunder or under any other law, a the Designated Court may convict such person of such other offence and pass any sentence authorised by this Act or such rule or, as the case may be, such other law, for the punishment thereof.

13. Public Prosecutors: (1) For every Designated Court, the Central Government or, as the case may be, the State Government, shall appoint a person to be the Public Prosecutor and may appoint one or more persons to be the Additional Public Prosecutor or Additional Public Prosecutors:

Provided that the Central Government or, as the case may be, the State Government, may also appoint for any case or class or group of cases a Special Public Prosecutor.

(2) A person shall not be qualified to be appointed as a Public Prosecutor or an Additional Public Prosecutor or a Special Public

Prosecutor under this section unless he has been in practice as an Advocate for not less than seven years or has held any post, for a period of not less than seven years, under the Union or a State, requiring special knowledge of law.

(3) Every person appointed as a Public Prosecutor or an Additional Public Prosecutor or a Special Public Prosecutor under this section shall be deemed to be a Public Prosecutor within the meaning of clause *(u)* of Section 2 of the Code and the provisions of the Code shall have effect accordingly.

14. Procedure and Powers of Designated Courts: A Designated Court may take cognisance of any offence, without the accused being committed to it for trial, upon receiving a complaint of facts, which constitute such offence, or upon a police report of such facts.

(2) Where an offence triable by a Designated Court is punishable with imprisonment for a term not exceeding three years or with fine or with both, the Designated Court may, notwithstanding anything contained in sub-section (1) of Section 260 or Section 262 of the Code, try the offence in a summary way in accordance with the procedure prescribed in the Code and the provisions of Section 263 to 265 of the Code, shall, so far as may be, apply to such trial:

Provided that when, in the course of a summary trial under this sub-section, it appears to the Designated Court that the nature of the case is such that it is undesirable to try it in a summary way, the Designated Court shall recall any witnesses who may have been examined and proceed to re-hear the case in the manner provided by the provisions of the Code for the trial of such offence and the said provisions shall apply to and in relation to a Designated Court as they apply to and in relation to a Magistrate:

Provided further that in the case of any conviction in a summary trial under this section, it shall be lawful for a Designated Court to pass a sentence of imprisonment for a term not exceeding two years.

(3) Subject to the other provisions of this Act, a Designated Court shall, for the purpose of trial of any offence, have all the powers of a Court of Session and shall try such offence as if it were a Court of Session so far as may be in accordance with the procedure prescribed in the Code for the trial before a Court of Session.

(4) Subject to the other provisions of this Act, every case transferred to a Designated Court under sub-section (2) of Section 11 shall be dealt with as if such case had been transferred under Section 406 of the Code to such Designated Court.

(5) Notwithstanding anything contained in the Code, a Designated Court may, if it thinks fit and for reasons to be recorded by it, proceed with the trial in the absence of the accused or his pleader and record the

evidence of any witness, subject to the right of the accused to recall the witness for cross-examination.

15. Certain Confessions Made to Police Officers to be Taken into Consideration: (1) Notwithstanding anything in the Code or in the Indian Evidence Act, 1872, but subject to the provisions of this section, a confession made by a person before a police officer not lower in rank than a Superintendent of Police and recorded by such police officer either in writing or on any mechanical device like cassettes, tapes or sound tracks from out of which sounds or images can be reproduced, shall be admissible in the trial of such person[6] [or co-accused, abettor or conspirator] for an offence under this Act or rules made thereunder:

Provided that co-accused, abettor or conspirator is charged and tried in the same case together with the accused.[7]

(2) The police officer shall, before recording any confession under sub-section (1), explain to the person making it that he is not bound to make a confession and that, if he does so, it may be used as evidence against him and such police officer shall not record any such confession unless upon questioning the person making it, he has reason to believe that it is being made voluntarily.

16. Protection of Witnesses: (1) [8] Notwithstanding anything contained in the Code, the proceedings under this Act may be held in camera if the Designated Court so desires.

(2) A Designated Court may, on an application made by a witness in any proceedings before it or by the Public Prosecutor in relation to such witness or on its own motion, take such measures as it deems fit for keeping the identity and address of any witness secret.

(3) In particular, and without prejudice to the generality of the provisions of sub-section (2), the measures, which a Designated Court may take under that sub-section, may include,

(a) the holding of the proceedings at a place to be decided by the Designated Court;

(b) the avoiding of the mention of the names and addresses of the witnesses in it orders or judgments or in any records of the case accessible to public;

(c) the issuing of any directions for securing that the identity and addresses of the witnesses are not disclosed.

(d) that it is in the public interest to order that all or any of the proceedings pending before such a court shall not be published in any manner.

(4) Any person who contravenes any direction issued under sub-section (3) shall be punishable with imprisonment for a term, which

may extend to one year and with fine, which may extend to one thousand rupees.

17. Trial by Designated Courts to have Precedence: The trial under this Act of any offence by a Designated Court shall have precedence over the trial of any other case against the accused in any other court (not being a Designated Court) and shall be concluded in preference to the trial of such other case and accordingly the trial of such other case shall remain in abeyance.

18. Power to Transfer Cases to Regular Courts: Where, after taking cognisance of any offence, a Designated Court is of opinion that the offence is not triable by it, it shall, notwithstanding that it has no jurisdiction to try such offence, transfer the case for the trial of such offence to any court having jurisdiction under the Code and the court to which the case is transferred may proceed with the trial of the offence as if it had taken cognisance of the offence.

19. Appeal: (1) Notwithstanding anything contained in the Code, an appeal shall lie as a matter of right from any judgment, sentence or order, not being an interlocutory order, of a Designated Court to the Supreme Court both on facts and on law.

(2) Except as aforesaid, no appeal or revision shall lie to any court from any judgment, sentence or order including an interlocutory order of a Designated Court.

(3) Every appeal under this section shall be preferred within a period of thirty days from the date of the judgment; sentence or order appealed from:

Provided that the Supreme Court may entertain an appeal after the expiry of the said period of thirty days if it is satisfied that the appellant had sufficient cause for not preferring the appeal within the period of thirty days.

CHAPTER IV
MISCELLANEOUS

20. Modified Application of Certain Provisions of the Code: (1) Notwithstanding anything contained in the Code or any other law, every offence punishable under this Act or any rule made thereunder shall be deemed to be a cognisable offence within the meaning of clause (c) of Section 2 of the Code, and "cognisable case" as defined in that clause shall be construed accordingly.

(2) Section 21 of the Code shall apply in relation to a case involving an offence punishable under this Act or any rule made thereunder subject to the modification that the reference to "the State Government" therein

shall be construed as a reference to "the Central Government or the State Government".

(3) Section 164 of the Code shall apply in relation to a case involving an offence punishable under this Act or any rule made thereunder, subject to the modification that the reference in subsection (1) thereof to "Metropolitan Magistrate or Judicial Magistrate" shall be construed as a reference to Metropolitan Magistrate, Judicial Magistrate, Executive Magistrate or Special Executive Magistrate.

(4) Section 167 of the Code shall apply in relation to a case involving an offence punishable under this Act or any rule made thereunder subject to the modifications that,

(a) the reference in sub-section (1) thereof to "Judicial Magistrate" shall be construed as a reference to Judicial Magistrate or Executive Magistrate or Special Executive Magistrate;

(b) the reference in sub-section (2) thereof to "fifteen days," "ninety days" and "sixty days," wherever they occur, shall be construed as references to "sixty days."[9] [one hundred and eighty days] and [one hundred and eighty days], respectively; and

(bb) sub-section (2-A) thereof shall be deemed to have been omitted.

(bbb)[10] in sub-section (2), after the proviso, the following proviso shall be inserted, namely:

Provided further that, if it is not possible to complete the investigation within the said period of one hundred and eighty days, the Designated Court shall extend the said period up to one year, on the report of the Public Prosecutor indicating the progress of the investigation and the specific reasons for the detention of the accused beyond the said period of one hundred and eighty days.

(5) Section 268 of the Code shall apply in relation to a case involving an offence punishable under this Act or any rule made thereunder subject to the modifications that

(a) the reference in sub-section(1) thereof

(i) to "the State Government" shall be construed as a reference to "the Central Government or the State Government";

(ii) to "order of the State Government" shall be construed as a reference to "order of the Central Government or the State Government, as the case may be"; or

(b) the reference in sub-section (2) thereof, to "State Government" shall be construed as a reference to "Central Government or the State Government, as the case may be".

(6) Sections 366 to 371 and Section 392 of the Code shall apply in relation to a case involving an offence triable by a Designated Court subject

to the modifications that the references to "Court of Session" and "High Court", wherever occurring therein, shall be construed as references to "Designated Court" and "Supreme Court", respectively.

(7) Nothing in Section 438 of the Code shall apply in relation to any case involving the arrest of any person on an accusation of having committed an offence punishable under this act or any rule made thereunder.

(8) Notwithstanding anything contained in the Code, no person accused of an offence punishable under this Act or any rule made thereunder shall, if in custody, be released on bail or on his own bond unless,

(a) the Public Prosecutor has been given an opportunity to oppose the application for such release, and

(b) where the Public Prosecutor opposes the application, the Court is satisfied that there are reasonable grounds for believing that he is not guilty of such offence and that he is not likely to commit any offence while on bail.

(9) The limitations on granting of bail specified in sub-section (8) are in addition to the limitations under the Code or any other law for the time being in force on granting of bail.

20-A. Cognisance of Offence: (1) Notwithstanding, anything contained in the Code, no information about the commission of an offence under this Act shall be recorded by the police without the prior approval of the District Superintendent of Police.

(2) No court shall take cognisance of any offence under this Act without the previous sanction of the Inspector-General of Police, or as the case may be, the Commissioner of Police.

21. Presumption as to Offences under Section 3: (1) In a prosecution for an offence under sub-section (1) of Section 3, if it is proved—

(a) that the arms or explosives or any other substances specified in Section 3 were recovered from the possession of the accused and there is reason to believe that such arms or explosives or other substances of similar nature, were used in the commission of such offence; or

(b). that by the evidence of an expert the fingerprints of the accused were found at the site of the offence or on anything including arms and vehicles used in connection with the commission of such offence.

(c) [* * *][12]

(d) [* * *]

(2) In a prosecution for an offence under sub-section 3 of Section 3, if it is proved that the accused rendered any financial assistance to a person accused of, or reasonably suspected of, an offence under that section, the

Designated Court shall presume, unless the contrary is proved, that such person has committed the offence under that sub-section.

22. Identification of Accused: Where a person has been declared a proclaimed offender in terrorist case, the evidence regarding his identification by witnesses on the basis of his photograph shall have the same value as the evidence of a test identification parade.

23. Saving: (1) Nothing in this Act shall affect the jurisdiction exercisable by, or the procedure applicable to, any Court or other authority under any law relating to the naval, military or air forces or other armed forces of the Union.

(2) For the removal of doubts, it is hereby declared that for the purposes of any such law as is referred to in sub-section (1), a Designated Court shall be deemed to be a Court of ordinary criminal justice.

24. Saving as to Orders: Where an order purports to have been made and signed by any authority in exercise of any power conferred by or under this Act, a Court shall, within the meaning of the Indian Evidence Act, 1872, presume that such order was so made by that authority.

25. Overriding Effect: The provisions of this Act or any rule made thereunder or any order made under any such rule shall have effect notwithstanding anything inconsistent therewith contained in any enactment other than this Act or in any instrument having effect by virtue of any enactment other than this Act.

26. Protection of Action Taken under this Act: No suit, prosecution or other legal proceeding shall lie against the Central Government or State Government or any other authority on whom powers have been conferred under this Act or any rules made thereunder, for anything which is in good faith done or purported to be done in pursuance of this Act or any rules made thereunder or any order issued under any such rule.

27. Power of the Supreme Court to Make Rules: The Supreme Court may, by notification in the Official Gazette, make such rules, if any, as it may deem necessary for carrying out the provisions of this Act relating to Designated Court.

28. Power to Make Rules: (1) Without prejudice to the powers of the Supreme Court to make rules under Section 27, the Central Government may, by notification in the Official Gazette, make rules for carrying out the provisions of this Act.

(2) In particular, and without prejudice to the generality of the foregoing power, such rules may provide for all or any of the following matters namely:

(a) regulating the conduct of persons in respect of areas the control of which is considered necessary or expedient and the removal of such persons from areas.

(b) The entry into, and search of,
   (i) any vehicle, vessel or aircraft; or
   (ii) any place, whatsoever,

   reasonably suspected of being used for committing the offence referred to in Section 3 or Section 4 or for manufacturing or storing anything for the commission of any such offence.

(c) conferring powers upon,
   (i) the Central Government;
   (ii) a State Government;
   (iii) an Administrator of a Union Territory under Article 239 of the Constitution;
   (iv) an officer of the Central Government not lower in rank than of a Joint Secretary; or
   (v) an officer of a State Government not lower in rank than that of a District Magistrate,

   to make general or special orders to prevent or cope with terrorist acts or disruptive activities;

(d) the arrest and trial of persons contravening any of the rules or any order made thereunder;

(e) the punishment of any person who contravenes or attempts to contravene or abets or attempts to abet the contravention of any rule or order made thereunder with imprisonment for a term which may extend to seven years or for a term which may not be less than six months but which may extend to seven years or with fine or with imprisonment as aforesaid and fine;

(f) Providing for the seizure and detention of any property in respect of which such contravention, attempt or abetment as is referred to in Clause (e) has been committed and for the adjudication of such seizure and detention, whether by any court or by any other authority.

29. Rules to be Laid before Houses of Parliament: Every rule made by the Central Government under this Act shall be laid, as soon as may be after it is made, before each House of Parliament, while it is in session, for a total period of thirty days which may be comprised in one session or in two or more successive sessions, and if, before the expiry of the session immediately following the session or the successive sessions aforesaid, both Houses agree in making any modification in the rule or both Houses agree that the rule should not be made, the rule shall thereafter have affect only in such modified form or be of no effect, as the case may be; so, however, that any such modification or annulment shall be without prejudice to the validity of anything previously done under that rule.

30. Repeal and Saving: (1) The Terrorist and Disruptive Activities (Prevention) Ordinance, 1987 (2 of 1987) is hereby repealed.

(2) Notwithstanding such repeal, anything done or any action taken under the said Ordinance shall be deemed to have been done or taken under the corresponding provisions of this Act.

ENDNOTES

1. The Act received the assent of the President on 3 September, 1987; published in the Gazette of India, (Extra.), Part II, Section 1, pp. 1 to 15, dated 3 September, 1987
2. Subs. by Act 16 of 1989, Section 2, for the words "two years", re-subs. by Act 35 of 1991, for "four years", (wef. 2.5.1991) and again subs. by Act 43 of 1993, Section 2, for "six years".
3. Ins. by Act 43 of 1993, Section 3.
4. Ins. by Act 43 of 1993, Section 4.
5. Ins. by Act 43 of 1993, Section 5.
6. Ins. by Act 43 of 1993, Section 6(a).
7. Ins. by Act 43 of 1993, Section 6(b).
8. Ins. by Act 43 of 1993, Section 7.
9. Subs. by Act 43 of 1993, Section 8(a).
10. Ins. by Act 43 of 1993, Section 8(b)
11. Ins. by Act 43 of 1993, Section 9.
12. Clauses (c) and (d), omitted by Act 43 of 1993, Section 10

Memorandum of Understanding with Tripura National Volunteers

[*After three years of insurgency, Bejoy Kumar Hrankhawl of the Tripura National Volunteers signed a Memorandum of Understanding with the Government of India*]

Preamble: Government of India has been making efforts to bring about a satisfactory settlement of the problems of tribals in Tripura by restoring peace and harmony in areas where disturbed conditions prevailed.

The Tripura National Volunteers (TNV), through their letter dated 4 May 1988, addressed to the Governor of Tripura and signed by Shri Bejoy Kumar Hrankhawl, stated that keeping in view the Prime Minister Shri Rajiv Gandhi's policy of solution of problems through negotiations, TNV have decided to abjure violence, give up secessionist demand and to hold negotiations for a peaceful solution of all the problems of Tripura within the Constitution of India. The TNV also furnished its by-laws which conform to the laws in force. On this basis, a series of discussions were held with representatives of TNV.

The following were the outcome of the discussions:

Deposit of Arms and Ammunition and stopping of underground activities by TNV.

The TNV undertakes to take all necessary steps to end underground activities and to bring out all undergrounds of the TNV with their arms, ammunition and equipment within one month of signing of this memorandum. Details for given effect to this part of settlement will be worked out and implemented under the supervision of the Central Government.

The TNV further undertakes to ensure that it does not resort to violence and to help in restoration of amity between different sections of the population.

The TNV undertakes not to extend any support to any other extremist group by way of training, supply of arms or providing protection or in any other manner.

Rehabilitation of Undergrounds

Suitable steps will be taken for the resettlement and rehabilitation of TNV undergrounds coming over ground in the light of the schemes drawn up for the purpose.

Measures to Prevent Infiltration

Stringent measures will be taken to prevent infiltration from across the border by strengthening arrangements on the border and construction of roads along vulnerable sections of the Indo-Bangladesh border in Tripura section for better patrolling and vigil. Vigorous action against such infiltrators would also be taken under the law.

Reservation of Seats in the Tripura Legislative Assembly for Tribals

With a view to satisfying the aspirations of tribals of Tripura for a greater share in the governance of the State, legislative measures will be taken including those for the enactment of the Bill for the amendment of the Constitution.

The Constitutional amendments shall provide that notwithstanding anything contained in the Constitution, the number of seats in the Legislative Assembly of Tripura reserved for scheduled tribes shall be such number of seats as bears to the total number of seats, a proportion not less than the number, as on the date of coming into force of the constitutional amendment, of members belonging to the scheduled tribes in the existing Assembly bears to the total number of seats in the existing Assembly.

The Representation of the People's Act, 1950, shall be amended to provide for reservation of 20 seats for the scheduled tribes in the Assembly of Tripura. However, the amendments shall not effect any representation in the existing Assembly of Tripura until its dissolution.

Restoration of Alienated Lands of Tribals

It was agreed that following measures will be taken:

(i) Review of rejected applications for restoration of tribal land under the Tripura Land Revenue and Land Reforms Act, 1960;

(ii) Effective implementation of the law for restoration;

(iii) Stringent measures to prevent fresh alienation;

(iv) Provision of soil conservation measures and irrigation facilities in tribal areas; and

(v) Strengthening of the agricultural credit system so as to provide for an appropriate agency with adequate tribal representation to ensure easy facilities for both consumption and operational credit to tribals.

Redrawing of the Boundaries of Autonomous District Council Area

Tribal majority villages which now fall outside the autonomous district council area and are contiguous to such areas will be included in the autonomous district and similarly placed non-tribal majority villages presently in the autonomous district and on the periphery may be excluded.

Measures for Long-run Economic Development of Tripura

Maximum emphasis will be placed on extensive and intensive skill-formation of the tribal youths of Tripura so as to improve their prospects of employment including self-employment in various trades such as motor workshops, pharmacies, electronic goods, carpentry, tailoring, stationary, weaving, rice and oil mills, general stores, fishery, poultry, piggery, horticulture, handloom and handicrafts.

Special intensive recruitment drives will be organised for police and paramilitary forces in Tripura with a view to enlisting as many tribal youths as possible.

All India Radio will increase the duration and content of their programmers in tribal languages or dialects of Tripura. Additional transmitting stations will be provided for coverage even of the remote areas of the State.

The demands relating to self-employment of tribals, issue of permits for vehicles to tribals for commercial purposes, visits of tribal men and women to such places in the country as may be of value for the viewpoint of inspiration, training and experience in relevant fields will be considered sympathetically by the government.

At least 2,500 *Jhumia* families will be rehabilitated in five centres or more in accordance with model schemes based on agriculture, horticulture including vegetable growing, animal husbandry, fisheries and plantations, with a view to weaning them away from *Jhum* cultivation. The scheme would also provide for housing assistance.

In the autonomous district council area of Tripura, rice, salt and kerosene oil will be given at subsidised rates during lean months for a period of three years.

Conscious effort will be made for effective implementation of the provisions of the Sixth Schedule of the Constitution in so far as it relates to Tripura.

All Bodo Students' Union and Government of India (Memorandum of Settlement)

[The Memorandum of Settlement on the fixed "Bodoland" issue was signed on 20 February 1993. With the signing of the memorandum, an important chapter of the six-year old movement for a separate "Bodoland," which started on 2 March 1987, ended, albeit temporarily]

MEMORANDUM OF SETTLEMENT
(BODO ACCORD)

1. Preamble: (i) Both the Government of India and the Government of Assam have been making earnest efforts to bring about an amicable solution to the problems of the Bodos and other Plains Tribals living in the north bank of river Brahmaputra within Assam.

(ii) Towards this end, the Government of India held a series of meetings with the State Government as well as with leaders of All Bodo Students' Union (ABSU) and Bodo Peoples' Action Committee (BPAC). The State Government has also separately held discussions with the Bodo leaders. As a result, it has been considered necessary to set-up an administrative authority within the State of Assam under a scheme, the details of which are outlined in the succeeding paragraphs.

2. Objective: The objective of this scheme is to provide maximum autonomy within the framework of the Constitution to the Bodos for social, economic, educational, ethnic and cultural advancement.

3. (a) Name [Bodoland Autonomous Council (BAC)]: There shall be formed, by an Act of Assam Legislative Assembly, a Bodoland Autonomous Council (BAC) within the State of Assam comprising contiguous geographical areas between river Sankosh and Mazbat river Pasnoi. The land records authority of the State will scrutinize the list of villages furnished by ABSU, BPAC having 50 per cent and more of tribal population, which shall be included in the BAC. For the purpose of providing a contiguous area, even the villages having less than 50 per cent tribal population shall be included. BAC will also include Reserve Forests as per the guidelines laid by Ministry of Defence and Ministry of

Environment and Forest, Government of India, not otherwise required by the Government for manning the international border and tea gardens located completely within the BAC contiguous area.

(b) *Powers*: The BAC will comprise of a General Council comprising 40 members, 35 elected on the basis of adult suffrage and having a life of five years. The Government will have powers to nominate 5 members to the Council, particularly from groups, which could not otherwise be represented. This Council will have powers to make by-laws, rules and orders for application within the BAC area on the subjects enumerated in Schedule "A."

(c) The Executive authority of the BAC would be exercised in its Executive Body to be known as Bodoland Executive Council (BEC). The BEC will be responsible for implementation within the BAC area of the laws on subjects enumerated in Schedule "A."

(d) The General Council and the BEC will hold office during the pleasure of the Governor of Assam. Consultation with the State Law Department of Government of Assam would be necessary if the Governor proposes to dissolve either the General Council or the BEC before the expiry of its term in accordance with the provisions of law. The executive authority of the BEC will be exercised by the party enjoying a simple majority in the General Council. On completion of elections, the Governor would invite the leader of the majority party to constitute the BEC.

4. Finances: (i) (a) The finances for the BAC will be earmarked under a separate sub-head within the State budget, in keeping with the guidelines laid down by the Government of India from time to time. The government of Assam would have no powers to divert this earmarked allocation to other heads/areas except in exigencies when there is unavoidable overall Budget cut.

(b) The provisions made in 4 (i) (a) regarding allocation of funds should be in line with spirit of the Constitution (Seventy Second and Seventy Third) amendment.

(ii) The BAC would also receive grant-in aid from time to time within the principles and policies enunciated by the Government of India.

(iii) The General Council will have powers to raise finances from levies/fees/taxes etc on subjects mentioned in Schedule "A" subject to Constitutional amendment mentioned above.

(iv) The finances for the BAC will be managed exclusively by its General Council and the statement of its annual audited accounts will be laid on the table of the State Assembly.

5. Powers of Appointments: The Bodoland Executive Committee would have powers to appoint Class III and Class IV staff within its jurisdiction for implementation of schemes connected with the subjects enumerated in Schedule "A."

6. Reservation of Seats: The Election Commission of India will be requested by the BAC to consider seat reservation and delimitation of constituencies, both Lok Sabha and State Assembly, within the BAC area to the extent permitted by the Constitution and the law.

7. Special Provisions for the BAC Area: The General Council shall be consulted and its views shall be given due regard before any law made on the following subjects, is implemented in the BAC area:

(i) for religious or social practice of the Bodos,
(ii) The Bodo customary laws and procedures, and
(iii) The ownership and transfer of land within the BAC.

8. Special Status for the Bodoland Autonomous Council: The BAC shall, within the laws of the land, take steps to protect the demographic complexion of the areas falling within its jurisdiction.

9. Special Courts: Action will be taken in consultation with the Gauhati High Court to set up within BAC area Special Courts as specified below to try suits and cases between parties all of whom belong to Scheduled Tribe or Tribes in accordance with the tribal customary laws and procedure, if any:

(a) Village Courts,
(b) Subordinate District Customary Law Courts within a civil Sub-Divisional Territory, and
(c) District Customary Law Court.

10. Appointment in the Central Bodies: The claims of the Bodos shall be considered for appointment to the North-Eastern Council.

11. Official Language: The General Council can lay down policy with regard to use of Bodo language as medium of official correspondences within the BAC area. However, while correspondence will have to be in bilingual form in accordance with Article 345 of the Constitution and the provision of law in this behalf.

12. Changes in Geographical Boundary: The geographical area of the Bodoland Autonomous Council as agreed upon can be changed with the mutual consent of the BAC and the Government of Assam.

13. Revision of List of Scheduled Castes and Scheduled Tribes: The scheduling and re-scheduling of Scheduled Castes and Scheduled Tribes residing within the Bodo areas will be done as per the Commission appointed by the Government of India under the Constitution.

14. Trade and Commerce: The General Council will have powers to regulate trade and commerce within its jurisdiction in accordance with the existing law. For this purpose, it can issue permits and licences to individuals within the BAC area, The Government of Assam and the Union Government while considering allotment of permits to people residing within the BAC area will give preference to the Bodos.

15. Employment Opportunities: The BAC will have powers to reserve jobs for Scheduled Tribes within its jurisdiction. However, exercise of such powers shall be in accordance with the existing constitutional and legal provisions.

16. Civil and Police Services:

(i) The Government of Assam may from time to time post officers of the rank of Class II and above to posts within the BAC in accordance with the exigencies. While making these postings due regard will be given to the views of BAC about officers being so posted.

(ii) The officers posted to the BAC area will be accountable to the BAC for their performance and the assessment of their work recorded by the BEC authorities, will be incorporated to their ACRs by the State Government.

(iii) The Central Government, while making recruitments from the State of Assam to the Army, para-military forces and police units, will hold special recruitment drives within the BAC area.

17. Appointment of Interim Bodoland Executive Council: The Government of Assam will take steps for the formation of an Interim Bodoland Executive Council for the BAC from amongst the leaders of the present Bodoland movement who are signatories to this settlement, during the transition period, i.e. prior to the holding of elections. Such Interim Council would be formed before a prescribed date mutually agreed between the Central and State Government.

18. Relief and Rehabilitation:

(i) ABSU-BPAC leaders will take immediate steps to bring over ground and deposit with the District authorities all arms, ammunition and explosives in the possession of their own supporters and will cooperate with the administration in bringing over ground all Bodo militants along with their arms and ammunition etc. within one month of the formation of the Interim BEC. In order to ensure the smooth return to civil life of the cadre and to assist in the quick restoration of peace and normalcy, such surrenders made voluntarily will not attract prosecution.

(ii) The Government of Assam will consider sympathetically the withdrawal of all cases against persons connected with the Bodoland Movement excluding those relating to heinous crimes.

(iii) The Government of India will initiate steps for review of action against the Bodo employees of Government of India and subordinate offices as well as in respect of Central Government Undertakings. Similar action would be taken by the Government of Assam.

(iv) The Government of Assam will initiate immediate steps for suitable rehabilitation of the Bodo militants coming over ground as a result of this settlement. Similarly, the Government will organize ex gratia payments as per rules to next of the kin killed during the Bodo agitation.

19. Share in Collection of Excise Duty on the Tea: The Government of Assam will deposit in the BAC Fund revenue collected from the tea gardens falling within the BAC area.

20. Protection of Rights of Non-Tribals: The Government of Assam and the BAC will jointly ensure that all rights and interests of the non-tribals as on date living in BAC area in matters pertaining to land as well as their language are protected.

21. Ad-hoc Central Grant for Launching the BAC: After the signing of this settlement, an ad-hoc Budget on reasonable basis will be prepared by Interim BEC and discussed with the State and Central Governments for necessary financial support.

Sd/-
S.K. Bwiswamutiary
President. ABSU

Sd/-
K.S. Rao
Addl. Chief Secretary
Govt. of Assam

Sd/-
Rabi Ram Brahma
General Secretary, ABSU

Sd/-
Subhash Basumatary
Chairman, BPAC

In the presence of

Sd/-Rajesh Pilot
Minister of State (Internal Security)
Ministry of Home Affairs
Govt. of India

Sd/-Hiteswar Saikia
Chief Minister of Assam
Govt. of Assam

List of Subjects and Departments Over which BAC will have Control within the BAC area

1. Cottage Industry
2. Animal Husbandry and Veterinary
3. Forests
4. Agriculture
5. P.W.D.
6. Sericulture
7. Education
   (a) Adult Education
   (b) Primary Education
   (c) Up to Higher Secondary including vocational training
8. Cultural Affair
9. Soil Conservation
10. Co-operation
11. Fisheries
12. Panchayat and Rural Development.
13. Handloom and Textiles
14. Health and Family Welfare
15. Public Health Engineering
16. Irrigation
17. Social Welfare
18. Flood Control scheme for protection of villages (not of highly technical nature)
19. Supports and Youth Welfare
20. Weights and Measures
21. Library Services
22. Museums and Archaeology
23. Urban Development-Town and Country Planning
24. Tribal Research Institute
25. College Education (General)
26. Land and Revenue
27. Publicity/Public Relations
28. Printing and Stationery
29. Tourism
30. Transport
31. Any other matter connected with development
32. Municipal Corporation, Improvement Trusts, district Boards and other local authorities

33. Tribal Welfare
34. Markets and Fairs
35. Lotteries, Theatres, Dramatic performances and Cinemas
36. Vital Statistics including registration of births and deaths
37. Food and Civil Supplies
38. Intoxicating liquors, opium and derivatives etc.

The SAARC Convention (Suppression of Terrorism) Act

[*Enacted on 26 April 1993*]

1. Act Objective: An Act to give effect to the South Asian Association for Regional Cooperation Convention on Suppression of Terrorism and for matters connected therewith or incidental thereto. WHEREAS a Convention on the Suppression of Terrorism was signed on behalf of the Government of India at Kathmandu on the 4th day of November, 1987; AND WHEREAS India, having ratified the said Convention, should make provisions for giving effect thereto and for matters connected therewith or incidental thereto; BE it enacted by Parliament in the Forty-fourth Year of the Republic of India as follows:

2. Definitions: In this Act, unless the context otherwise requires:

(a) "Convention" means the South Asian Association for Regional Cooperation Convention on Suppression of Terrorism signed at Kathmandu on the 4th day of November 1987 as set out in the Schedule;

(b) "Convention country" means a country in which the Convention is for the time being in force.

3. Application of the Convention: Notwithstanding anything to the contrary contained in any other law, the provisions of Articles I to VIII of the Convention shall have the force of law in India.

4. Hostage-taking: (1) Whoever, by force or threat of force or by any other form of intimation, seizes or detains any person and threatens to kill or injure that person with intent to cause a Convention country to do or abstain from doing any act as the means of avoiding the execution of such threat, commits the offence of hostage-taking.

(2) Whoever commits the offence of hostage taking shall be punished with imprisonment for a term, which may extend to ten years, and shall also be liable to fine.

5. Provisions as to Extradition Act: For the purposes of the Extradition Act, 1962 (34 of 1962), in relation to a Convention country, an offence under sub-section (1) of section 4 or any other offence specified in Article I of the Convention, shall not be considered to be an offence of a political character.

6. Offences Committed Outside India: (1) When an offence under sub-section (1) of section 4 or any other offence specified in Article I of the Convention is committed outside India,—(a) by a citizen of India, whether on the high seas or elsewhere; (b) by a person, not being such citizen, on any ship or aircraft, registered in India; or (c) by a person, not being such citizen, in a Convention country, he may be dealt with in respect of such offence as if it had been committed at any place within India at which he may be found.

(2) Notwithstanding anything contained in sub-section (1), the Central Government may, by general or special order published in the Official Gazette, direct that the offence under sub-section (1) of section 4 or any other offence specified in Article I of the Convention may be inquired into or tried at any place within India.

7. Previous Sanction Necessary for Prosecution: No prosecution for an offence under this Act shall be instituted except with the previous sanction of the Central Government and the sanction granted under this section shall be deemed to be a sanction granted under section 188 of the Code of Criminal Procedure, 1973 (2 of 1974).

8. Protection of Action Taken in Good Faith: (1) No suit, prosecution or other legal proceeding shall lie against any person for anything which is in good faith done or intended to be done in pursuance of the provisions of this Act.

(2) No suit or other legal proceeding shall lie against the Central Government for any damage caused or likely to be caused for anything which is in good faith done or intended to be done in pursuance of the provisions of this Act.

Ceasefire Ground Rules between Government of India and the National Socialist Council of Nagalim (Isaac-Muivah)

[*In December 1997, the Union Government and the NSCN-IM finalised a set of 11 ground rules to undertake steps for "effective and unambiguous implementation of the prevailing cease-fire in Nagaland"*]

1. There would be no offensive operations like ambush, raid and attack leading to death/injury/damage or loss of property against the NSCN by the Indian Army, paramilitary forces and the police.
2. Patrolling by the Indian Army, paramilitary forces and the police would continue to prevent infiltration of militants and arms as earlier.
3. Protection of convoys and patrolling of roads would continue to be undertaken by the Indian Army, paramilitary forces and the police.
4. The Indian Army, paramilitary forces and police would issue instructions to their formations, not to use masks to cover their faces during the period of ceasefire.
5. The NSCN would not undertake offensive operations like ambush raid, sniping, and attack leading to death/injury/damage or loss of property.
6. In the interest of promoting peace process, there would be no parading (either in groups or individually) or NSCN cadres in uniform and/or with arms.
7. There would be no blockade of roads and communications, disruption of economic or developmental activities as well as essential services by the NSCN;
8. It is mutually agreed that no safe haven or sanctuary to any armed group or elements will be maintained by anyone.
9. On the Government of India side, a concern was expressed that forcible collection of money on essential supplies and intimidation of individuals including government officials were taking place in the State. The NSCN representatives stated that theirs being a people's organization, they did not resort to such activities.

10. It was further agreed that implementation of these ground rules and modalities will be monitored by a group constituted for this purpose comprising of representatives of NSCN, NGOs and representatives nominated by the Government of India.

On the Government of India side a concern was expressed about reports of forced recruitment of armed cadres. The NSCN representatives stated that they have not and do not resort to forced recruitment.

Scheme for Surrender-Cum-Rehabilitation of Militants in the North East

[*The Government of Assam announced a comprehensive scheme in 1998 for the surrender and rehabilitation of militants of various organisations. The second such package announced in the state, the first one was instituted during the Hiteswar Saikia government. The earlier package was called the "100 per cent Special Money Margin Scheme" and was implemented between 1 June 1992 and 31 March 1997, prior to the institution of the present scheme*]

Objectives of the Scheme

1. The objective of the Scheme is to wean away the misguided youth and hardcore militants that have strayed into the folds of militancy and now find themselves trapped into that net. The Scheme also seeks to ensure that the militants who have surrendered do not find it attractive to join militancy again.

Eligibility Criteria

2. The Scheme is applicable to those militants who surrender at least with one weapon as mentioned in para 6. However, in exceptional and deserving cases, militants, who surrender without arms, may also be considered for rehabilitation under the Scheme. The names of such militants would be scrutinised by the Screening Committee and a final view taken by Unified Headquarters or similar body at the State Government headquarters.

Benefits under the Scheme

3. Persons eligible under the Scheme will be initially lodged in a Rehabilitation Camp where they will be imparted training in a trade/ vocation of their liking or befitting their aptitude.

4. They shall be paid a monthly stipend for a period of 12 months. The stipend in respect of a surrenderee shall not exceed Rs. 2000 per month. The scale of stipend for various categories of surrenderees will be decided by the State Government in consultation with the Government of India.

5. Board and lodging at the Rehabilitation Camp will be free.

Note 1: The stay of a surrenderee in a Rehabilitation Camp shall not exceed one year. All attempts shall be made to settle the surrenderees during this period. In case of settlement of any surrenderee before the expiry of one year, the stipend shall be stopped with effect from the date of settlement.

Note 2: Minor crime cases against successfully rehabilitated surrenderees will be withdrawn.

Note 3: The surrenderees who have committed heinous crimes like murder, rape, abduction etc. will be subject to the due process of law and surrender shall not imply amnesty from the crimes.

Note 4: A surrenderee who indulge in crime while under rehabilitation shall forfeit the benefits under the Scheme.

Note 5: The agency for rehabilitation may be a suitable NGO and/or the State Government. In case it is an NGO, it will run the Rehabilitation Camp with support from the Security Forces and the Government where required. (A suitable NGO, which has good credentials and willing to work in this sphere, will have to be identified and provided necessary support from the Government). Necessary infrastructure for board, lodging and training of surrenderees shall be provided to the NGO at Government cost.

Incentives for Weapons

6. The following incentives have been built into the Scheme for the surrendered weapons/ammunitions:

(i)	Rocket Launchers/UMG/GPMG/PIMCA/ Sniper Rifle	Rs.25, 000 per weapon
(ii)	AK 47/56/74 Rifle	Rs.15, 000 per weapon
(iii)	.303 Rifles/Pistol/Revolver and other service weapon	Rs.3, 000 per weapon
(iv)	Rocket	Rs.1, 000 per weapon
v)	Grenade/Hand grenade/Stick grenade	Rs.500 per grenade
(vi)	Remote Control device	Rs.3000 each
(vii)	Ammunition of all types	Rs.3 per round
(viii)	Wireless Sets:	
	a. Short range	Rs.1000 each
	b. Long range	Rs.5000 each set
(ix)	IED	Rs.3000 each
(x)	Explosive material	Rs.1000 per kg.

However, the incentive given for surrender of the aforesaid arms shall be deposited in the form of a Fixed Deposit in the joint name of surrenderee and the NGO/State Government nominee and shall be given to the surrenderee at the time of his leaving the Rehabilitation Camp.

7. The State Governments of the North East shall implement the Scheme. However, the Government of India shall provide 100 per cent reimbursement for expenditure incurred on the rehabilitation of surrenderees. In view of the financial position of insurgency affected States and also the fact that the NGO's who may undertake rehabilitation work would immediately need some money in advance, it was felt that there shall be provision for giving a part of the rehabilitation money in advance and the rest as reimbursement. Details would be worked out by the Ministry of Home Affairs in consultation with the Ministry of Finance.

8. The Government of India shall have the right to inspect any of the Camps set up for rehabilitation or transit and to verify any record in this regard.

Procedure

9. The following agencies will be involved in the process of surrender and rehabilitation:

- (i) IG (Special Branch) will act as the Surrender and Rehabilitation Officer (S&RO) under the Scheme
- (ii) Army
- (iii) Central Para Military Force
- (iv) A nominated NGO

10. Each of the Security Forces will identify one officer of the rank of DIG or equivalent officer as the nodal officer for coordinating surrender and rehabilitation work of militants with respect to their organisation.

11. A militant shall be free to surrender before any unit of the Army/ CPMFs, District Magistrate, District SP, Range DIG, IG (Ops), IG (Special Branch), DIG (Special Branch), SPs (Special Branch), SDM, Sub Divisional Police Officers and other notified officers. The officers for this purpose shall be notified by the State Governments with due approval of the Government of India. A militant may also surrender before any unit if the Army or the CPMFs outside the State. The officer receiving the surrender shall get the details as informed by the surrenderee filled into a prescribed proforma and send the same to the S&R Officer and to the nodal officer of the three forces. The nodal officer of each of the organisations will verify the antecedents of the militants from its own sources and his activities and send its specific recommendations to the S&R Officer stating whether the individual could be taken in as surrenderee or not.

12. The officer receiving the surrender will provide immediate security to the surrendered militant and, after getting necessary details for filling up the proforma, send him to the Transit Camp to be maintained by the

S&R Officer. The board and lodging expenses for the person lodged in the Transit Camp will be borne by the Government. The maximum period within which the decision about a person should be taken would be 15 days.

13. On receiving reports from the four organisations regarding the activities of surrendered person as militant, a Screening Committee headed by the S&R Officer and comprising nodal offices of the four organisations would formally consider the surrender of militant and if accepted, transfer him to the Rehabilitation Camp.

14. Impact assessment of the policy would be done every year to ensure corrective action if required. If the percentage of surrenderees who are successfully rehabilitated at the rehabilitation centre is below 80 per cent, the NGO should be changed.

15. The expenditure during the current financial year, i.e. 1998-99 will be meted out of the sanctioned Budget.

Date of Effect

16. The Scheme will be applicable to those militants who have surrendered/surrender after 1-4-1998. However, the Scheme will have only prospective effect so far as the payment of monthly stipend to the surrenderees is concerned. Similarly, the facilities to be provided to the NGO will be with prospective effect.

Modification in the Scheme

17. The Ministry of Home Affairs may carry out such modifications in the Scheme as may be considered necessary in public interest. The Ministry of Finance will be consulted if any such modification involves financial implications.

Illegal Migration into Assam

[*Prepared by a former Governor of Assam, Lt Gen (Retd) S.K. Sinha, PVSM for submission to the then President of India, K.R. Narayanan, the seminal report provides detailed description and analysis of the magnitude of the illegal migration problem in Assam*]

Report on
Illegal migration into Assam

Submitted to
The President of India

By
The Governor of Assam
8 November 1998

Raj Bhawan, Guwahati

D.O.No.GSAG.3/98/
November 8, 1998

Dear Adarniya Rashtrapatiji,

Large-scale illegal migration from East Pakistan/Bangladesh over several decades has been altering the demographic complexion of this State. It poses a grave threat both to the identity of the Assamese people and to our national security. Successive Governments at the Centre and in the State have not adequately met this challenge.

As Governor of Assam, I feel it is my bounden duty, both to the Nation and the State I have sworn to serve, to place before you this report on the dangers arising from the continuing silent demographic invasio. I have also formulated my recommendations for dealing with this issue of vital importance. I earnestly hope that this matter will receive due consideration and suitable action taken to avert the grave danger that has been building up for some time.

With profound regards.
Yours sincerely,
(Lt Gen (Retd) S.K. Sinha, PVSM)

CHAPTER I
INTRODUCTION

1. The unabated influx of illegal migrants from Bangladesh into Assam and the consequent perceptible change in the demographic pattern of the State has been a matter of grave concern. It threatens to reduce the Assamese people to a minority in their own State, as happened in Tripura and Sikkim.
2. Illegal migration into Assam was the core issue behind the Assam student movement. It was also the prime contributory factor behind the outbreak of insurgency in the State. Yet we have not made much tangible progress in dealing with this all-important issue.
3. There is a tendency to view illegal migration into Assam as a regional matter, affecting only the people of Assam. Its more dangerous dimension of greatly undermining our national security is ignored. The long cherished design of Greater East Pakistan/Bangladesh, making inroads into the strategic land link of Assam with the rest of the country, can lead to severing the entire land mass of the North East, with all its rich resources, from the rest of the country. This will have disastrous strategic and economic consequences.
4. I have held prolonged discussions about illegal migration with a large number of people in Assam of different background and with different shades of opinion. This has included politicians, leaders of the minority community, journalists, lawyers, Government officials, both serving and retired, social workers and so on. I have also discussed this issue at length with the Indian High Commissioner at Dhaka. Besides, I have extensively toured the border areas of Assam with Bangladesh, visiting a number of land and riverine Border Out-Posts (BOPs) of the Border Security Force (BSF). Further, I have studied the relevant literature and statistics on this subject. On this basis, I have formulated my views and recommendations contained in this report. Different aspects connected with the illegal migration have been examined. Recommendations have been made for more effectively arresting the ongoing influx of illegal migrants and taking practical steps to soften the adverse fallouts from the large-scale infiltration that has already taken place.

CHAPTER II
MIGRATION INTO ASSAM

Historical Background

1. Illegal migration from Bangladesh into Assam should be viewed

against the backdrop of past history, present realities and future designs. Migration into Assam has been taking place from the dawn of history. However, after the British annexed Assam, large-scale population movement from the South (Bengal, East Pakistan and now Bangladesh) has been an ongoing phenomenon for over a century. Initially, this movement was for economic reasons only but with the approach of Independence, it started developing both communal and political overtones. After Independence, it acquired an international dimension and it now poses a grave threat to our national security.

2. The British developed the tea industry in Assam. They imported labour from Bihar and other provinces to work in the tea gardens. The Assamese people living mostly in Upper Assam and cultivating one crop per year were not interested in working as labour in the tea gardens nor in increasing or expanding land cultivation to meet the additional requirement of food for the large labour population employed in the tea gardens. Therefore, the British encouraged Bengali Muslim peasants from present Bangladesh to move into Lower Assam for putting virgin land under cultivation. This set in motion a movement pattern which despite changed conditions, has been continuing to this day.

3. When Lord Curzon partitioned erstwhile Bengal Presidency in 1905, Assam was a Chief Commissioner's province. It was merged with the new Muslim majority province of East Bengal. This led to tremendous popular resentment in the country and it ushered political awareness, ultimately culminating in India's Independence. In 1911, the British Government annulled the partition of Bengal. Assam was restored its status as a province and was now placed under a Lieutenant Governor. The Assamese fear of losing their identity and being swamped by Bengalis goes back to this merger and even earlier. This fear had been aroused both by the Bengali Hindus dominating the administration and the professions, and the Bengali Muslims altering the demography of the province. The Bengali Muslims were hard working peasants who occupied vacant land and put virgin areas under cultivation. They made a significant contribution to the agricultural economy of Assam.

4. With Constitutional Reforms, the country started advancing towards democracy, which is a game of numbers. The Muslim League now came up with its demand for Partition, on the basis of religion. This added a new twist to this population movement. During Sir Mohammad Sadulla's Muslim League Ministry, a concerted effort was made to encourage the migration of Bengali Muslims into Assam for political reasons. The Viceroy, Lord Wavell wrote in the Viceroy's Journal, "The chief political problem is the desire of the Muslim Ministers to increase this immigration

into the uncultivated Government lands under the slogan of Grow More Food but what they are really after, is Grow More Muslims."

5. When the demand for Partition was raised, it was visualised that Pakistan would comprise Muslim majority provinces in the West and Bang-e-Islam comprising Bengal and Assam, in the East. Mr. Moinul Haque Chowdhary the Private Secretary of Jinnah, who after Independence became a Minister in Assam and later at Delhi, told Jinnah that he would "present Assam to him on a silver platter". Jinnah confidently declared at Guwahati that Assam was in his pocket. The Cabinet Mission Plan placed Assam in Group C with Bengal. Both the Congress High Command and the Muslim League accepted the grouping plan but Lokapriya Gopinath Bordoloi vehemently opposed it. He was supported by Mahatma Gandhi. The grouping plan was foiled and Assam was saved from becoming a part of Pakistan.

6. Partition brought about a sea change in the situation. An international border now separated Assam and East Pakistan. Population movement from East Pakistan continued but it was initially mostly of Hindu refugees, fleeing from religious persecution. Unlike the West, where refugee movement lasted for a few months only, in the case of the East, this spread over several years and is still continuing. Hindu population in East Pakistan started declining steeply. In 1947 it was 27 per cent, by 1971 it got reduced to 14 per cent and by 1991 it was down to 10 per cent. Along with Hindu refugees, Muslim infiltrators continued migrating into Assam for economic reasons. The movement of Hindu refugees into Assam got largely arrested due to anti-Bengali riots and as a result of violence in the wake of insurgency in the State. However, Hindu refugee movement from Bangladesh has continued to Tripura and West Bengal. Illegal migrants from Bangladesh into Assam are now almost exclusively Muslims.

7. Failure to get Assam included in East Pakistan in 1947 remained a source of abiding resentment in that country. Zulfiqar Ali Bhutto in his book, Myths of Independence wrote, "It would be wrong to think that Kashmir is the only dispute that divides India and Pakistan, though undoubtedly the most significant. One at least is nearly as important as the Kashmir dispute, that of Assam and some districts of India adjacent to East Pakistan To these Pakistan has very good claims." Even a pro-India leader like Sheikh Mujibur Rahman in his book, Eastern Pakistan: Its Population and Economics, observed, "Because Eastern Pakistan must have sufficient land for its expansion and because Assam has abundant forests and mineral resources, coal, petroleum etc., Eastern Pakistan must include Assam to be financially and economically strong".

8. Leading intellectuals in Bangladesh have been making out a case for "lebensraum" (living space) for their country. Mr. Sadeq Khan, a former

diplomat wrote in *Holiday* of October 18, 1991, "All projections, however, clearly indicate that by the next decade, that is to say by the first decade of the 21st century, Bangladesh will face a serious crisis of lebensraum... if consumer benefit is considered to be better served by borderless competitive trade of labour, there is no reason why regional and international co-operation could not be worked out to plan and execute population movements and settlements to avoid critical demographic pressure in pockets of high concentration.... A natural overflow of population pressure is there very much on the cards and will not be restrainable by barbed wire or border patrol measures. The natural trend of population over-flow from Bangladesh is towards the sparsely populated lands in the South East in the Arakan side and of the North East in the Seven Sisters side of the Indian sub-continent". Mr. Abdul Momin, former Foreign Secretary and Bangladesh's first Ambassador to China writing in the same magazine in its issue of November 22, 1991 stated, "The runaway population growth in Bangladesh resulting in suffocating density of population in a territorially small country, presents a nightmarish picture". Urging that along with borderless circulation of goods and commodities there should be borderless competitive trade of labour, he proposed that "if we in Bangladesh ingratiate ourselves with the hill tribes within our borders, our bulging population might find a welcome in adjacent land inhabited by kindred peoples". The views of Jinnah, Zulfiqar Ali Bhutto, Sheikh Mujibur Rahman, Sadeq Khan and Abdul Momin have a common thread running through them. No matter how friendly our relations with Bangladesh, we can ill afford to ignore the dangers inherent in demographic invasion from that country.

Contributory Factors

9. Illegal migration from Assam has been taking place primarily for economic reasons. Bangladesh is the world's most densely populated country with a population density of 969 per square kilometre. The growth rate of population in that country is 2.2 per cent and its population is growing at the rate of 2.8 million per year. Each year nearly one third of Bangladesh gets inundated by floods, displacing 19 million people. 70 million people constituting 60 per cent of the population live below the poverty line. The per capita income in Bangladesh is 170 dollars per year, which is much lower than the per capita income in India. The border between India and Bangladesh is very porous. In these circumstances, the continued large-scale population movement from Bangladesh to India is inevitable, unless effective measures are taken to counter it.

10. Besides the above considerations, there are other contributory factors facilitating infiltration from Bangladesh. Ethnic, linguistic and

religious commonality between the illegal migrants and many people on our side of the border, enables them to find shelter. It makes their detection difficult. Some political parties have been encouraging and even helping illegal migration, with a view to building vote banks. These immigrants are hard working and are prepared to work as cheap labour and domestic for lower remuneration, than the local people. This makes them acceptable. Moreover, with corruption being all pervasive, corrupt officials, are bribed to provide help. Recently, a racket has been busted in Lakhimpur. Four individuals were found to have been providing forged citizenship certificates and other documents to illegal migrants for the last 14 years.

11. There is no evidence of Bangladesh authorities organising the movement of population but they certainly have made no attempts to prevent it and indeed, may be welcoming it, to ease their problem of bursting population. Thus, there is now even an attempt to cover up this movement. Prime Minister Sheikh Hasina has recently asserted that no Bangladeshi is illegally living in India.

Illegal Migrants

12. Illegal migrants have been defined in Assam Accord as those who infiltrated illegally after 24 December 1971. However, the stream that infiltrated illegally between 1 January 1966 and 24 December 1971 was not to be deported and was to be given Indian citizenship after a lapse of ten years. No doubt, Hindus required special consideration at the time of Partition and had to be treated as refugees, but this cannot be allowed to continue forever. Post 1971 Hindu illegal migrants cannot justifiably claim refugee status.

13. No census has been carried out to determine the number of these illegal migrants. Precise and authentic figures are not available but on the basis of estimates, extrapolations and various indicators, their number runs into millions.

14. Mr. S.C. Mullan, ICS, Census Superintendent of Assam, wrote in 1931, "Probably the most important event in the province during the last twenty five years—an event, moreover, which seems likely to alter permanently the whole future of Assam and to destroy more surely than did the Burmese invaders of 1829, the whole structure of Assamese culture and civilisation—has been the invasion of a vast horde of land hungry Bengali immigrants; mostly Muslims, from the districts of Eastern Bengal sometime before 1911 and the census report of that is the first report which makes mention of the advancing host. But, as we now know, the Bengali, immigrants censused for the first time on their char islands of Goalpara in 1921 were merely the advance guard—or rather the scouts—of a huge army following closely at their heels. By 1921 the first army corps had

passed into Assam and had practically conquered the district of Goalpara... Where there is wasteland thither flock the Mymensinghias. In fact, the way in which they have seized upon the vacant areas in the Assam valley seems almost uncanny. Without fuss, without tumult, without undue trouble to the district revenue staffs, a population which must amount to over half a million has transplanted itself from Bengal into the Assam Valley during the last twenty-five years. It looks like a marvel of administrative organisation on the part of Government but it is nothing of the sort; the only thing I can compare it to is the mass movement of large body of ants... it is sad but by no means improbable that in another thirty years Sibsagar district will be the only part of Assam in which an Assamese will find himself at home". The Census Report of 1931 has graphically shown the growth of Mymensinghias in the three undivided districts of Goalpara, Kamrup and Nowgong from 1911 to 1931, as follows:

Goalpara			*Kamrup*			*Nowgong*		
1911	1921	1931	1911	1921	1931	1911	1921	1931
30,000	70,000	80,000		30,000	90,000		50,000	100,000

15. I have quoted the 1931 census report in extensio for three reasons. First, it contains precise figures for migration from Bengal into Assam even when this did not involve any movement across international border. Unfortunately, today we have no census report on the basis of which we can accurately define the contours of trans-border movement. Thus we have to rely on broad estimates of theatrical extrapolations to work out the dimension of illegal migration that has taken place from East Pakistan/Bangladesh. Second, Mr. Mullan described this invasion using military terminology, which in present geo-strategic context underscores the strategic aspect of the problem. It is unfortunate that to this day, after half a century of Independence, we have chosen to remain virtually oblivious to the grave danger to our national security arising from this unabated influx of illegal migrants. Third, the prophecy that except in Sibsagar District, the Assamese people will not find themselves at home in Assam, is well on its way to becoming true as reflected by the present demographic pattern of Assam.

16. Shri Indrajit Gupta, the then Home Minister of India stated in the Parliament on 6 May 1997 that there were 10 million illegal migrants residing in India. Quoting Home Ministry/Intelligence Bureau source, the 10 August 1998 issue of India Today has given the breakdown of these illegal migrants by States—West Bengal 5.4 million, Assam 4 million, Tripura 8 million, Bihar 0.5 million, Maharashtra 0.5 million, Rajasthan 0.5 million and Delhi 0.3 million making a total of 10.83 million.

17. On 10 April, 1992, Shri Hiteswar Saikia, the then Chief Minister of Assam stated that there were 3 million Bangladeshi illegal migrants in Assam but two days later, he committed a volte face and declared that there were no illegal migrants in Assam. However, one can see for oneself, the large-scale infiltration of Bangladeshis that has taken place into Assam. Looking at the population in the border areas of Assam, sometimes one wonders whether one is in Assam or in Bangladesh. Shri E.N. Rammohan, DG, BSF, who is an IPS officer of Assam cadre, in his report of 10 February 1997 has stated, "As Additional SP in 1968 in Nagaon, I did not see a single Bangladeshi village in Jagiroad or in Kaziranga. In 1982, when I was posted as DIGP, Northern Range, Tezpur, five new Bangladeshis Muslim villages had come up near Jagiroad and hundreds of families had built up their huts encroaching into the land of the Kaziranga Game Sanctuary". He mentioned that in 1971 the large island of Chawalkhoa comprising 5000 Bighas of land was being cultivated by Assamese villagers from Gorukhut and Sanuna and went on the state, "In 1982 when I was posted as DIGP, Tezpur, there was a population of more than 10,000 immigrant Muslims on the island. The pleas of the Assamese villagers to the District Administration to evict those people from the island fell on deaf ears. Any honest young IAS, SDO of Mangaldoi Sub-division who tried to do this, found himself transferred. In 1983 when an election was forced on the people of Assam... the people of the villages living on the banks of the Brahmaputra opposite Chawalkhoa attacked the encroachers on this island, when they found that they had been given voting rights by the Government. It is of interest that Assamese Muslims of Sanuna village attacked the Bengali Muslim encroachers on this island. I am a direct witness to this."

18. The following indicators of the dimension of illegal migration taking place are relevant:

(a) Bangladesh census records indicate a reduction of 39 lakh Hindus between 1971 and 1981 and another 36 lakh between 1981 and 1989. These 75 lakh (39+36) Hindus have obviously come into India. Perhaps most of them have come into States other than Assam.

(b) There were 7.5 lakh Bihari Muslims in refugee camps in Bangladesh in 1971. At the instance of Saudi Arabia, Pakistan was persuaded to accept 33,000 Bihari Muslims. There are at present only 2 lakh Bihari Muslims in refugee camps in Bangladesh. The unaccounted for 5.17 lakh must have infiltrated into India, as there is little possibility or evidence of them having merged into Bangladesh society.

(c) In 1970 the total population of East Pakistan was 7.5 crore but in 1974 it had come down to 7.14 crore. On the basis of 3.1 per cent annual population growth rate of that period, the population in 1974 should have been 7.7 crore. The shortfall of 6 million people can be explained only by large-scale migration.

19. Assam specific figures of illegal migrants have been worked out from available statistics as follows:

(a) Recent enumeration of electors list in Assam by the Election Commission shows more than 30 per cent increase in 17 Assembly constituencies and more than 20 per cent increase in 40 constituencies between 1994 and 1997. Whereas the All India average growth for a three-year period intervening the two intensive revisions in 1994 and 1997 is 7 per cent, the growth in Assam for this period is 16.4 per cent.

(b) Relative decadal percentage growth of population of Assam, All India and Bangladesh is as follows:

	Year	Assam	All India	Bangladesh
(i)	1901-1911	16.99	5.75	9.1
(ii)	1911-1921	20.48	-0.31	5.4
(iii)	1921-1931	19.91	11.00	7.06
(iv)	1931-1941	20.40	14.22	17.6
(v)	1941-1951	34.98	21.51	0.1
(vi)	1951-1961	34.95	24.80	29.83
(vii)	1971-1981	23.8	24.66	31.83
(viii)	1981-1991	23.8	23.85	22.00

Explanatory Notes:

(i) There was no census in Assam in 1981. The figures indicated have been worked out on the basis of 1971-91 growth rate.

(ii) There was no census in Bangladesh in 1971. It was carried out in 1974. The population grew by 40.4 per cent between 1961-74 and another 21.9 per cent during 1974-81.

(iii) The much higher percentage of growth rate in Assam from 1911 to 1971 over the All India and Bangladesh figures indicate migration into Assam. The All India growth rate for 1921 should be treated as an aberration but even in that decade Assam's growth rate was higher than neighbouring Bengal districts which now constitute Bangladesh.

(iv) The reduced percentage of growth rates for Assam in 1971-91 presents a distorted picture unless one relates it to community-wise percentage of growth in Assam as compared to All India figures. This is shown at sub-para (c) below.

(c) Community-wise Growth:

Year	*Assam*		*All India*	
	Hindus	*Muslims*	*Hindus*	*Muslims*
(i) 1951-1961	33.71	38.35	20.29	25.61
(ii) 1961-1971	37.17	30.99	23.72	30.85
(iii) 1971-1991	41.89	77.42	48.38	55.04

Explanatory Note:

The decadal growth rate for both Hindus and Muslims for the period 1951-61 and 1961-71 was higher than their respective All India growth rate, indicating migration of both communities into Assam. However, during the period 1971-91 Hindu growth rate in Assam was much less than the All India figure. Possibly, this was due to large-scale population movement of non-Assamese Hindus out of Assam during the Students movement and subsequent militancy in the State. In the case of Muslims the Assam growth rate was much higher than the All India rate. This suggests continued large scale Muslim illegal migration into Assam.

(d) Muslim population of Assam has shown a rise of 77.42 per cent in 1991 from what it was in 1971. Hindu population has risen by nearly 41.89 per cent in this period.

(e) Muslim population in Assam has risen from 24.68 per cent in 1951 to 28.42 per cent in 1991. As per 1991 census, four districts (Dhubri, Goalpara, Barpeta and Hailakandi) have become Muslim majority districts. Two more districts (Nagaon and Karimganj) should have become so by 1998 and one district (Morigaon) is fast approaching this population.

20. The growth of Muslim population has been emphasised in the previous paragraph to indicate the extent of illegal migration from Bangladesh to Assam because as stated earlier, the illegal migrants coming into India after 1971 have been almost exclusively Muslims.

21. Pakistan's ISI has been active in Bangladesh supporting militant movements in Assam. Muslim militant organisations have mushroomed

in Assam and there are reports of some 50 Assamese Muslim youth having gone for training to Afghanistan and Kashmir.

Consequences

22. The dangerous consequences of large-scale illegal migration from Bangladesh, both for the people of Assam and more for the Nation as a whole, need to be emphatically stressed. No misconceived and mistaken notions of secularism should be allowed to come in the way of doing so.

23. As a result of population movement from Bangladesh, the spectre looms large of the indigenous people of Assam being reduced to a minority in their home State. Their cultural survival will be in jeopardy, their political control will be weakened and their employment opportunities will be undermined.

24. This silent and invidious demographic invasion of Assam may result in the loss of the geo-strategically vital districts of Lower Assam. The influx of these illegal migrants is turning these districts into a Muslim majority region. It will then only be a matter of time when a demand for their merger with Bangladesh may be made. The rapid growth of international Islamic fundamentalism may provide the driving force for this demand. In this context, it is pertinent that Bangladesh has long discarded secularism and has chosen to become an Islamic State. Loss of Lower Assam will sever the entire landmass of the North East, from the rest of India and the rich natural resources of that region will be lost to the Nation.

CHAPTER III
PREVENTING INFILTRATION

Early Years

1. Assam has 262 km border with Bangladesh out of which 92 km is riverine. In 1947 with the emergence of two dominions on the Sub-Continent, India and Pakistan, this became an international border. For the first few years, unrestricted trans-border movement continued in this sector. Bengali Hindu refugees from East Pakistan fleeing from their homes poured across the border-seeking asylum. Concurrently, Bengali Muslims too continued to come across the border for economic reasons. There was also some movement of Muslims from Assam into East Pakistan.

2. Whereas in the West, the trans-border movement of refugees from India to Pakistan and vice versa was a deluge which lasted only a few months, in the East the situation was very different. Hindus from East Pakistan (Bangladesh) kept coming across for many years and indeed they still continue to come. Muslims from Assam going to East Pakistan were relatively in much less number. The traditional influx of Bengali Muslims into Assam continued unabated. The large-scale movement of Bengali population, both

Hindus and Muslims into Assam, caused considerable resentment among the Assamese people and there were instances of anti-Bengali riots.

3. Initially, the State Police with its limited resources policed this border but they could not stem the trans-border movement. The large influx into Assam was a matter of great concern. Government of India evolved the PIP (Prevention of Infiltration from Pakistan) scheme, which came into operation in 1964. 159 Watch Posts, 15 Patrol Posts and 6 Passport Check Posts were set up. A Police force of 1914 personnel under a DIGP was deployed to check infiltration. After the 1965 war, when the Border Security Force came into being, responsibility for guarding the border was taken over by that Force. The Border organisation set up under the PIP scheme was now deployed in the interior to identify and deport illegal migrants. In 1987 this organisation was augmented by 1280 officers and men provided by Government of India and 806 by Government of Assam, making a total of 4000 personnel. Currently, this organisation is functioning under an Additional DG Police of Assam.

4. Neither the BSF on the border nor the Border organisation in the interior could prevent large-scale illegal migration from Bangladesh. The border is very porous and the illegal migrants enjoyed political patronage. Efforts to prevent their ingress or to deport them were not very successful. Nevertheless in the first flush as per JIC Paper No 04/95 of 3 January 1995, 1.5 lakh illegal migrants were pushed back but many managed to re-enter from different points on the border. There were reports of police excesses and high-handedness, as also allegation of harassment of genuine Indian Muslims.

5. The Chief Election Commissioner, Shri S.L. Shakhdher told a conference of State Chief Electoral Officers in 1978, "In one State (Assam), the population in 1971 recorded an increase as high as 34.98 per cent, over the 1961 figures and this increase was attributed to the influx of a very large number of persons from the neighbouring countries. The influx has become a regular feature. I think it may not be a wrong assessment to make, on the basis of the increase of 34.98 per cent between the two censuses, the increase that is likely to be recorded in 1991 census would be more than 100 per cent over the 1961 census. In other words, a stage would be reached when the State would have to reckon with the foreign nationals who may probably constitute a sizeable percentage, if not the majority of the population of the State. Another disturbing factor in this regard is the demand made by the political parties for the inclusion in the electoral rolls of the names of such migrants who are not Indian citizens, without even questioning and properly determining the citizenship status". A few months later a by-election was to be held at Mangaldoi in which there were complaints about 70,000 illegal migrants figuring in the voter's

list. The people got convinced that illegal migration on a colossal scale had been taking place and this sparked the anti-foreigner's movement in Assam. Government of India forced the 1983 election in Assam on the basis of a defective voters list. This was done on the plea that there was not enough time to revise the electoral rolls before the election. There was widespread violence during this agitation including the infamous massacre of 1700 Bengali Muslims at Nellie by the Lalung tribe.

6. After years of a massive agitation, demanding detection, deletion and deportation of foreigners, the agitators reached a settlement with Government of India. Assam Accord was signed in 1985. Besides other issues agreed on, Assam Accord stipulated fencing of the border with Bangladesh, to prevent ingress of illegal migrants.

Border Fencing

7. A border fence may be a foolproof method of preventing infiltration but there is no better way of doing so. To be effective, border fencing has to be supplemented by vigorous patrolling and other measures. The motivating factors behind infiltration must be addressed. If this can be done successfully, then a permanent solution of the problem can be found.

8. Border policing in both Punjab and Assam should prevent trans-border movement of smugglers, militants and infiltrators. In the case of Assam, infiltration has a much bigger and a more dangerous dimension. Despite this, the measures to counter trans-border movement in Assam appear to have been given a lower priority than in Punjab. This is evident from the following facts:

(a) The decision to fence the border was taken in 1985 and reflected in Assam Accord but the work on fencing started seven years later in 1992. 13 years have elapsed since this Accord and fencing has not yet been completed. Whereas in Dhubri sector of Assam it is nearly complete, in the Cachar sector only a little over half has been completed. As against this, fencing in Punjab started in 1988 and was completed in 3 years by 1991.

(b) The quality of fencing in Punjab is superior. It is two feet taller. Observation towers and lighting of the fence have been provided in Punjab, all along the border. In Assam observation towers have been constructed in Dhubri sector only and there are none in Cachar sector. There is no lighting of the fence anywhere in Assam.

(c) The density of troops guarding the fence is higher in Punjab. A BSF battalion in Punjab holds a frontage of approximately 30 kilometres. In Assam, BSF Battalions in Dhubri sector are deployed over frontages of 70 kilometres and in Cachar sector over a frontage of 40 Km.

9. Border fencing in Assam must be completed forthwith on a war footing. In terms of cost outlay, it may not now be possible to provide border fencing of the same height as in Punjab but there must be lighting arrangements for the fence. Observation towers must be provided in Cachar Sector.

10. Additional BSF battalions should be provided in the East with each battalion having a frontage of 30 kilometres. It is understood that one reason for thin deployment of BSF in the East is the fact that 16 battalions are deployed on counter insurgency tasks. Such diversion of forces from border policing to other duties, when the battle against illegal migrants is on, cannot but have adverse effect. The shortage of BSF units must be made up on priority through new raising.

11. The present arrangement of guarding the riverine border with some speedboats and out-board fitted country boats, is not adequate. There is a need to have floating BOPs on medium watercraft with four to five speedboats attached to them. A proposal for nine medium crafts has been put up by DG BSF. This should be sanctioned soon.

12. All country boats plying on the river near the border must be registered with their registration number marked on them and the registration papers available with the crew for verification, when required.

Other Measures

13. Certain other measures are also required to be taken to deal with illegal migration. These are as follows:

(a) Our nationals in the border districts and for that matter in the whole State should be provided multipurpose photo identity card. This task should be completely on high priority.

(b) Effective arrangements must be made for registration of births and deaths in the State.

(c) The 1950 National Register of Citizens should be updated. Computerisation will facilitate this process. A separate register for illegal migrants (Stateless citizens) should also be maintained.

14. The Brahmaputra is normally 5 to 7 Km wide and during floods has only one water channel. However, In lean season, there are two, three or even more water channels throwing up chars (river islands). Due to changing river configurations, it is difficult to survey the chars. The Bangladeshi Muslims settle on these chars. They are hardy and are prepared to face difficult living conditions, particularly when the chars gets submerged for a few days during floods, which come three to four times in a season. Chickens are put on roofs, cattle herded on platforms above the water level and in emergent situation men and cattle live in boats. This

hardy community has been living on chars in the Brahmaputra from Dhubri (near the international border) to Lakhimpur. There are still several chars, which are uninhabited. These should be handed over to the Forest Department and notified as forestland. Trees, which can withstand 1 to 3 feet of water during the flood season, should be planted on them.

Developments in Bangladesh

15. The measures recommended to arrest the influx of illegal migrants may not completely stop their ingress but will certainly go a long way in reducing it to a small trickle. A more lasting and effective solution can come about through economic development in Bangladesh. This will remove the motivation behind trans-border migration. Lately, there have been welcome developments in this regard in Bangladesh. There are signs of the economy picking up in that country through the unique experiment of Grameen Bank supported by a large amount of international funding and the efforts of the Government and other NGOs. The Grameen Bank has been targeting the women. Its membership has swelled to over 2 million, and of these, 93 per cent are women. It is providing micro-credit loans without any collateral. These run into several billions and they have a record recovery rate of 98 per cent. This is bringing about a perceptible change in the rural areas. Targeting women for economic development provides multi-benefits. It adds to the earning of the family, encourages gender justice, promotes women's education, which acts as a curb on population growth, and liberated women become bulwark against the spread of Islamic fundamentalism. All these benefits suit the interests of India. India should, as far as possible, be prepared to assist in socio-economic development of Bangladesh.

Implementation

16. The various measures recommended to stop illegal migration are non-controversial. No political party or organisation within the country can legitimately protest and demand that these steps should not be taken. Through these measures, we can bring about a sea change in the situation and trans-border migration will become a trickle. If we do not take effective measures to stop this movement and allow trans-border migration to continue unabated, then it may spell the doom of Assam and put our national security in grave jeopardy.

CHAPTER IV
DETECTION AND DEPORTATION

Conflicting Viewpoints

1. Measures to stem illegal migration can be undertaken without any

controversy but any alternation of status quo in regard to detection and deportation of these migrants will result in strident assertion of conflicting viewpoints. The "secular" parties and the minorities do not see any danger from illegal migration. They believe that most of the so-called illegal migrants are Bengali speaking Indian Muslims and this issue has been unnecessarily blown out of proportion. They fear that in the garb of deporting foreigners, Indian Muslims will be harassed. Thus they are for the continuance of IM (DT) Act in its present form. On the other hand, the majority community of Assam and the political parties dubbed as "communal" by the "secularists" have a diametrically opposite viewpoint. They are gravely concerned about the large influx of illegal migrants and want their ingress stopped. They also want that the highly discriminating IM (DT) Act be repealed forthwith. There appears to be no meeting ground between these opposing views. Notwithstanding this, it is in our national interest to work out a mutually acceptable solution to this burning problem, which not only affects the people of Assam but the entire Nation.

2. The furore raised over the attempt by Maharashtra Government to deport 34 Bangladeshis from Mumbai in accordance with the due process of law, underscored the sharp divide in the country over this issue. The ugly incidents in Calcutta, the stalling of the proceedings of the Parliament and the outraged feelings so strongly expressed in the Press, showed how sensitivities got aroused on this issue. In the past few years, many illegal migrants from different States, including Maharashtra, were being pushed back into Bangladesh—4895 in 1993, 5782 in 1994, 3612 in 1995, 2791 in 1996, 4222 in 1997 and 1597 up to September 1998. In other words such deportation had been a common feature and no protests were being raised on that account. The point about Government of West Bengal not being given prior information does not hold much water. The deportation had to be effected by a central agency, the BSF. No doubt the illegal migrants escorted by Maharashtra Police had to transit through West Bengal but for that matter, they had also to transit through other States en route. On that basis, each State Government en route could ask for prior information of their deportation. It is pertinent that during the days of terrorism in Punjab, Policemen from that State had to come to Calcutta and had picked up suspected terrorists without any intimation to West Bengal Government. The protest made about that action was almost mute compared to what happened in the case of the attempted deportation of the Bangladeshis from Mumbai. Understandably there was sharp reaction in Bangladesh. The Bangladeshi Press was highly critical of the designs of the "Hindu fundamentalist Government" in India, trying to throw out innocent Indian Muslims and dump them in Bangladesh. One newspaper went to the extent of demanding that Bangladesh should seek assistance

from the USA to deal with India. Prime Minister, Sheikh Hasina, a known friend of India, issued a statement that no Bangladeshi was illegally living in India. Her predecessor, not known to be so friendly towards India, had agreed to a Joint Working Group of India and Bangladesh to be set up for examining the issue of illegal migrants. This had implied acceptance of the existence of this problem, which was now being so summarily dismissed.

Deportation

3. International law does not provide for unilateral deportation in defiance of the views of the country to which the deportation is to take place. With the stand now taken by Bangladesh, it will not be possible for India to deport millions of illegal migrants to Bangladesh. From 1993 to September 1998, the BSF tried to hand over 39,746 illegal migrants to Bangladesh Rifles. The latter accepted only 9.253 and refused to accept 30.493. The acceptance figures by Bangladesh declined from 5799 in 1993 to only 55 in 1998 (up to 30 September). With the recent developments in the wake of the attempt to deport 34 Bangladeshi Muslims from Mumbai and the statement of the Prime Minister of Bangladesh, it is unlikely that Bangladesh Rifles will now accept Bangladeshi migrants. Moreover, the bursting population of Bangladesh creates a Malthusian nightmare and is not conducive to that country accepting them. Further, our capability to identify and deport over ten million such people is questionable. In these circumstances, deportation of these illegal migrants is not now a practical proposition.

IM (DT) Act

4. IM (DT) Act was enacted at the height of the anti-foreigner's movement in Assam. The large-scale violence during the movement including the Nellie massacre, had led to understandable apprehension among the minorities of harassment and victimisation. A large number of illegal migrants had been pushed back in previous years. It is possible that in this process, some genuine Indian citizens had been harassed and pushed back. Be that as it may, the fact is that on the plea of protecting genuine Indian citizens, the IM (DT) Act was formulated but in practice, it has been found to be primarily serving the interests of the illegal migrants.

5. The Act provided for two individuals living within a radius of 3 km of a suspected illegal migrant to file a complaint accompanied with a deposit sum of Rs. 25. The 3 Km restriction was modified and now the complainant can be from the same police station area as the individual being complained against. The deposit fee has been reduced from Rs. 25

to Rs. 1 0. The Police can also suo moto initiate action. Elaborate time consuming procedures have been laid down for screening, for examination by District Tribunals and for appeal to the Appellate Tribunal. The 3 km restriction

6. Proponents of IM (DT) maintain that unwarranted fears have been aroused about the large influx of population from Bangladesh when in actual fact their number is very small. They want to retain this Act at all costs. They feel that otherwise, the minorities would face great hardship and harassment.

7. The opponents of this Act demand its immediate repeal, as it is a highly discriminatory legislation applying only to Assam and not to any other State. They argue that such a legislation should not have been on the statute of any sovereign State. It gives freedom to an alien to enter this country, secure in the knowledge that the country he has entered illegally, will have to prove that he is an illegal migrant to deny him citizenship. Under the Foreigners Act which applies to the rest of the country and which is in consonance with the practice followed the world over, it is for the foreigner to prove that he is an Indian national to claim Indian citizenship. The IM (DT) Act shifts the burden of proof on the complainant or the Police, to establish that the person complained against is a foreigner.

8. This Act caters for an Appellant Tribunal of two retired High Court Judges, sixteen district Tribunals of two retired District/Additional District Judges with supporting staff. The Border organisation of 4000 Policemen processes the cases of alleged illegal migrants. The efforts of these agencies maintained at cost of hundreds of crore to the Exchequer, extending over a period of 15 years, has led to the identification of only 9,599 illegal migrants. Out of these only 1,454 could be deported. These statistics amply establish the futility of continuing with the IM (DT) Act in its present form.

9. Apart from the conflicting views of the proponents and opponents of the IM (DT) Act, those working for executing its provisions have been facing difficulties as indicated below:

(a) The Tribunals have been starved of funds and resources. Out of 16 District Tribunals only 5 are functioning. The remaining 11 tribunals have only one person each on the bench and as such are non-functional. Salaries and TA bills of the staff are not paid in time. Essential facilities, like transport and telephone are lacking and funds are often not available to buy even postage stamps.

(b) The Border Organisation required to process these cases has been encountering difficulties at every step. Often by the time a complaint is received or the Police initiates inquiry against a suspect, that individual shifts to another location and is not traceable. When the individual is available, he insists he is an Indian national and while the Police tries to collect evidence, he often disappears. The process of absconding also occurs at two subsequent stages—before the case is heard by the Tribunal and during the 30 days period allowed to the person to appear to the higher tribunal or face expulsion. Under this Act, the Police does not have the powers of search, seizure or arrest as available under the Foreigners Act. During trial by Tribunals, prosecution witnesses do not appear because there is no provision for paying them their travelling expense.

10. Any move to repeal the IM (DT) Act is likely to encounter strong opposition from the minorities and their supporters, for vested and opportunistic reasons. Some of these have begun to suggest that to remove the allegation of discrimination connected with this Act, its provisions should be extended to other States. They argue that the Foreigners Act of 1946 is a legacy of the British era and were meant to deal with foreign national who were ethnically and culturally different from Indians. The requirements for dealing with Bangladeshis, who have ethnic, cultural, linguistic and religious affinities with our population, are different. This requires a different legislation. This line of argument ignores similarities between the Tamil people of Sri Lanka and of Tamil Nadu or for that matter, the similarities among the people living on either side of the Indo-Nepal border. It is further argued that the meagre number of foreigners detected under the IM (DT) Act is not due to any infirmities of this Act or in the procedures being followed, but due to the very small numbers of illegal migrants in the country. This argument flies in the face of all available statistics and other indicators, establishing the presence of a very large number of illegal Bangladeshi migrants in the country.

11. As deportation of such a large number of illegal migrants is no longer a viable option and because of the numerous infirmities in the IM (DT) Act, which have rendered its continuation, a wasteful exercise, it is imperative that this Act be repealed. It should be replaced by a more just, workable and fair enactment.

Replacing IM (DT) Act

The IM (DT) Act does not exclusively apply to any religious community. It is applicable as much to Bengali Hindus as to Bengali Muslims. Providing asylum to minorities fleeing from their home country was a Partition liability for both India and Pakistan. Yet in Assam no distinction has been made between Hindus and Muslims. Those migrants who came into Assam up to 24 March 1971 have been given Indian citizenship, irrespective of the religious community to which they belong. However, the ground reality is that of late almost all the illegal migrants now coming into Assam are Muslims.

12. The repeal of IM (DT) Act and its replacement by another Act, must take into account the legitimate fears of the minorities. They should be assured that the new Act will be fair, just and transparent, leading to expeditious disposal of cases. The following aspects have to be noted:

(a) Partition liability of India in relation to refugees from East Pakistan/Bangladesh is only in respect of the minority community of that country. However, this liability should not be extended beyond a reasonable time frame. A quarter of a century is adequate for this purpose. Any Hindu migrant coming to India after 24 March 1971 without valid papers should be classified as an illegal migrant.

(b) Although India had no Partition liability for East Pakistani Muslims, Assam Accord caters for Indian citizenship being granted to all East Pakistani Muslims who came across illegally between 15 August 1947 and 24 March 1971, with a special provision that those who came between 1 January 1966 and 24 March 1971 would be eligible for this, only after a lapse of ten years of being identified as foreigners.

(c) As per JIC Paper No. 04/95 of 3 January 1995, even after legitimising pre-1971 illegal migrants, 18 per cent of the population of Assam in 1991 comprises illegal migrants. Since deportation is being ruled out as a viable option, even those, whether Hindus or Muslims, who came in illegally after 24 March 1971, will now not be deported. Thus the scope for harassment gets considerably reduced and the main sting in the whole process gets taken out.

13. Although illegal migrants, who came in after 24 March 1971 will not be deported, they must be identified and after identification denied voting rights and certain other facilities like acquisition of immovable property. A suitable process for doing so which may have acceptability and command credibility should be evolved. This exercise should be completed expeditiously. This process for doing so should be on the following lines:

(a) Ground survey teams each under a Magistrate assisted by the Border Organisation, should extensively tour the areas allotted to them, to identify illegal migrants. To ensure maximum objectivity and freedom from local pressures, political or otherwise, Magistrates from outside Assam be deputed for this task. The survey should be completed in a fixed time frame of a few months. Inducting Magistrates from outside will be on the lines of what happened in 1983 elections, when officers were brought into Assam from different States on temporary deputation.

(b) Individuals identified as illegal migrants should be allowed the right of appeal before Foreigners Tribunal set up under the Foreigners Act. This will provide necessary judicial sanctity to this exercise.

(c) Foreigners' identity as illegal migrants should be denied voting rights and their children born in India should not automatically become eligible for Indian citizenship. Disenfranchisement may be a big issue for political parties who so assiduously try to build vote banks but is no hardship to the immigrant. The denial of voting rights to these migrants can by no stretch be deemed to be unjust. Over 1 lakh Hindu and Sikh refugees from West Pakistan, who settled in Jammu region in 1947, have to this day, after a lapse of over 50 years, not been given voting rights. However, refugees from West Pakistan who settled in other States were given full citizenship rights and many amongst them became Union Cabinet Ministers and one became Prime Minister

14. The proposed arrangement should adequately assuage the legitimate fears of the minority community and will also be a humane measure for the illegal migrants. Pre-1971 illegal migrants stand already legitimised and the post-1971 illegal migrants, not now to be deported, will be partially legitimised.

15. The minority community in Assam now comprises nearly 30 per cent of the population and with their tendency to vote as a bloc, they can hardly be considered a minority, in real terms. They have come to acquire a decisive role in Assam's democratic polity, which the majority community with its split votes, cannot match. So far as the majority community is concerned, they may resent the decision not to deport the illegal migrants but in the present circumstances, there is no other alternative. They should get reconciled to it. Illegal migrants up to 24 March 1971 have been made Indian citizens and this has been accepted by them. Illegal migrants of post-24 March 1971 vintage will not be deported but will be made Stateless citizens. The minority community should appreciate that the repeal of IM (DT) Act and its replacement by a just, fair, transparent and expeditious act will provide adequate safeguards against harassment and victimisation. This will also reduce political patronage for illegal migration and will be yet another disincentive for prospective illegal migrants.

CHAPTER V
CONCLUSION

1. A silent and invidious invasion of Assam has been taking place for several decades and successive Governments have failed to stem this demographic onslaught. It started as a purely economic movement contributing to the development of Assam's agricultural economy. As Independence approached, it acquired communal and political contours. And today, an international dimension with security overtones has got added to this population movement.

2. Hitherto the intrusion of illegal migrants has generally been looked upon as a local problem affecting only the people of Assam. The myopic view accounts for the more sinister and dangerous aspects being overlooked. The views expressed by Jinnah, Bhutto, Sheikh Mujib-ur-Rahman and the present day intellectuals in Bangladesh cannot be ignored. Assam can provide the much-desired lebensraum for Bangladesh. This fact coupled with Assam's geo-strategic importance, Bangladesh's bursting population and growing international Islamic fundamentalism, underscore the volatile situation created by this ongoing demographic intrusion from across the border. We must not allow any misconceived notions of secularism to blind us to these realities.

3. Although Bangladeshi illegal migrants have come into several States of India and they are more numerous in West Bengal than in Assam, they pose a much greater threat in Assam than in any other State. If not effectively checked, they may swamp the Assamese people and may sever the North East landmass from the rest of India. This will lead to disastrous strategic and economic results.

4. Political parties have been underplaying the grave importance of this problem and have been viewing it as something affecting only the Assamese people. Thus an issue of great concern for national security has been made into a partisan affair and a matter of vote banks. It must be lifted above the mire of party politics and viewed as a national security issue of great importance. There is an imperative need to evolve a national consensus on this all-important threat facing the Nation.

5. Concrete steps must be taken on war footing to ensure that the borders are as nearly sealed as possible and the unabated flood of infiltration, reduced to a trickle. Concurrently, the highly discriminatory IM (DT) Act, which during the last 15 years has proved to be an exercise in futility, should be repealed. With deportation of illegal migrants to Bangladesh no longer a viable option, a new legislation needs to be introduced which will ensure a just, fair, practical and expeditions approach to detecting illegal migrants and declaring them Stateless citizens without voting rights, and without the right to acquire immovable property.

6. A summary of recommendations is attached as an appendix to this report.

Lt. Gen. (Retd.) S.K. Sinha, PVSM
Governor of Assam
Guwahati
8 November 1998

APPENDIX
SUMMARY OF RECOMMENDATIONS

1. Awareness should be promoted about illegal migration into Assam being not only a threat to the identity of the Assamese people but what is more, being a grave threat to our national security.
2. Border fencing in Assam should be completed on a war footing. Observation towers and lighting should be provided on the same scale as in Punjab.
3. BSF battalions deployed in Assam should not be given responsibility to hold unduly extended frontages. As in the case of Punjab, BSF battalions should hold a frontage of 30 Km. Additional BSF battalions should be provided for this purpose.
4. Diversion of BSF battalions from the border in Assam for other tasks, when the battle against infiltrators is on, must be scrupulously avoided.
5. All country boats, plying in the river near the border should be registered and their registration numbers marked on them.
6. Medium crafts for floating BOPs with adequate speedboats for the riverine sector should be made available as early as possible.
7. Multi-purpose photo identity cards should be provided to all our nationals. Districts bordering Bangladesh should be accorded higher priority.
8. Effective arrangements should be made for registration of births and deaths.
9. The National Register of Citizens (NRC) should be updated and computerised. A separate register of Stateless citizens should also be maintained.
10. Vacant Chars in the river should be handed over to the Forest Department and trees planted on them.
11. As far as possible, we should assist in the process of economic development in Bangladesh. Socio-economic programmes designed to improve the lot of women should be given priority due to its multiple beneficiary spin offs—improving the family's income, women's education curbing population growth and

educated women becoming a bulwark against the spread of Islamic fundamentalism.

12. Hindu illegal migrants who have infiltrated after 24 March 1971 should not be given refugee status. They should be treated as illegal migrants.
13. While maximum effort must be made to stem the ingress of illegal migrants, those who have already infiltrated after 24 March 1971 to date, may not be deported.
14. The IM (DT) Act should be repealed and replaced by a new legislation, which should provide for detection for illegal migrants in a just, fair and expeditious manner, with due judicial sanctity accorded to the process. Those identified, as illegal migrants should be allowed to stay in the country as Stateless citizens with no voting right nor the right to acquire immovable property.
15. Survey teams working under Magistrates on deputation from other States assisted by policemen of Border Organisation should identify illegal migrants in a fixed time frame of short duration. Those identified as foreigners by these teams should be given the right of appeal to tribunals set up under Foreigners Act.

ISI Activities in Assam

[A detailed statement pertaining to the activities of Pakistan's secret service organisation, the Inter Services Intelligence in Assam was laid on the table of the Assam Legislative Assembly on 6 April 2000 by the then Chief Minister of Assam, Prafulla Kumar Mahanta. The report showcased evidence collected by the Assam Police, which proves the Pakistan intelligence agency's involvement in fomenting violence, communalism and terror in Assam. It also exposed Pakistan's agenda of attempting to wound India with a "thousand cuts"]

Statement Laid on the Table of the House of Assam Legislative Assembly Under Item No. 12 Dated 6.4.2000

By Shri Prafulla Kumar Mahanta
Chief Minister, Assam

ISI Activities in Assam

During the recent past, Assam Police has gathered sufficient evidence to prove that the Pakistani intelligence agency, Inter Services Intelligence (ISI) has been actively involved in fomenting violence and terrorism in the State. These activities are mainly in the following areas:

1. Promoting indiscriminate violence in the State by providing active support to the local militant outfits.
2. Creating new militant outfits along ethnic and communal lines by instigating ethnic and religious groups.
3. Supply of explosives and sophisticated arms to various terrorist groups.
4. Causing sabotage of oil pipelines and other installations, communication lines, railways and roads.
5. Promoting fundamentalism and militancy among local Muslim youth by misleading them in the name of "jihad".
6. Promoting communal tension between Hindu and Muslim citizens by way of false and highly inflammatory propaganda.

Support to Militancy and Terrorism in Assam

Assam Police is in possession of plenty of evidence to show that the top ULFA leadership is in touch with certain officials of the Pakistani High

Commission in Dacca. The ULFA leaders have been travelling to Pakistan regularly. Pakistani agencies have already imparted arms training to hundreds of ULFA cadres. According to the statement of scores of arrested ULFA leaders including their self-styled Vice Chairman Pradip Gogoi, the Pakistani officials in their High Commission in Dacca arrange for their passport in various Muslim names and send them to Karachi. From Karachi airport, they are whisked away in unmarked vehicles to the training centres. Specific evidence to such trips by dozens of ULFA leaders is already available.

ISI has procured different passports for Paresh Barua, the self-styled C-in-C of ULFA in different names. Assam Police has been able to procure a copy of one passport issued to Paresh Barua in the name of Kamaruddin Zaman Khan. Documentary evidence suggests that this Bangladeshi passport has been obtained by fraudulent means with the help of an official of the Pakistani High Commission.

During the recent Kargil conflict, the ULFA issued a statement condemning Indian Government's role in Kashmir. The language of the above statement was exactly the same as that issued by the Harkat-ul-Mujahideen, a Pakistan based terrorist outfit controlled by the ISI. This shows that even the drafting of the above statement was probably made by Pakistani agencies.

Terrorism on Religious Lines

Assam Police arrested the following four persons in Guwahati on August 10, 1999 while they were found moving about under suspicious circumstances and contacting certain persons in different parts of the State.

1. Md. Fasih Ullah Hussaini @ Hamid Mahmood @ Khalid Mehmood, son of Syed Habibulla, resident of Hyderabad, Sind, Pakistan.
2. Md. Javed Wakhar @ Md. Musaffar @ Md. Mehraj @ Abdul Rahman Danish, resident of Karachi, Pakistan.
3. Maulana Hafiz Md. Akram Mallick @ Musaffar Hassain @ Atabulla @ Bhaijan @ Abdul Awal, son of Md. Abdul Aziz of Village Mukam Shahwali, Kupwara, Jammu and Kashmir (J&K) State.
4. Qari Salim Ahmed @ Abdul Aziz @ Sadat, son of Abdul Rashid, resident of Village Mehilki, Dist. Muzaffarnagar, UP.

These persons had arrived in Dacca from Karachi by Pakistan International Airlines (PIA) flight on different dates in the third week of July 1999 and had meetings with the ISI officials based in Dacca to arrange for onward despatch of a consignment of explosives to Assam.

Subsequently, they travelled to Sylhet and crossed over to India through illegal channels somewhere near Karimganj.

Spread of Harkat-ul-Mujahideen (HuM) in Assam

During interrogation of the arrested persons, it came to light that the Harkat-ul-Mujahideen, a dreaded Pakistan-based terrorist outfit, has recruited and despatched a number of youths from Assam for training in Pakistan. Based on the information provided by them, Assam Police arrested a large number of persons who have returned after training in Pakistan, including some of the top most activists of the Assam unit of the Harkat-ul-Mujahideen. The chief organiser of HuM in Assam, Md. Muslimuddin was also arrested. It has come to light that the Naib Amir of HuM in India, Maulana Md. Fakruddin @ Akram Master also hails from Goalpara district of Assam. He is at present based in Pakistan.

Efforts to Repatriate Funds from Pakistan for Defending the Case of ISI Operatives

Md. Fasih Ullah Hussaini and Javed Wakhar, Pakistani nationals (top activists of Pakistan based Harkat-ul-Mujahideen) who were arrested in Guwahati in August 1999, are now lodged in Goalpara jail. Recently Fasih Ullah moved the Chief Judicial Magistrate of Goalpara for permission to write to the Pakistani High Commissioner in Delhi to obtain a sum of Rs. 3 lakh for meeting their legal expenses to defend their case. The CJM passed an order dated November 16, 1999, agreeing to the prayer and accordingly Md. Fasih Ullah wrote to Mr. Ashraf Jahangir Qazi, the Pakistani High Commissioner stating that he along with his colleagues have been arrested by Assam Police and asking him to obtain a sum of Rs. 3 lakh from his "guardian" in Islamabad. The telephone number of the "guardian" provided in the application – 414446 – is the personal telephone of Fazlur Rahman Khalil, the Chief Amir of Harkat-ul-Mujahideen.

Militant Outfits Organised along Religious Lines

During the last few years, a large number of Muslim militant outfits have mushroomed in the State. The outfits that have come to notice are:

- Muslim United Liberation Front of Assam (MULFA)
- Muslim Liberation Tigers of Assam (MLTA)
- Islamic Liberation Army of Assam (ILAA)
- United Muslim Liberation Front of Assam (UMLFA)
- United Reformation Protest of Assam (URPA)
- People's United Liberation Front (PULF)
- Muslim Volunteer Force (MVF)
- Adam Sena (AS)

- Islamic Sevak Sangha (ISS)
- Harkat-ul-Mujahideen (HuM)
- Harkat-ul-Jihad (HuJ)

These outfits have been actively engaged in extortion of money, recruitment of cadres and training in handling arms and explosives. During the last two years, Assam Police have arrested 101 MLTA activists, 60 other cadres belonging to other outfits noted above.

Misuse of Madrassas and Mosques

Although some of the top arrested militants have been connected with the activities of Mosques or Madrassas, nobody should jump to a conclusion that all these sacred religious institutions have been maligned. While it is necessary to take legal action against those criminals involved in anti-national activities, care should be taken not to bring bad name to the sacred religious institution or to the Muslim community in general. Care has been taken to see that Muslim police officers alone are deputed for such enquiry in religious places.

Inflammatory Propaganda

A number of audiocassettes of speeches by Maulana Masood Azhar have been found in circulation in various parts of the State. The contents of these speeches have been found to be highly inflammatory and communally sensitive.

Profiles of Some of the Arrested Activists

1. Salim Ahmed @ Abdul Aziz, @ Qari Salim (30), S/o, Abdul Rashid of village Mehelki, Dist. Muzaffar Nagar, UP worked as a teacher in a Madrassa and then as Alim in Durul Ulum Shawala Madrassa in Dist. Kupwara in J&K. Salim went to Bangladesh with Faruque in May 1997 through Karimganj border. On May 29, 1997, Salim travelled from Dacca to Pakistan in a PIA flight with one Qasim, a HuM activist. In Pakistan Salim met Chief Amir HuM who advised him to organise HuM in UP, J&K and in Assam by recruiting local Muslim youths for undergoing arms and explosive training in Pakistan. He has visited Assam several times and has stayed with many important people in Assam during such trips. He has been the main inspiring force in recruiting large numbers of Muslim youths from Goalpara, Dhubri and Barpeta Districts after which he organised their trip to Pakistan via Bangladesh for imparting arms and explosive training organised by HuM through ISI operatives. During his stay in Dacca on his return from Pakistan Salim received an explosive consignment of 34 Kg of RDX, 9 timer devices, 30 pieces of detonators, 3 time pencils and 5 blasting machines from an ISI operative located in

Bangladesh. Salim brought the consignment to Rajshahi and handed over the same to Maulana Abdul Jabbar an Imam of Rajshahi in Bangladesh. This consignment was intercepted near the Indo-Bangladesh border by a joint team of Assam and West Bengal Police after it was smuggled into India on August 14, 1999.

2. Javed Wakhar @ Md. Musaffa is another ISI operative and HuM activist arrested at Guwahati. He originally hailed from UP and subsequently obtained Pakistani citizenship. He is an explosive expert of the HuM and was sent to Assam and other States of India for causing large-scale sabotage through a series of bomb explosions.

3. Md. Akram Malik @ Muzaffar Hussain @ Attaullah @ Bhaijan @ Abul Awal @ Jaffar Alam (30) S/o. Abdul Aziz Malik, vill. Mukam Sahwali, District Kupwara, J&K worked as a teacher in Durul Ulum Mukam Sahwali Madrassa from 1993 to 1997 and subsequently joined the HuM. He went over to Pakistan for arms training and was being used by the ISI for creating large-scale disturbances in various States in India. After arrival in Bangladesh, on July 17, Akram accompanied by Salim and Abdul Rahman, Amir HuM, Mumbai, went to Rajshahi with a huge explosives consignment and kept it with Imam Abdul Jaffar of Rajshahi. On July 20, 1999 Akram, Fasiullah left Dacca for Sylhet and with Musaffa, crossed over to India via Karimganj border on 28 July 1999 and reached Guwahati on 29 July 1999.

4. Fasiullah @ Fasi @ Hamid Mahmood (30), S/o. Sayed Habibulla village Gulshan-e-Maymar, Karachi Pakistan, is a HuM activist. After joining the outfit 1991, he took arms training at Pak Afghan border. In 1993, Fasiullah, a commerce graduate, underwent an explosive training at Mansera NWFP in Pakistan. In March 1999, a 70-member group of Mujaheedins consisting of HuM, Lashkar-e-Toiba, Hizbul Mujahideen, Harkat-ul-Ansar, Al Fatah activists made three attempts of intrusion into J&K for Jihad but did not succeed due to stepped up security and vigil along the Line-of-Control (LoC). Fasiullah was one of the members of the above group of Mujaheedins, who was sponsored by ISI of Pakistan to make attempts to infiltrate into J&K for participating in Jihad. On 15 July 1999, under instructions from the ISI and Fazlur Rahman Khalil, Chief Amir HuM, Fasiullah travelled to Bangladesh by air. On his arrival at Dacca, Fasiullah was met and briefed by two ISI officers and later he crossed over to India via Zakiganj border on July 28/99 and reached Guwahati on July 29/99.

5. Muslimuddin @ Muslim Ali @ Abu Raihan, 39, S/o. Jonab Ali of village Paikan Part-II, Krishnai, Goalpara Dist. Assam, after obtaining MA degree in Arabic from Sharanpur, Uttar Pradesh (UP) joined as a teacher in Durul Ulum Madrassa, Habraghat, Krishani. In 1997, he was

forced to resign from his post following some dispute with the Managing Committee of the Madrassa over misappropriation of money. He was closely associated with Jamaat-Ul-Ulema-E-Hind and was the Vice President of Goalpara District JUUEH. It was Maulavi Fakruddin @ Akram Master of village Mainbari, Barpeta District, a HuM activist and ISI operative presently based at Islamabad Pakistan who motivated Muslimuddin to join HuM. Muslimuddin held a series of meeting with local youths of Goalpara and Kokrajhar districts and advised them to join the HuM to join the "jihad" for creating an Islamic State in Assam. As advised by Fakruddin, Muslim Ali along with Shah Alam, Abul Qasim left for Bangladesh in June '98 via Cooch Behar and stayed at Nurani Madrasa, Jatrabari, Dacca, which was the transit camp of all HuM activists making trans-border movement to Pakistan via Bangladesh. Muslimuddin underwent arms and explosive training at Batrasi with many other cadres from Assam. He also underwent training in arms and ammunition at Vaddi-E-Neliam in Pakistan-occupied Kashmir (PoK). After his return to India in June 1999, Muslimuddin circulated several inflammatory leaflets captioned *Farman-E-Rasul* in a fake name, Abu Raihan inciting the Muslim community of Assam to declare jihad against the non-Muslims and to establish a separate Muslim country in Assam. Apart from recruiting large number of local Muslim youth for joining the cadres of HuM, Muslimuddin has also been organising local training camps for these youth.

6. Zakir Hussain @ Md. Rafiqe S/o. Md. Golam Ali of Chandmari, District Goalpara, Assam is a HuM activist who first cross over to Bangladesh in June '98 with Shah Alam and Abul Qasim and Muslim Ali of Krishnai, Goalpara. It was Muslim Ali who motivated Zakir Hussain and took him and other two youths to Dacca. After staying at Nurani Madrassa which is a transit camp of HuM activists for about 20 days, Zakir and Shah Alam went to Batrasi HuM training centre in Pakistan being arranged by Abu Sayed @ Faruque, the ISI agent working in Bangladesh. Zakir underwent arms and explosives training for 40 days in Batrasi imparted by HuM. On completion of training he returned to India via Bangladesh. After his return to Assam Zakir stepped up his activities in collusion with other HuM activists of Goalpara, Dhubri and Barpeta districts.

7. Abul Qasim @ Osman S/o Altaf Hussain of Khoridhra, Krishani PS Dudhnoi, Dist Goalpara, Assam is a member of the HuM. Abul Qasim was motivated by Muslim Ali of Goalpara and Mina Fakruddin of Barpeta to join HuM. In the middle of 1998, Abul Qasim came to Dacca with Muslimuddin, Zakir Hussain and Shah Alam-all of Goalpara and stayed at Nurani Madrassa, Jatrabari, Dacca. At Nurani Madrassa Abul Qasim met Qari Salim, Yasin and Danish, all HuM activists of UP and Allauddin

and Hassam Mobia of Dhubri. On being arranged by Abu Sayed @ Faruque, the ISI agent working in Bangladesh, Abul Qasim left for Pakistan for arms and explosives training at Batrasi, Pakistan. After undergoing 45 days training in Pakistan, Abul Qasim returned to Assam via Bangladesh and started doing subversive activities along with other HuM activists of Goalpara, Dhubri and Barpeta districts.

8. Mainul Haque @ Jamaluddin S/o. Faizuddin of Rampur, Krishnai, district Goalpara, Assam is a Pak trained HuM activist. In 1998, when he went to Delhi with one Nazmul Haque of Krishani he met Abu Sayed @ Faruque, a Pak ISI agent who sent him to Bangladesh. After staying a few days in Nurani Madrassa, Jatrabari, he went to Pakistan with Nazmul Haque in the last part of 1998 for undergoing training at Batrasi, Pakistan. On completion of his training he returned to India and engaged himself in organisational work of HuM in collaboration with other HuM activists of Assam.

9. Saiful Islam @ Bulbul S/o/Md. Wazed Ali Khan of Pulkipara, Hawli, district Barpeta is a PULF activist, a Manipur based Muslim militant outfit. Saiful Islam, who is a graduate, underwent arms training imparted by PULF under the auspices of NSCN (IM) at Laisen Khulen, Phungyar sub-division, district Ukhrul, Manipur. After his arms training Saiful Islam with two other PULF activists viz. Faruque and Saddam made an abortive attempt to kidnap the owner of Sarkar Medical Store, Mandia. In April 1999, he along with his associates kidnapped one Subhash Saha and after taking a ransom of 2 lakh for his release. At the time of kidnapping Saiful and his associates killed one Mainul who tried to intervene between the kidnappers and the kidnapped person.

10. Allauddin Ahmed @ Md. Omar @ Ashik Ahmed S/o. Md. Muktarur Rahman of Purani Bazar, Bilashipara, District Dhubri, Assam is a Pak trained activist. Maulana Fakruddin @ Akram Master of Barpeta who is a HuM activist, an ISI agent based in Islamabad, Pakistan met Allauddin Ahmed at Dhubri Bara Maszid during 1998. It was Fakruddin who motivated him to join HuM. Allauddin as per advice of Fakruddin came to Dacca in June 1998 and in Madrassa Nurani, Jatrabari he met Abu Sayed @ Faruque, Abdul Mannan @ Mainul Haque of Barpeta, Abu Bakkar Siddique @ Abdullah of Nalbari who were waiting in the said transit camp before they moved out to Pakistan for training. On being arranged by Faruque, all of them went to Pakistan and underwent 45 days arms and explosive training at Batrasi training camp. During the last part of December, Allauddin returned to Assam via Bangladesh.

11. Sajid @ Mainuddin S/o. Hazarat Ali of village Gorgori of Nalbari district, Assam was in Delhi in 1994 for studying Qari after completion of Hafiji in Durul Ulum Madrassa, Deoband, UP in 1990. During his stay in

Delhi in 1994 he along with Omar Syed Sheikh and Sahji Mahmood etc. got involved in a kidnapping case of one American Bela Joseph Naos and three British nationals (Rhys Curzel Partridge, Paul Benjamin Rideout and Christopher Milis Gosten). The foreigners were kidnapped by Harkat ul Ansar activists from Connaught Place in a bid to secure the release of dreaded leader Maulana Masood Azhar belonging to the said outfit. (Incidentally, Omar Syed Sheikh and Masood Azhar were the terrorists who had to be released by Government of India on December 31, 1999 in exchange for the passengers of the Indian Airlines flight). Ever since his involvement in kidnapping of the foreign nationals, Nurul Amin became a fugitive and went to Bangladesh twice. During his stay in Bangladesh Nurul Amin underwent arms and explosive training imparted by Harkat-Ul-Jihad-Al-Islami-Arakan, a Bangladesh based militant organisation

12. Kifayetullah S/o. Liyakatullah of Bidyanagar, Garigaon, District Kamrup, Guwahati was identified by arrested Qari Salim as their local ISI contact. Abdul Mannan of vill. Moinbori, PS. Barpeta Road (a HuM activist) and Nurul Amin of Nalbari (Since arrested) are his ex-students. Kifayetullah also disclosed that in January 1997 Md. Nurul Amin came to the bookstall of Kifayetullah accompanied by a youth who was introduced as Nadeem of Delhi. Nurul gave Kifayetullah a paper packet that contained a bundle containing a huge amount of US dollars and some loose Indian currency of Rs. 500/- denomination and Nurul requested him to keep the currency notes in a safe custody as it belonged to Nadeem who spent the night at Hotel Lisa, Lakhtokia, Guwahati. Next day, they collected the money from Kifayetullah and proceeded to Bangladesh. After some days Nadeem came to his house and gave him a water cooler having a capacity of 10/15 litres in which some RDX explosives was kept concealed, for keeping it in safe custody. Next day both Nurul and Nadeem came to his bookstall and collected the water cooler. Within a few days Kifayetullah came to know from newspaper report that Nadeem had been caught in New Delhi Railway Station for carrying RDX inside a water cooler. Kifayetullah also disclosed that Nurul Amin was a frequent visitor to Garigaon Madrassa and met Mufti Nazrul Islam. Kifayetullah disclosed that in the last week of July/99, the state committee of JEI assembled at Lucknow and paid homage to the Muslim jawans/officers of the Indian Army who lost their lives in Kargil. The meeting also decided to deter the Muslim youths from joining the Indian Army.

13. Md. Akbar Ali, S/o. Md. Amir Ali of Josihatipara, PS. Barpeta Road, Dist. Barpeta. In September 1998, Saiful Islam Khan (Since arrested) told him about Peoples' United Liberation Front (PULF). In October 1998, Rubul the leader of PULF, came to his house and told that the aim of PULF is to form an Islamic country in the North Eastern region of India

by Armed struggle against the Govt. of India. He told that the instructors of NSCN (I-M) imparted arms training to the members of PULF in Manipur. Then Md. Akbar Ali joined PULF. Md. Muslim Ali, Sahidul Islam (of Joshihatipara, Barpeta), Rubul of Nagaon, Mansur Rahman, Abul Qasim (the leader of HuM, Assam) and Md. Akbar Ali assembled in the house of Qasim Ali of Khoridhara (PS, Dudhnoi, Goalpara) and held a closed-door meeting in this context. In February 1999 Rubul, Md. Akbar Ali, Maulana Muslim Ali, Abul Qasim, Sahidul Islam, Mansur Rahman, Abu Bakkar Siddique @ Abdullah of Rampur (PS. Barpeta) held discussion in the house of Md. Akbar Ali. Rubul told that he possessed stengun, carbine and pistol. In April 1999 Moinul Haque came to the house of Md. Akbar Ali and told him and Rubul that he had brought 20 Kg of explosive substances from Bangladesh, but he did not tell about the place where he had kept the consignment. In February 1999 Akbar Ali recruited and produced the following youth before Rubul in the house of the subject for arms training in Manipur and Myanmar. They were (1) Sahidul Islam S/o. Harmoj Ali of Josihatipara PS, Barpeta (2) Jahidul Islam S/o. Afsar Ali Ahmed of Moirajhar, Howly (PS Barpeta,) (Since arrested) (3) Mansur Rahman S/o. Abdul Kader of Dhakali Yapara (PS, Barpeta)

14. Md. Tazrul Islam joined the Harkat-ul-Mujahideen on 03-06-1998 on being asked by Allauddin, an activist of HuM (since arrested) of Bilashipara. One Allauddin and one Md. Juber alias Makbul Maulana of Lakhiganj (Bilashipara) took Md. Tazrul Islam to Bangladesh on 03-06-1998 through a clandestine route by boat. Md. Tazrul Islam, Allauddin and Juber reached Ronmari Bazar (Bangladesh) and subsequently they left for Dhaka by bus and reached Nurani Madrassa of Jatrabari and stayed there for three days. Md. Tazrul Islam stated that one Abu Sayed of Nurani Madrassa and Jubor inspired him to undergo Arms training and they were shifted to another location where Md. Tazrul Islam also stated that during his 40 days stay at Jatrabari he met Asrab, Rafique, Osman Muslimuddin @ Jubor Mulla (since arrested) of Goalpara Dist. Tazrul Islam stated that their names were changed there. He was renamed as Tahidul and Allauddin was also renamed as Ashik. Abu Sayeed arranged two passports and visas for both of them. Md. Tazrul Islam further stated that on 24/07/98 Abu Sayeed sent him to Pakistan (Karachi) by air with a jackfruit (for his identification). Tazrul Islam was imparted arms training (Tachuchia) in Batrasi training centre for 20 days and he was taught how to handle AK-47, G-2, G-3, SLR, T.T. pistol, carbine. There he underwent training with the following HuM activists of Assam. Tazrul Islam had to undergo another arms training in a secret place/training centre (name not known) where they learnt the art of handling LMG, Rocket Launcher, Telescopic weapons etc. for 20 days. Thereafter, he had to undergo "Khususi" explosive training

and learnt saddle charge (remote control device) and chip charge besides making and exploding bombs using C-4, C-3 explosives. He also stated that such explosions were useful to blow up pipelines and bridges. It was also revealed by Md. Tazrul Islam that the training instructor namely "Baba" told them that the trainees would be engaged where necessary after training in their native place. Md. Tazrul Islam further stated that after the training their Master told them to organise meetings in their local places and to form organisations giving different names selecting office bearers and they were instructed to run such organisations like NDFB and ULFA extremists for the cause of the Muslims.

15. Md. Abdul Mukit Choudhury S/o. Late Motahir Choudhury of Sowajpur, Kakirabazar, PS & Dist. Karimganj. He has been helping the ISI operatives and other militant outfits controlled by the ISI in crossing over between India and Bangladesh, via Karimganj border.

16. Haji Billaluddin Ahmed S/o. Late Haji Sahid Ali of Manugram, PS & Dist. Karimganj. He has been helping the ISI operatives and other militant outfits controlled by the ISI in crossing between India and Bangladesh, via Karimganj border.

Jehirul Islam (23) S/o. Late Ahad Ali of Dhumarpathar, PS, Barpeta Road. Jehirul Hoque @ Jahu @ Saddam Hussain @ Mithun joined PULF in the last part of 1997. The subject stayed in the training camp in the deep jungles of Ukhrul District of Manipur for 8 months along with Faruque, Bulbul and Ratel. After 8 months he stayed with Anwar Sadat (Jorhat), Raju Ahmed, Jitu Ali and Jahir @ Aphel (all of Jorhat Saulkhowa). Jehirul Hoque further disclosed that the aim and object of PULF was to safeguard the Muslim community. He stated that PULF cadres were imparted training in Ukhrul Dist. of Manipur run by NSCN.

Tripartite Talks to Review the Implementation of the Assam Accord: Report of the Ministry of Home Affairs, Government of India

[*A tripartite talk with officials and representatives of Government of Assam, Ministry of Home Affairs, Government of India and representatives of the All Assam Students' Union was held in New Delhi on 31 May 2000. The meeting was held to assess the progress in implementation of the 1985 Assam Accord. The discussion revolved around issues related to general socio-economic development of Assam, border management, problems emerging out of the influx of migrants from Bangladesh etc. with reference to the Assam Accord similar exercise was undertaken in May 2005, in which certain important decisions were taken, including that of the updating of the National Register of Citizens. The prime minister was also a participant in the 2005 tripartite talks such talks are continuing*]

Dr. P.D. Shenoy, Additional Secretary (Home), Ministry of Home Affairs held a meeting with the office bearers of the All Assam Students Union (AASU) and the representatives of the Government of Assam in connection with the tripartite talks on 31.05.2000. The Govt. of India team comprises Shri G.K. Pillai, Joint Secretary (NE) and Shri Jatinder Bir Singh, Director (Assam). Shri M.K. Barooah, Home Secretary, Assam along with senior officials of Govt. of Assam also attended the meeting. Shri Prabin Boro, President, AASU, Shri Amiya Kr. Bhuyyan, General Secretary, AASU Shri Samujjal Kumar Bhattacharya, Adviser, AASU along with senior office bearers participated in the deliberation. The meeting took place in a cordial atmosphere. The welcome speech of AS (H), MHA is annexed herewith.

The tripartite talks inter-alia focused on devising (a) effective border management for containing influx of illegal migrants from Bangladesh; (b) strengthening of Prevention of' Infiltration of Foreigners Scheme in Assam; (c) consolidation of creation of second line of defence to check the illegal migrants (d) expediting the raising of 2 IR Bn in Assam, (e) facilitating the functioning of the Foreigners Tribunals constituted under the Illegal Migrants (Determination by Tribunals) Act, 1983, and (f) Preservation and Updating of the National Register of Citizens.

The Govt. of Assam was urged upon to vigorously take follow-up action on the decisions taken in the meeting in a time bound manner. It was also assured that the Central Govt. will take all necessary measures to accelerate the socio-economic development of Assam. The meeting concluded with a vote of thanks to the Chair.

Welcome Address by Dr. P.D. Shenoy, Additional Secretary, MHA and Chairman of the Tripartite Committee on Assam Accord

On behalf of Government of India, I extend a warm welcome to the Office bearers of the All Assam Students Union (AASU) and the representatives of the Government of Assam to the tripartite talks on May 31, 2000. I also take this opportunity to reiterate the commitment of the Central Government for implementation of the Assam Accord.

Friends, the last few months have witnessed growing popular mandate for peace and development in Assam. In the general elections to the 13th Lok Sabha, more than 71 per cent of the electorate had voted despite a boycott call of various militant outfits. This is a vivid example of popular faith in democracy. Similarly, nearly 750 militants have surrendered this year reflecting the urge of youth to return to the national mainstream. The Bodo Liberation Tigers have also come for peace negotiations within the Four Corners of the Constitution of India abjuring the cult of violence. As a goodwill gesture, the Government has suspended operations by security forces against the BLT. We fervently hope that other militant outfits will also realize the futility of violence in a democratic society and will soon return to the path of peaceful living.

Government of India have sanctioned the construction of balance 797 Kms border roads and 2429 Kms border fencing on the Indo-Bangladesh border at a total cost of Rs. 1334 crore. The work on this project would start this year and would be completed by March 2007. Under this scheme, in Assam 77.5 Kms of road and 71.5 Kms. of fence have been sanctioned at a tentative cost of Rs. 167 crore.

Friends, the Prime Minister visited Shillong leading a high level team consisting of Senior Union Cabinet Ministers to address the security and developmental needs of North East on January 21-22, 2000. On January 22, Prime Minister announced Rs. 10,271 crore agenda for Socio-Economic Development in the North-East and Sikkim. This major national initiative, inter alia envisages (a) coverage of all the 446 blocks in the North-East under information technology programme in next two years with an allocation of Rs. 100 crore (b) Excise concession in new industrial policy to Numaligarh Refinery in Assam with an annual concession of around Rs. 200 crore and (c) an allotment of Rs. 30 crore per annum for next 3 years for the development of infrastructure and other facilities in the Bodo Autonomous Council Areas. This special focus on the development of Assam will certainly give a boost to infrastructural development in Assam.

The flow of funds under the Non-lapsable pool has been further consolidated. An amount of Rs. 20 crore has been sanctioned for installation of one-lakh shallow tube-wells in Assam. The last meeting of the tripartite sub-committee on Clause VI and VII of the Assam Accord had taken place on April 10, 2000 at Guwahati. After the Committee submits its report further action will be taken.

I hope that the deliberations of this tripartite meeting will sharpen our focus on the developmental and social needs of Assam.

Achievements of Assam Accord

The Government of India is fully committed to the implementation of the Assam Accord, 1985. Various measures have been taken in this regard. These include, inter-alia, the following:

Foreigners' Issue

The Citizenship Act, 1955, Citizenship Rules, 1956 and Foreigners (Tribunals) Order, 1964, were amended.

Eleven Tribunals under the Foreigners (Tribunals) Order, 1964 have been created in Assam for Identifying foreigners of 1966-71 stream. 24,376 persons declared as foreigners by the Tribunals.

Special Registration officers have been appointed. Sanction was also accorded for the creation of 1280 additional posts under the prevention of Infiltration of Foreigners Scheme.

Sixteen Tribunals under the Illegal Migrants (Determination by Tribunals) Act, 1983 have been created in Assam.

A Sub-Committee involving representatives of Ministry of Law and Justice, Ministry of Finance, Govt. of Assam, All Assam Students Union (AASU) has been Constituted to examine the proposal submitted by AASU and Govt. of Assam under clause VI and VII of the Assam Accord.

Inauguration of Srimanta Sankaradeva Kalakshetra, Guwahati was inaugurated by Hon'ble President of India in November 1998. (A sum of Rs. 18.05 crore has been released).

Jyoti Chitrabon (Film) Studio at Guwahati at a cost of Rs. 8.79 crore has been modernised and inaugurated b the Chief Minister, Assam in April 1999.

Numaligarh Refinery, set up at a cost of Rs. 2,500 crore, and inaugurated by the Prime Minister in July, 1999

Two Central Universities, one at Tezpur and the other at Silchar, have been set up.

An IIT (Indian Institute of Technology) has been set up at Guwahati.

Rail-cum-road bridge at Jogighopa has been commissioned and inaugurated by Prime Minister in April 1998. This has opened road traffic from Jogighopa to Guwahati via South Bank of Brahmaputra.

Kathalguri Power Project 60 (MW) has been commissioned.

LPG Bottling Plan at Bongaigaon has been set up at an estimated cost of Rs. 30.68 crore.

3 industrial growth centres at a cost of Rs. 20 crore each have been sanctioned at Chariduar, Matia and Sonapur.

The power to issue citizenship certificates now vests only with the Central Government. 94 per cent of sanctioned border fencing of 152.31 Kms has been completed on Assam-Bangladesh border.

Ex-gratia payment was made to the next of kin of persons killed in the course of the agitation.

Disciplinary cases against employees in connection with the agitation were reviewed.

In the matter of recruitment, orders were issued by the Central Government for relaxation in upper age limit up to a maximum of six years in the case of candidates who had ordinarily resided in the state of Assam during the period 1.1.1980 to 15.8.1985.

NSA detenues detained in connection with agitation were released.

Revised Ground Rules for Ceasefire between Government of India and NSCN-IM

[*On 13 January 2001 representatives of the Government of India and the National Socialist Council of Nagaland (Isaac-Muivah) finalised, in New Delhi, a new set of ground rules to govern the existing ceasefire between the two parties. The main features of the revised agreed ground rules are provided below*]

Main Features

Main features of the Revised Agreed Ground Rules for Cease Fire finalized on 13th January 2001 would be as follows:

NSCN would not undertake offensive operations like ambush, raid, sniping, and attack leading to death/injury/damage or loss of property. NSCN would also act in a manner as not to cause harassment/damage or loss of property or injury to the civilian population. There would be no blockade of roads and communications, disruption of economic or developmental activities as well as essential services by the NSCN.

NSCN will notify list of all its camps to the CFMG who after due consultation would declare them as the designated camps. In the interest of promoting peace process, there would be no parading "(either in groups or individually) of NSCN cadres in uniform and/or with arms. For the present, this would cover all populated areas, public transport and Highways.

For the movement of NSCN armed cadres from one designated camp to another, the concerned Army/para military forces post would be given prior intimation. While proceeding through a village, the arms will be concealed. The modalities of this would be finalized in the CFMG. Persons from NSCN requiring to move frequently will have photo identity cards, which would be issued in the format mutually agreed upon. These identity cards, not to exceed 60 at present, would be issued by the NSCN and be countersigned by the Chairman, CFMG. The holder of these identity cards would, for their personal security, be entitled to have one NSCN armed cadre each accompany them at all times. The weapons would be carried in a concealed fashion.

The concern that forcible collection of money on essential supplies and intimidation of individuals including Government officials were taking place was denied by the NSCN. However, in the interest of promoting the peace process, the NSCN representatives agreed that the above activities would be prevented.

On the reports of forced recruitment of armed cadres the NSCN representatives stated that they have not and do not resort to forced recruitment. However, in the interest of promoting the peace process, it was agreed that if there are any reports of forced recruitment, they should be discussed in the Monitoring Group.

It is mutually agreed that no safe haven or sanctuary or assistance to any armed group or elements will be provided by anyone. No new Armed Forces Post would be set up within two Kms. of a designated camp.

There would be no offensive operations by the Security Forces against the NSCN and that the Security Forces would act in a manner as not to cause harassment/damage of loss of property or injury to the civilian population however, patrolling by the Security Forces would continue to prevent infiltration of militants and arms as hitherto fore but patrolling within 1 Km of NSCN designated camps will be carried out with intimation to them. The designated camps will not be located in populated areas, and/or near Highways, SF posts. Protection of convoys and patrolling of roads would continue to be undertaken by the Security Forces.

For implementation of the ground rules it was agreed that modalities will be monitored by a group constituted for this purpose comprising of representatives of NSCN, NGOs and representatives nominated by the Government of India. However, it was also agreed that any accidental encounter or violation should not be allowed to jeopardise the peace process and the effect of any such incident should be localised through mutual consultations. All cases of violation of these ground rules would be referred to the Monitoring Groups, so that the reasons for violation are identified and steps to be taken to prevent such violation in future are suggested. Notwithstanding the above, the Security Forces will act in an impartial and unbiased manner against any group causing public disturbances or when there is imminent danger to public safety or peace.

Text of Cease-fire Ground Rules Agreed upon between the Government of India and the National Socialist Council of Nagaland-Khaplang (NSCN-K)

[*On 28 May 2001, the Government of India declared a ceasefire agreement with the National Socialist Council of Nagaland (Khaplang) for a period of one year. This followed a round of discussion between the Centre's representatives led by the then Additional Secretary, Ministry of Home Affairs, Dr. P.D. Shenoy and representatives of the NSCN (K) led by Mr. Tongmeth Wangnao Konyak. The ground rules to be observed by both sides are provided below*]

These ground rules will be valid only for the State of Nagaland.

Enforcement of ground rules will be the responsibility of the GOI. The GOI and the NSCN will jointly implement the ground rules. Contentious issues relating to the implementation of the ground rules will be resolved by a Ceasefire Supervisory Board (CFSB) comprising five representatives each of GOI and NSCN and a Chairman to be nominated by the GOI.

The NSCN would not undertake offensive operations like ambush, raid, sniping and attack leading to death/injury/damage or loss of property against anybody. The NSCN would also act in a manner as not to cause harassment/damage or loss of property or injury to the civilian population.

There would be no offensive operations like ambush, raid and attack leading to death/injury/damage or loss of property against the NSCN by the Indian Army, Paramilitary Forces and the Police. However, the Government of India reserves its right to continue operations against all other militant groups who are not a party to the "Ceasefire."

NSCN will notify to the CFSB, the list of all their camps. The CFSB would, after due scrutiny, finalise the list of the "designated camps" where all the armed cadres of the NSCN would be located within three months.

In the interest of promoting the peace process, there will be no movement in uniform and/or with arms outside "designated camps".

Movement of NSCN cadres from one "designated camp" to another will be carried out for mutually agreed purposes and with intimation to the Security Forces and CFSB. The modalities of this would be finalised by the CFSB.

The NSCN would refrain from blockade of roads and communications and from any activity which would disturb the functioning of local and, State Governments and of economic or developmental activities as well as essential services.

The NSCN will refrain from extending any form of support or assistance to other militant groups.

During the course of the cease-fire, the NSCN will refrain from acquiring any additional arms/ammunition military equipment.

The NSCN will refrain from extortions, forcible collection of money and supplies and intimidation of individuals including Government officials.

The NSCN will refrain from forcible recruitment of armed cadres.

Patrolling by the Indian Army, Paramilitary Forces and the Police would continue to prevent infiltration of militants and arms as hithertofore. However, patrolling within one Km of the "designated camps" decided after due consultation in the Ceasefire Supervisory Board (CFSB) will be carried out, with intimation to them. It is noted that no such camps are located/will be located in populated areas, and/or near Highways, Indian Army/Para Military Forces Posts, Police Station/Police Posts etc.

Protection of convoys and patrolling of roads would continue to be undertaken by the Indian Army, Para Military Forces and Police.

Security Forces will retain the right to enforce measures necessary to uphold the laws of the land and prevent any disturbance to peace.

The Prevention of Terrorism Ordinance

[*The Prevention of Terrorism Ordinance was enacted in 2001 and was later replaced by the Prevention of Terrorism Act, 2002*]

Promulgated by the President in the Fifty-second Year of the Republic of India. An Ordinance to make provisions for the prevention of, and for dealing with, terrorist activities and for matters connected therewith.

WHEREAS Parliament is not in session and the President is satisfied that circumstances exists which render it necessary for him to take immediate action;

NOW, THEREFOR, in exercise of the powers conferred by clause (1) of article 123 of the Constitution, the President is pleased to promulgate the following Ordinance:

CHAPTER I
PRELIMINARY

1. (1) This Ordinance may be called the Prevention of Terrorism Ordinance, 2001.

(2) It extends to the whole of India.

(3) Every person shall be liable to punishment under this Ordinance for every act or omission contrary to the provisions thereof, of which he is held guilty in India.

(4) Any person who commits an offence beyond India which is punishable under this Ordinance shall be dealt with according to the provisions of this Ordinance in the same manner as if such act had been committed in India.

(5) The provisions of this Ordinance apply also to

(a) Citizens of India outside India,

(b) Persons in the service of the Government, wherever they may be, and

(c) Persons on ships and aircrafts, registered in India, wherever they may be

(6) It shall come into force at once and shall remain in force for a period of five years from the date of its commencement, but its expiry under the operation of this sub-section shall not affect—

(a) The previous operation of, or anything duly done or suffered under this Ordinance, or

(b) Any right, privilege, obligation or liability acquired, accrued or incurred under this Ordinance, or

(c) Any penalty, forfeiture or punishment incurred in respect of any offence under this Ordinance, or

(d) Any investigation, legal proceeding or remedy in respect of any such right, privilege, obligation, liability, penalty, forfeiture or punishment as aforesaid, and, any such investigation, legal proceeding or remedy may be instituted, continued or enforced and any such penalty, forfeiture or punishment may be imposed as if this Ordinance had not expired.

2. Definitions: (1) In this Ordinance, unless the context otherwise requires,-

(a) "Code" means the Code of Criminal Procedure, 1973,

(b) "Designated Authority" shall mean such officer of the Central Government not below the rank of Joint Secretary to the Government, or such officer of the State Government not below the rank of Secretary to the Government, as the case may be, as may be specified by the Central Government or as the case may be, the State Government, by a notification published in the Official Gazette;

(c) "Proceeds of terrorism" shall mean all kinds of properties which have been derived or obtained from commission of any terrorist act or have been acquired through funds traceable to a terrorist act, and shall include cash, irrespective of person in whose name such proceeds are standing or in whose possession they are found;

(d) "Property" means property and assets of every description, whether corporeal or incorporeal, movable or immovable, tangible or intangible and deeds and instruments evidencing title to, or interest in, such property or assets;

(e) "Public Prosecutor" means a Public Prosecutor or an Additional Public Prosecutor or a Special Public Prosecutor appointed under section 28 and includes any person acting under the directions of the Public Prosecutor.

(f) "Special Court" means a Special Court constituted under section 23;

(g) "Terrorist act" has the meaning assigned to it in sub-section (1) of section 3, and the expression "terrorist" shall be construed accordingly;

(h) "State Government", in relation to a Union territory, means the Administrator thereof;

(i) Words and expressions used but not defined in this Ordinance and defined in the Code shall have the meanings respectively assigned to them in the Code.

(2) Any reference in this Ordinance to any enactment or any provision thereof shall, in relation to an area in which such enactment or such provision is not in force, be construed as a reference to the corresponding law or the relevant provision of the corresponding law, if any, in force in that area.

CHAPTER II
PUNISHMENT FOR, AND MEASURES FOR DEALING WITH, TERRORIST ACTIVITIES

3. (1) Whoever,

(a) With intent to threaten the unity, integrity, security or sovereignty of India or to strike terror in the people or any section of the people does any act or thing by using bombs, dynamite or other explosive substances or inflammable substances or fire arms or other lethal weapons or poisons or noxious gases or other chemicals or by any other substances (whether biological or otherwise) of a hazardous nature or by any other means whatsoever, in such a mariner as to cause or likely to cause, death of; or injuries to any person or persons or loss of, or damage to, or destruction of, property or disruption of any supplies or services essential to the life of the community or causes damage or destruction of any property or equipment used or intended to be used for the defence of India or in connection with any other purposes of the Government of India, any State Government or any of their agencies, or detains any person and threatens to kill or injure such person in order to compel the Government or any other person to do or abstain from doing any act;

(b) Is or continues to be a member of an association declared unlawful under the Unlawful Activities (Prevention) Act, 1967 or voluntarily does an act aiding or promoting in any manner the objects of such association and in either case is in possession of any unlicensed firearms, ammunition, explosive or other instrument or substance capable of causing mass destruction and commits any act resulting in loss of human life or grievous injury to any person or causes significant damage to any property, commits a terrorist act.

Explanation: For the purposes of this sub-section, "a terrorist act" shall include the act of raising funds intended for the purpose of terrorism-

(2) Whoever commits a terrorist act, shall,

(i) If such act has resulted in the death of any person, be punishable with death or imprisonment for life and shall also be liable to fine;

(ii) In any other case, be punishable with imprisonment for a term which shall not be less than five years but which may extend to imprisonment for life and shall also be liable to fine.

(3) Whoever conspires or attempts to commit, or advocates, abets, advises or incites or knowingly facilitates the commission of, a terrorist act or any act preparatory to a terrorist act, shall be punishable with imprisonment for a term which shall not be less than five years but which may extend to imprisonment for life and shall also be liable to fine.

(4) Whoever voluntarily harbours or conceals, or attempts to harbour or conceal any person knowing that such person is a terrorist shall be punishable with imprisonment for a term which shall not be less than three years but which may extend to imprisonment for life and shall also be liable to fine:

Provided that this sub-section shall not apply to any case in which the harbour or concealment is by the husband or wife of the offender.

(5) Any person who is a member of a terrorist gang or a terrorist organisation, which is involved in terrorist acts, shall be punishable with imprisonment for a term which may extend to imprisonment for life or with fine which may extend to rupees ten lakh or with both.

Explanation: For the purposes of this sub-section, "terrorist organisation" means an organisation, which is concerned with or involved in terrorism.

(6) Whoever knowingly holds any property derived or obtained from commission of any terrorist act or has been acquired through the terrorist funds shall be punishable with imprisonment for a term which may extend to imprisonment for life or with fine which may extend to rupees ten lakh or with both.

(7) Whoever threatens any person who is a witness or any other person in whom such witness may be interested, with violence, or wrongfully restrains or confines the witness, or any other person in whom the witness may be interested, or does any other unlawful act with the said intent, shall be punishable with imprisonment which may extend to three years and fine.

(8) A person receiving or in possession of information which he knows or believes to be of material assistance

(i) In preventing the commission by any other person of a terrorist act, or

(ii) In securing the apprehension, prosecution or conviction of any other person for an offence involving the commission, preparation or instigation of such an act, and fails, without reasonable cause, to disclose that information as soon as reasonably practicable to the police, shall be punishable with imprisonment for a term which may extend to one year or with fine or with both:

Provided that a legal practitioner of the accused shall not be bound to disclose such information, which he might have received while defending the accused.

4. Where any person is in unauthorized possession of any,

(a) Arms or ammunition specified in columns (2) and (3) of Category I or Category III (a) of Schedule I to the Arms Rules, 1962, in a notified area,

(b) Bombs, dynamite or hazardous explosive substances or other lethal weapons capable of mass destruction or biological or chemical substances of warfare in any area, whether notified or not, he shall be guilty of terrorist act notwithstanding anything contained in any other law for the time being in force, and be punishable with imprisonment for a term which may extend to imprisonment for life or with fine which may extend to rupees ten lakh or with both.

Explanation: In this section "notified area," means such area as the State Government may, by notification in the Official Gazette, specify.

5. Enhanced Penalties: (1) If any person with intent to aid any terrorist contravenes any provision of, or any rule made under, the Arms Act, 1959, the Explosives Act, 1884, the Explosive Substances Act, 1908 or the Inflammable Substances Act, 1952, he shall, notwithstanding anything contained in any of the aforesaid Acts or the rules made thereunder, be punishable with imprisonment for a term which may extend to imprisonment for life and shall also be liable to fine.

(2) For the purposes of this section, any person who attempts to contravene or abets, or does any act preparatory to the contravention of any provision of any law, rule or order, shall be deemed to have contravened that provision, and the provisions of sub-section (I) shall, in relation to such person, have effect subject to the modification that the reference to "imprisonment for life" shall be construed as a reference to "imprisonment for ten years."

6. (1) No person shall hold or be in possession of any proceeds of terrorism.

(2) Proceeds of terrorism, whether held by a terrorist or by any other person and whether or not such person is prosecuted or convicted under this Ordinance, shall be liable to be forfeited to the Central Government

or the State Government, as the case may be, in the manner provided under this Chapter.

7. Powers of Investigating Officers: (1) If an officer (not below the rank of Superintendent of Police) investigating an offence committed under this Ordinance, has reason to believe that any property in relation to which an investigation is being conducted, represents proceeds of terrorism, he shall, with the prior approval in writing of the Director General of the Police of the State in which such property is situated, make an order seizing such property and where it is not practicable to seize such property, make an order of attachment directing that such property shall not be transferred or otherwise dealt with except with the prior permission of the officer making such order, or of the Designated Authority, or the Special Court, as the case may be, before whom the properties seized or attached are produced and a copy of such order shall be served on the person concerned.

(2) The investigating officer shall duly inform the Designated Authority or, as the case may be, the Special Court, within forty-eight hours of the seizure or attachment of such property.

(3) It shall be open to the Designed Authority or the Special Court before whom the seized or attached properties are produced either to confirm or revoke the order of attachment so issued:

Provided that an opportunity of making a representation by the person whose property is being attached shall be given.

(4) In the case of immovable property attached by the investigating officer, it shall be deemed to have been produced before the Designated Authority or the Special Court, as the case may be, when the investigating officer notifies his report and places it at the disposal of the Designated Authority or the Special Court, as the case may be.

(5) The investigating officer may seize and detain any cash to which this Chapter applies if he has reasonable grounds for suspecting that-

(a) It is intended to be used for the purposes of terrorism;
(b) It forms the whole or part of the resources of an organisation declared as terrorist organisation under this Ordinance:

Provided that the cash seized under this sub-section by the investigating officer shall be released not later than the period of forty-eight hours beginning with the time when it is seized unless the matter involving the cash is before the Designated Authority, or as the case may be, the Special Court and such authority or, as the case may be, the Court passes an order allowing its retention beyond forty-eight hours.

Explanation: For the purposes of this sub-section "cash" means

(a) Coins and notes in any currency;
(b) Postal orders;

(c) Traveler's cheques;
(d) Banker's drafts, and
(e) Such other monetary instruments as the Central Government, or as the case may be, the State Government may specify by an order made in writing.

8. Where any property is seized or attached in the belief that it constitutes proceeds of terrorism and is produced before the Designated Authority, it shall, on being satisfied that the said property consists of proceeds of terrorism, order forfeiture of such property, whether or not the person from whose possession it is seized or attached, is prosecuted in a Special Court for an offence under this Ordinance.

9. (1) No order forfeiting any proceeds of terrorism shall be made under section 8 unless the person holding or in possession of such proceeds is given a notice in writing informing him of the grounds on which it is proposed to forfeit the proceeds of terrorism and such person is given an opportunity of making a representation in writing within such reasonable time as may be specified in the notice against the grounds of forfeiture and is also given a reasonable opportunity of being heard in the matter.

(2) No order of forfeiture shall be made under sub-section (I), if such person establishes that he is a bonafide transferee, of such proceeds for value without knowing that they represent proceeds of terrorism,

(3) It shall be competent for the Designated Authority to make an order in respect of property seized or attached,

(a) Directing it to be sold if it is a perishable property and the provisions of section 459 of the Code shall, as nearly as may be practicable, apply to the net proceeds of such sale;
(b) Nominating any officer of the Central or State Government, in the case of any other property, to, perform the function of the Administrator of such property subject to such conditions as may be specified by the Designated Authority.

10. Appeal: (1) Any person aggrieved by an order of forfeiture under section 8 may, within one month from the date of the receipt of such order, appeal to the High Court within whose jurisdiction, the Designated Authority, who passed the order appealed against, is situated.

(2) Where an order under section 8 is modified or annulled by the High Court or where in a prosecution instituted for the contravention of the provisions of this Ordinance, the person against whom an order of forfeiture has been made under section 8 is acquitted, such property shall be returned to him and in either case if it is not possible for any reason to return the forfeited property, such person shall be paid the price therefore as if the property had been sold to the Central Government with reasonable

interest calculated from the day of seizure of the property and such price shall be determined in the manner prescribed.

11. The order of forfeiture made under this Ordinance by the Designated Authority, shall not prevent the infliction of any other punishment to which the person affected thereby is liable under this Ordinance.

12. (1) Where any claim is preferred, or any objection is made to the seizure of any property under section 7 on the ground that such property is not liable to seizure, the Designated Authority, or as the case may be, the Special Court, before whom such property is produced, shall proceed to investigate the claim or objection:

Provided that no such investigation shall be made where the Designated Authority or the Special Court considers that the claim or objection was designed to cause unnecessary delay.

(2) In case claimant or objector establishes that the property specified in the notice issued under section 9 is not liable to be attached or forfeited under the Ordinance, the said notice shall be withdrawn or modified accordingly.

13. The Designated Authority, acting under the provisions of this Ordinance, shall have all the powers of a Civil Court required for making a full and fair enquiry into the matter before it.

14. (1) Notwithstanding anything contained in any other law, the officer investigating any offence under this Ordinance, with prior approval in writing of an officer not below the rank of a Superintendent of Police, may require any officer or authority of the Central Government or a State Government or a local authority or a Bank, company, or a firm or any other institution, establishment, organisation or any individual to furnish information in their possession in relation to such offence, on points or matters, where the investigating officer has reason to believe that such information will be useful for, or relevant to the purposes of this Ordinance.

(2) Failure to furnish the information called for under sub-section (1), or deliberately furnishing false information shall be punishable with imprisonment for a term, which may extend to three years or with fine or with both.

(3) Notwithstanding anything contained in the Code, the offence under sub-section (1) shall be tried as a summary case and the procedure prescribed in Chapter XXI of the said Code [except sub-section (2) of section 262] shall be applicable thereto.

15. Where, after the issue of an order under section 7 or issue of a notice under section 9, any property referred to in the said order or notice is transferred by any mode whatsoever, such transfer shall, for the purpose of the proceedings under this Ordinance, be ignored and if such property is subsequently forfeited, the transfer of such property shall be deemed to be null and void.

16. (1) Where any person is accused of any offence under this Ordinance, it shall be open to the Special Court trying him to pass an order that all or any of the properties, movable or immovable or both belonging to him, shall, during the period of such trial, be attached, if not already attached under this Ordinance.

(2) Where a person has been convicted of any offence punishable under this Ordinance, the Special Court may, in addition to awarding any punishment, by order in writing, declare that any property, movable or immovable or both, belonging to the accused and specified in the order, shall stand forfeited to the Central Government or the State Government, as the case may be, free from all encumbrances.

17. Where any shares in a company stand forfeited to the Central Government or the State Government, as the case may be, under this Ordinance, then, the company shall on receipt of the order of the Special Court, notwithstanding anything contained in the Companies Act, 1956, or the articles of association of the company, forthwith register the Central Government or the State Government, as the case may be, as the transferee of such shares.

CHAPTER III
TERRORIST ORGANISATIONS

18. (l) For the purposes of this Ordinance an organisation is a terrorist organisation if.

(a) It is listed in the Schedule, or
(b) It operates under the same name as an organisation listed in that Schedule.

(2) The Central Government may by order, in the Official Gazette—

(a) Add an organisation to the Schedule;
(b) Remove an organisation from that Schedule:
(c) Amend that Schedule in some other way.

(3) The Central Government may exercise its power under clause (a) of sub-section (2) in respect of an organisation only if it believes that it is involved in terrorism.

(4) For the purposes of sub-section (3) an organisation shall be deemed to be involved in terrorism if it

(a) Commits or participates in acts of terrorism,
(b) Prepares for terrorism,
(c) Promotes or encourages terrorism, or
(d) Is otherwise involved in terrorism.

19. (1) An application may be made to the Central Government for the exercise of its power under clause (b) of sub-section (2) of section 18 to remove an organisation from the Schedule.

(2) An application may be made by

(a) The organisation, or

(b) Any person affected by inclusion of the organisation in the Schedule as a terrorist organisation.

(3) The Central Government may make rules to prescribe the procedure for admission and disposal of an application made under this section.

(4) Where an application under sub-section (I) has been refused, the applicant may apply for a review to the Review Committee constituted by the Central Government under sub-section (1) of section 59 within one month from the date of receipt of the order by the applicant.

(5) The Review Committee may allow an application for review against refusal to remove an organisation from the Schedule, if it considers that the decision to refuse was flawed when considered in the light of the principles applicable on an application for judicial review.

(6) Where the Review Committee allows review under sub-section (5) by or in respect of an organisation, it may make an order under this sub-section.

(7) Where an order is made under sub-section (6), the Central Government shall as soon as the certified copy of the order is received by it, make an order removing the organisation from the list in the Schedule.

20. (1) A person commits an offence if he belongs or professes to membership belong to a terrorist organisation:

Provided that this sub-section shall not apply where the person charged is able to prove-

(a) That the organisation was not declared as a terrorist organisation at the time when he became a member or began to profess to be a member; and

(b) That he has not taken part in the activities of the organisation at any time during its inclusion in the Schedule as a terrorist organisation.

(2) A person guilty of an offence under this section shall be liable, on conviction, to imprisonment for a term not exceeding ten years or with fine or with both.

21. (1) A person commits an offence if

(a) He invites support for a terrorist organisation, and

(b) The support is not, or is not restricted to, the provision of money or other property within the meaning of section 22.

(2) A person commits an offence if he arranges, manages or assists in arranging or managing a meeting, which he knows, is

(a) To support a terrorist organisation,
(b) To further the activities of a terrorist organisation, or
(c) To be addressed by a person who belongs or professes to belong to a terrorist organisation.

(3) A person commits an offence if he addresses a meeting for the purpose of encouraging support for a terrorist organisation or to further its activities.

(4) A person guilty of an offence under this section shall be liable on conviction, to imprisonment for a term not exceeding ten years or with fine or with both.

Explanation: For the purposes for this section, the expression "meeting" means a meeting of three or more persons whether or not the public are admitted.

22. (1) A person commits an offence if he

(a) Invites another to provide money or other property, and
(b) Intends that it should be used, or has reasonable cause to suspect that it may be used, for the purposes of terrorism.

(2) A person commits an offence if he-

(a) Receives money, or other property, and
(b) Intends that it should be use or has reasonable cause to suspect that it may be used, for the purposes of terrorism.

(3) A person commits an offence if he

(a) Provides money or other property, and
(b) Knows or has reasonable cause to suspect that it will or may be used for the purposes of terrorism.

(4) In this section, a reference to the provision of money or other property is a reference to its being given, lent or otherwise made available, whether or not for consideration.

(5) A person guilty of an offence under this section shall be liable on conviction, to imprisonment for a term not exceeding fourteen years, or with fine or with both.

CHAPTER IV
SPECIAL COURTS

23. (1) The Central Government or a State Government, may, by notification in the Official Gazette, constitute one or more Special Courts for such area or areas, or for such case or class or group of cases, as may be specified in the notification.

(2) Where a notification constituting a Special Court for any area or areas or for any case or class or group of cases is issued by the Central Government under sub-section (1), and a notification constituting a Special Court for the same area or areas or for the same case or class or group of cases has also been issued by the State Government under that sub-section, the Special Court constituted by the Central Government, whether the notification constituting such Court is issued before or after the issue of the notification constituting the Special Court by the State Government, shall have, and the Special Court constituted by the State Government shall not have, jurisdiction to try any offence committed in that area or areas or, as the case may be, the case or class or group of cases and all cases pending before any Special Court constituted by the State Government shall stand transferred to the Special Court constituted by the Central Government.

(3) Where any question arises as to the jurisdiction of any Special Court, it shall be referred to the Central Government whose decision in the matter shall be final.

(4} A Special Court shall be presided over by a judge to be appointed by the Central Government or, as the case may be, the State Government, with the concurrence of the Chief Justice of the High Court.

(5) The Central Government or, as the case may be, the State Government may also appoint, with the concurrence of the Chief' Justice of the High Court, additional judges to exercise jurisdiction of a Special Court.

(6) A person shall not be qualified for appointment as a judge or an additional judge of a Special Court unless he is. Immediately before such appointment, a sessions Judge or an additional sessions judge in any State.

(7) For the removal of doubts, it is hereby provided that the attainment, by a person appointed as a judge or an additional judge of a Special Court, of the age of superannuation under the rules applicable to him in the service to which he belongs, shall not affect his continuance as such judge or additional judge.

(8) Where any additional judge or additional judges is or are appointed in a Special Court, the judge of the Special Court may, from time to time, by general or special order, in writing, provide for the distribution of business of the Special Court among all judges including himself and the additional judge or additional judges and also for the disposal of urgent business in the event of his absence or the absence of any additional judge.

24. A Special Court may, on its own motion, or on an application made by the Public Prosecutor and if it considers it expedient or desirable so to do, sit for any of its proceedings at any place other than its ordinary place of sitting:

Provided that nothing in this section shall be construed to change the place of sitting of a Special Court constituted by a State Government to any place outside that State.

25. (1) Notwithstanding anything contained in the Code, every Jurisdiction of offence punishable under any provision of this Ordinance, shall be triable only by the Special Court within whose local jurisdiction it was committed or, as the case may be, by the Special Court constituted for trying such offence under section 23.

(2) If, having regard to the exigencies of the situation prevailing in a State.

(i) It is not possible to have a fair, impartial or speedy trial; or
(ii) It is not feasible to have the trial without occasioning the breach of peace or grave risk to the safety of the accused, the witnesses, the Public Prosecutor and a judge of the Special Court or any of them; or
(iii) It is not otherwise in the interests of justice, the Supreme Court may transfer any case pending before a Special Court to any other Special Court within that State or in any other State and the High Court may transfer any case pending before a Special Court situated in that State to any other Special Court within the State.

(3) The Supreme Court or the High Court, as the case may be, may act under this section either on the application of the Central Government or a party interested and any such application shall be made by motion, which shall, except when the applicant is the Attorney-General of India, be supported by an affidavit or affirmation.

26. (1) When trying any offence, a Special Court may also try any other offence with which the accused may, under the Code, be charged at the same trial if the offence is connected with such other offence.

(2) If, in the course of any trial under this Ordinance of any offence, it is found that the accused person has committed any other offence under this Ordinance or under any other law, the Special Court may convict such person of such other offence, and pass any sentence or award punishment authorized by this Ordinance or such rule or, as the case may be, under such other law.

27. (1) When a police officer investigating a case requests the Court of a Chief Judicial Magistrate or the Court of a Chief Metropolitan Magistrate in writing for obtaining samples of hand writing, finger prints, foot prints, photographs, blood, saliva, semen, hair, voice of any accused person, reasonably suspected to be involved in the commission of an offence under this Ordinance, it shall be lawful for the Court of a Chief Judicial Magistrate or the Court of a Chief Metropolitan Magistrate to direct that such samples be given by the accused person to the police officer either through a medical practitioner or otherwise, as the case may be.

(2) If any accused person refuses to give samples as provided in sub-section (1), the court shall draw adverse inference against the accused.

28. (1) For every Special Court, the Central Government or, as the case may be, the State Government, shall appoint a person to be the Public Prosecutor and may appoint one or more persons to be the Additional Public Prosecutor or Additional Public Prosecutors;

Provided that the Central Government or, as the case may be, the State Government, may also appoint for any case or class or group of cases, a Special Public Prosecutor.

(2) A person shall not be qualified to be appointed as a Public Prosecutor or an Additional Public Prosecutor or a Special Public Prosecutor under this section unless he has been in practice as an Advocate for not less than seven years or has held any post, for a period of not less than seven years, under the Union or a State, requiring special knowledge of law.

(3) Every person appointed as a Public Prosecutor or an Additional Public Prosecutor or a Special Public Prosecutor under this section shall be deemed to be a Public Prosecutor within the meaning of clause (u) of section 2 of the Code, and the provisions of the Code shall have effect accordingly.

29. (7) Subject to the provisions of section 49, a Special Court may take cognizance of any offence, without the accused being committed to it for trial, upon receiving a complaint of facts that constitute such offence or upon a police report of such facts.

(2) Where an offence triable by a Special Court is punishable with imprisonment for a term not exceeding three years or with fine or with both, the Special Court may, notwithstanding anything contained in sub-section (1) of section 260 or section 262 of the Code, try the offence in a summary way in accordance with the procedure prescribed in the Code and the provisions of sections 263 to 265 of the Code, shall so far as may be, apply to such trial:

Provided that when, in the course of a summary trial under this sub-section, it appears to the Special Court that the nature of the case is such that it is undesirable to try it in a summary way, the Special Court shall recall any witnesses who may have been examined and proceed to re-hear the case in the manner provided by the provisions of the Code for the trial of such offence and the said provisions shall apply to and in relation to a Special Court as they apply to and in relation to a Magistrate:

Provided further that in the case of any conviction in a summary trial under this section, it shall be lawful for a Special Court to pass a sentence of imprisonment for a term not exceeding one year and with fine, which may extend to rupees five lakh.

(3) Subject to the other provisions of this Ordinance, a Special Court shall, for the purpose of trial of any offence, have all the powers of a Court of Session and shall try such offence as if it were a Court of Session so far as may be in accordance with the procedure prescribed in the Code for the trial before a Court of Session.

(4) Subject to the other provisions of this Ordinance, every case transferred to a Special Court under section 25 shall be dealt with as if such case had been transferred under section 406 of the Code to such Special Court.

(5) Notwithstanding anything contained in the Code, but subject to the provisions of section 299 of the Code, a Special Court may, if it thinks fit and for reasons to be recorded by it, proceed with the trial in the absence of the accused or his pleader and record the evidence of any witness, subject to the right of the accused to recall the witness for cross-examination.

30. (1) Notwithstanding anything contained in the Code, the proceedings under this Ordinance may, for reasons to be recorded in writing, be held in camera if the Special Court so desires.

(2) A Special Court, if on an application made by a witness in any proceeding before it or by the Public Prosecutor in relation to such witness or on its own motion, is satisfied that the life of such witness is in danger, it may, for reasons to be recorded in writing, take such measures as it deems fit for keeping the identity and address of such witness secret.

(3) In particular, and without prejudice to the generality of the provisions of sub-section (2), the measures, which a Special Court may take under that sub-section, may include

(a) The holding of the proceedings at a place to be decided by the Special Court;

(b) The avoiding of the mention of the names and addresses of the witnesses in its orders or judgments or in any records of the case accessible to public;

(c) The issuing of any directions for securing that the identity and address of the witnesses are not disclosed;

(d) A decision that it is in the public interest to order that all or any of the proceedings pending before such a court shall not be published in any manner.

(4) Any person who contravenes any decision or direction issued under sub-section (3) shall be punishable with imprisonment for a term, which

may extend to one year and with fine, which may extend to one thousand rupees.

31. The trial under this Ordinance of any offence by a Special Court shall have precedence over the trial of any other case against the accused in any other court (not being a Special Court) and shall be concluded in preference to the trial of such other case and accordingly the trial of such other case shall remain in abeyance.

32. (1) Notwithstanding anything in the Code or in the Indian Evidence Act, 1872, but subject to the provisions of this section, a confession made by a person before a police officer not lower in rank than a Superintendent of Police and recorded by such police officer either in writing or on any mechanical or electronic device like cassettes, tapes or sound tracks from out of which sound or images can be reproduced, shall be admissible in the trial of such person for an offence under this Ordinance or rules made thereunder.

(2) A police officer shall, before recording any confession made by a person under sub-section (1) explain to such person in writing that he is not bound to make a confession and that if he does so, it may be used against him;

Provided that where such person prefers to remain silent, the police officer shall not compel or induce him to make any confession.

(3) The confession shall be recorded in an atmosphere free from threat or inducement and shall be in the same language in which the person makes it.

(4) The person from whom a confession has been recorded under sub-section (1), shall be produced before the Court of a Chief Metropolitan Magistrate or the Court of a Chief Judicial Magistrate along with the original statement of confession, written or recorded on mechanical or electronic device within forty-eight hours.

(5) The Chief Metropolitan Magistrate or the Chief Judicial Magistrate, shall, record the statement, if any, made by the person so produced and get his signature or thumb impression and if there is any complaint of torture, such person shall be directed to be produced for medical examination before a Medical Officer not lower in rank than an Assistant Civil Surgeon and thereafter, he shall be sent to judicial custody.

33. Where, after taking cognizance of any offence, a Special Court is of the opinion that the offence is not triable by it, it shall, notwithstanding that it has no jurisdiction to try such offence, transfer the case for the trial of such offence to any court having jurisdiction under the Code and the court to which the case is transferred may proceed with the trial of the offence as if it had taken cognizance of the offence.

34. (1) Notwithstanding anything contained in the Code, an appeal shall lie from any judgment, sentence or order, not being an interlocutory order, of a Special Court to the High Court both on facts and on law.

Explanation: For the purposes of this section, "High Court" means a High Court within whose jurisdiction, a Special Court which passed the judgment, sentence or order, is situated.

(2) Every appeal under sub-section (1) shall be heard by a bench of two Judges of the High Court.

(3) Except as aforesaid, no appeal or revision shall lie to any court from any judgment, sentence or order including an interlocutory order of a Special Court.

(4) Notwithstanding anything contained in sub-section (3) of section 378 of the Code, an appeal shall lie to the High Court against an order of the Special Court granting or refusing bail.

(5) Every appeal under this section shall be preferred within a period of thirty days from the date of the judgment, sentence or order appealed from:

Provided that the High Court may entertain an appeal after the expiry of the said period of thirty days if it is satisfied that the appellant had sufficient cause for not preferring the appeal within the period of thirty days.

CHAPTER V
INTERCEPTION OF COMMUNICATION IN CERTAIN CASES

35. Definitions: In this Chapter, unless the context otherwise requires,

(a) "Electronic communication" means any transmission of signs, signals, writings, images, sounds, data or intelligence of any nature transmitted in whole or in part by a wire, radio, electromagnetic, photo electronic or photo optical system that affects inland or foreign commerce but does not include,
   - (i) The radio portion of a cordless telephone communication that is transmitted between the wireless telephone handset and the base unit,
   - (ii) Any wire or oral communication;
   - (iii) Any communication made through a tone only paging device; or
   - (iv) Any communication from a tracking device;

(b) "Intercept" means the aural or other acquisition of the contents by wire, electronic or oral communication through the use of any electronic, mechanical or other device;

(c) "Oral communication" means any oral communication uttered by a person exhibiting an expectation that such communication is not subject to interception under circumstances justifying such expectation but such term does not include any electronic communication;

(d) "Wire communication" means any aural transmission made in whole or part through the use of facilities for the transmission of communications by the aid of wire, cable or other like connection between the point of origin and the point of connection, between the point of origin and the point of reception (including the use of such connection in switching station) and such term includes any electronic storage of such communication.

36. The Central Government or the State Government, as the case may be, may appoint an officer not below the rank of Secretary to the Government in case of State Government and not below the rank of Joint Secretary to the Government in the case of Central Government, to be the Competent Authority for the purposes of this Chapter.

37. (1). A police officer not below the rank of Superintendent of Police supervising the investigation of any terrorist act under this Ordinance may submit an application in writing to the Competent Authority for an order authorizing or approving the interception of wire, electronic or oral communication by the investigating officer when he believes that such interception may provide, or has provided evidence of any offence involving a terrorist act.

(2) Each application shall include the following information:

(a) The identity of the investigating officer making the application, and the head of the department authorizing the application;

(b) A statement of the facts and circumstances relied upon by the applicant to justify his belief that an order should be issued, including—

  (i) Details as to the offence of terrorist act that has been, is being, or is about to be committed;

  (ii) A particular description of the nature and location of the facilities from which or the place where the communication is to be intercepted;

  (iii) A particular description of the type of communications sought to be intercepted; and

  (iv) The identity of the person, if known, committing the terrorist act whose communications are to be intercepted;

(c) A statement of the period of time for which the interception is required to be maintained, if the nature of the enquiry is such that the authorization of interception should not automatically terminate after the described type of communication has been first obtained;

(d) A particular description of facts establishing probable cause to believe that additional communications of the same type will occur thereafter; and

(e) Where the application is for the extension of an order, a statement setting forth the results thus far obtained from the interception, or a reasonable explanation of the failure to obtain such results.

(3) The Competent Authority may require the applicant to furnish additional oral or documentary evidence in support of the application.

38. (l) Upon such application, the Competent Authority may reject the application, or issue an order, as requested or as modified, authorizing or approving interception of wire, electronic or oral communications, if the Competent Authority determines on the basis of the facts submitted by the applicant that-

(a) There is a probable cause for belief that an individual is committing, has committed, or is about to commit a particular offence described and made punishable under sections 3 and 6 of this Ordinance;

(b) There is a probable cause of belief that particular communications concerning that offence may be obtained through such interception;

(c) There is probable cause of belief that the facilities from which, or the place where, the wire, electronic or oral communications are to be intercepted are being used or are about to be used, in connection with the commission of such offence, leased to, or are listed in the name of or commonly used by such person.

(2) Each order by the Competent Authority authorizing or approving the interception of any wire, electronic or oral communication under this section shall specify-

(a) The identity of the person, if known, whose communications are to be intercepted;

(b) The nature and location of the communication facilities as to which, or the place where, authority to intercept is granted;

(c) A particular description of the type of communication sought to be intercepted, and a statement of the particular offence to which it relates;

(d) The identity of the agency authorized to intercept the communications, and the person authorizing the application; and

(e) The period of time during which such interception is authorized, including a statement as to whether or not the interception shall automatically terminate after the described communication has been first obtained.

39. (1) The Competent Authority shall immediately after passing the order under sub-section (*l*) of section 38, but in any case not later than seven days from the passing of the order, submit a copy of the same to the Review Committee constituted under section 59 along with all the relevant underlying papers, record and his own findings, in respect of the said order, for consideration and approval of the order by the Review Committee.

(2) An order authorizing the interception of a wire, electronic or oral communication under this section shall, upon request of the applicant, direct that a provider of wire or electronic communication service, landlord, custodian or other person shall furnish to the applicant forthwith all information, facilities, and technical assistance necessary to accomplish the interception unobtrusively and with a minimum of interference with the services that such service provider, landlord, custodian, or person is providing to the person whose communications are to be intercepted.

40. (1) No order issued under this section may authorize or approve the interception of any wire, electronic or oral communication for any period longer than is necessary to achieve the objective of the authorization, nor in any event longer than sixty days and such sixty days period shall begin on the day immediately preceding the day on which the investigation officer first begins to conduct an interception under the order or ten days after order is issued whichever is earlier.

(2) The extension of an order may be granted, but only upon an application for an extension made in accordance with sub-section (1) of section 37 and the Competent Authority making the findings required by sub-section (1) of section 38, and the period of such extension shall be no longer than the Competent Authority deems necessary to achieve the purposes for which it was granted and in no event for longer than sixty days at a time.

(3) Every order and extension thereof shall contain a provision that the authorization to intercept shall be executed as soon as practicable and shall be conducted in such manner as to minimize the interception of communications not otherwise subject to interception under this section and shall terminate upon attainment of the authorized objective, or in any event on the expiry of the period of said order or extension thereof.

41. (1) An interception under this Chapter may be conducted in whole or in part by a public servant, acting under the supervision of the investigating officer authorized to conduct the interception.

(2) Whenever an order authorizing an interception is issued pursuant to this section, the order may require reports to be made to the Competent Authority who issued the order showing that progress has been made towards achievement of the authorized objective and the need for continued interception and such report shall be made at such intervals as the Competent Authority may require.

42. (1) Notwithstanding anything contained in any other provision of this section, an officer not below the rank of Additional Director General of Police or a police officer of equivalent rank who reasonably determines that—

(a) An emergency situation exists that involves:

(i) Immediate danger of death or serious physical injury to any person;

(ii) Conspiratorial activities threatening the security or interest of the State; or

(iii) Conspiratorial activities, characteristic of a terrorist act, that requires a wire, electronic or oral communication to be intercepted before an order from the Competent Authority authorizing such interception can, with due diligence, be obtained, and

(b) There are grounds, on which an order should be issued under this section to authorize such interception, may authorize, in writing, the investigating officer to intercept such wire, electronic or oral communication, if an application for an order approving the interception is made in accordance with the provisions of sub-sections (1) and (2) of section 37 within forty-eight hours after the interception has occurred, or begins to occur.

(2) In the absence of an order approving the interception made under sub-section (1), such interception shall immediately terminate when the communication sought is obtained or when the application for the order is rejected, whichever is earlier; and in the event of an application for permitting interception being rejected under sub-section (1) of section 38 or an application under sub-section (1) of section 42 for approval being rejected, or in any other case where the interception is terminated without an order having been issued, the contents of any wire, electronic or oral communication intercepted shall be treated as having been obtained in violation of this section.

43. (a) The contents of any wire, electronic or oral communication intercepted by any means authorized by this section shall as far as possible, be recorded on tape or wire or other comparable device and shall be done in such manner as to protect the recording from editing or other alterations.

(b) Immediately upon the expiration of the period of order, or extension thereof, such recording shall be made available to the

Competent Authority issuing such order and shall be sealed under his directions and kept in the custody of such person or authority as the Competent Authority orders, and such recordings shall not be destroyed except upon an order of the Competent Authority and in any event shall be kept for ten years.

(c) Applications made and orders issued under this section shall be sealed by the Competent Authority and custody of the applications and orders shall be kept in such manner as the Competent Authority directs, and shall not be destroyed except on an order of the Competent Authority, and in any event shall be kept for ten years.

44. Notwithstanding anything in the Code or in any other law for the time being in force, the evidence collected through the interception of wire, electronic or oral communication under this Chapter shall be admissible as evidence against the accused in the Court during the trial of a case:

Provided that, the contents of any wire, electronic or oral communication intercepted pursuant to this Chapter or evidence derived therefrom shall not be received in evidence or otherwise disclosed in any trial, hearing or other proceeding in any court unless each accused has been furnished with a copy of the order of the Competent Authority, and accompanying application, under which the interception was authorized or approved not less than ten days before trial, hearing or proceeding:

Provided further that, the period of ten days may be waived by the judge trying the matter, if he comes to the conclusion that it was not possible to furnish the accused with the above information ten days before the trial, hearing or proceeding and that the accused will not be prejudiced by the delay in receiving such information.

45. (1) The Review Committee constituted by the Central Government or the State Government, as the case may be, shall review every order passed by the Competent Authority under section 38.

(2) Every order passed by the Competent Authority under section 38, or disapproved by the officer under section 42, shall be placed before the Review Committee, which shall be considered by the Review Committee within ten days after its receipt, to decide whether the order, was necessary, reasonable and justified.

(3) The Review Committee, after examining the entire record and holding such enquiry, if any, deemed necessary may, by order in writing, either approve the order passed By the Competent Authority or may issue order disapproving the same.

(4) On issue of an order of disapproval by the Review Committee, the interception, if any, already commenced shall be forthwith discontinued and the intercepted communication, if any, in the form of tape, wire or

other device shall, thereupon, not be admissible as evidence in any case and shall be directed to be destroyed.

46. Except as otherwise specifically provided in section 38, any police officer who

(a) Intentionally intercepts, endeavours to intercept, or procures any other person to intercept or endeavour to intercept any wire, electronic or oral communication;

(b) Intentionally uses, endeavours to use, or procures any other person to use or endeavours to use any electronic, mechanical or other device to intercept any oral communication when

(i) Such device is affixed to or otherwise transmits a signal through a wire, cable, or other like connection used in wire communication; or

(ii) Such device transmits communications by radio, or interferes with the transmission of such communication;

(c) Intentionally discloses, or endeavours to disclose, to any other person, the contents of any wire, electronic or oral communication, knowing or having reason to know that the information was obtained through the interception of a wire, electronic or oral communication in violation of this Chapter,

(d) Intentionally uses, or endeavours to use, the contents of any wire, electronic or oral communication, knowing or having reason to know that the information was obtained through the interception' of a wire, electronic or oral communication in violation of this Chapter; or

(e) Intentionally discloses, or endeavours to disclose, to any other unauthorized person the contents of any wire, electronic or oral communication, intercepted by means authorized by section 38;

(f) Intentionally continues the interception of wire, electronic or oral communication after the issue of an order of rejection by the Competent Authority under this Chapter.

(g) Intentionally continues the interception of wire, electronic or oral communication after the issue of an order of disapproval by the Review Committee under sub-section (3) of section 45, shall for such violation be punishable with imprisonment for a term which may extend to one year and with fine up to rupees fifty thousand.

47. (1) The Central Government and the State Government, as the case may be, shall cause an annual report to be prepared giving a full account of.

(i) The number of applications for authorization of interceptions received by the Competent Authority from the Police Department in which prosecutions have been launched;

(ii) The number of such applications permitted or rejected;
(iii) The number of interceptions carried out in emergency situations and the number of approvals granted or rejected in such matters;
(iv) The number of prosecutions launched based on such interceptions and convictions resulting from such interceptions, along with an explanatory memorandum giving general assessment of the utility and importance of the interceptions authorized.

(2) An annual report shall be laid by the State Government before the State Legislature within three months of the completion of every calendar year:

Provided that, if the State Government is of the opinion that the inclusion of any matter in the annual report would be prejudicial to the security of the State or to the prevention or detection of any terrorist act, the State Government may exclude such matter from being included in such annual report.

(3) An annual report shall be laid by the Central Government before each House of Parliament within three months of the completion of every calendar year:

Provided that, if the Central Government is of the opinion that the inclusion of any matter in the annual report would be prejudicial to the security of the country or to the prevention or detection of any terrorist act, the Central Government may exclude such matter from being included in such annual report.

CHAPTER VI
MISCELLANEOUS

48. (1) Notwithstanding anything contained in the Code or any other law, every offence punishable under this Ordinance shall be deemed to be a cognizable offence within the meaning of clause (c) of section 2 of the Code, and "cognizable case" as defined in that clause shall be construed accordingly.

(2) Section 167 of the Code shall apply in relation to a case involving an offence punishable under this Ordinance subject to the modification that in sub-section (2).

(a) The references to "fifteen days", "ninety days" and "sixty days", wherever they occur, shall be construed as references to "thirty days", "ninety days" and "ninety days", respectively; and
(b) After the proviso, the following provisos shall be inserted, namely: "Provided further that if it is not possible to complete the investigation within the said period of ninety days, the Special Court shall extend the said period up to one hundred and eighty days, on the report of the Public Prosecutor indicating the progress

of the investigation and the specific reasons for the detention of the accused beyond the said period of ninety days;

Provided also that if the police officer making the investigation under this Ordinance, requests, for the purposes of investigation, for police custody from judicial custody of any person from judicial custody, he shall file an affidavit stating the reasons for doing so and shall also explain the delay, if any, for requesting such police custody."

(3) Section 268 of the Code shall apply in relation to a case involving an offence punishable under this Ordinance subject to the modification that

(a) The reference in sub-section (1) thereof

(i) To "the State Government" shall be construed as a reference to "the Central Government or the State Government",

(ii) To "order of the State Government" shall be construed as a reference, to "order of the Central Government or the State Government, as the case may be"; and

(b) The reference in sub-section (2) thereof, to "State Government" shall be construed as a reference to "Central Government or the State Government, as the case may be."

(4) Sections 366, 367 and 371 of the Code shall apply in relation to a case involving an offence triable by a Special Court subject to the modification that the reference to "Court of Session," wherever occurring therein, shall be construed as the reference to "Special Court."

(5) Nothing in section 438 of the Code shall apply in relation to any case involving the arrest of any person accused of having committed an offence punishable under this Ordinance.

(6) Notwithstanding anything contained in the Code, no person accused of an offence punishable under this Ordinance shall, if in custody, be released on bail or on his own bond unless the Court gives the Public Prosecutor an opportunity of being heard.

(7) Where the Public Prosecutor opposes the application of the accused to release on bail, no person accused of an offence punishable under this Ordinance or any rule made thereunder shall be released on bail until the court is satisfied that there are grounds for believing that he is not guilty of committing such offence:

Provided that after the expiry of a period of one year from the date of detention of the accused for an offence under this Ordinance, the provisions of sub-section (6) of this section shall apply.

(8) The restrictions on granting of bail specified in sub-sections (6) and (7) are in addition to the restrictions under the Code or any other law for the time being in force on granting of bail.

(9) Notwithstanding anything contained in sub-sections (6), (7) and (8), no bail shall be granted to a person accused of an offence punishable under this Ordinance, if he is not an Indian citizen and has entered the country unauthorisedly or illegally except in very exceptional circumstances and for reasons to be recorded in writing.

49. No Court shall take cognizance of any offence under this Ordinance without the previous sanction of the Central Government or as the case may be, the State Government.

50. Notwithstanding anything contained in the Code, no police officer,

(a) In the case of the Delhi Special Police Establishment, not below the rank of a Deputy Superintendent of Police or a police officer of equivalent rank;

(b) In the metropolitan areas of Mumbai, Kolkata, Chennai and Ahmedabad and any other metropolitan area notified as such under sub-section (1) of section 8 of the Code, not below the rank of an Assistant Commissioner of Police;

(c) In any other case not relatable to clause (a) or clause (b), not below the rank of a Deputy Superintendent of Police or a police officer of an equivalent rank, shall investigate any offence punishable under this Ordinance.

51. (1) Where a police officer arrests a person, he shall prepare a custody memo of the person arrested.

(2) The person arrested shall be informed of his right to consult a legal practitioner as soon as he is brought to the police station.

(3) Whenever any person is arrested, information of his arrest shall be immediately communicated by the police officer to a family member or in his absence to a relative of such person by telegram, telephone or by any other means and this fact shall be recorded by the police officer under the signature of the person arrested.

(4) The person arrested shall be permitted to meet the legal practitioner representing him during the course of interrogation of the accused person:

Provided that nothing in this sub-section shall entitle the legal practitioner to remain present throughout the period of interrogation

52. (1) In a prosecution for an offence under sub-section (1) of section 3, if it is proved

(a) That the arms or explosives or any other substances specified in section 4 were recovered from the possession of the accused and there is reason to believe that such arms or explosives or other substances of a similar nature, were used in the commission of such offence; or

(b) That the finger-prints of the accused were found at the site of the offence or on anything including arms and vehicles used in connection with the commission of such offence, the Special Court shall draw adverse inference against the accused.

(2) In a prosecution for an offence under sub-section (3) of section 3, if it is proved that the accused rendered any financial assistance to a person, having knowledge that such person is accused of, or reasonably suspected of, an offence under that section, the Special Court shall draw adverse inference against the accused.

53. No civil court or other authority shall have or, be entitled to, exercise any jurisdiction, powers or authority in relation to the matters referred to in section 19 and section 39 of the Ordinance.

54. (1) Nothing in this Ordinance shall affect the jurisdiction exercisable by, or the procedure applicable to, any court or other authority under any law relating to the naval, military or air forces or other armed forces of the Union.

(2) For the removal of doubts, it is hereby declared that for the purposes of any such law as is referred to in sub-section (1), a Special Court shall be deemed to be a court of ordinary criminal justice.

55. The provisions of this Ordinance shall have effect notwithstanding anything inconsistent therewith contained in any enactment other than this Ordinance or in any instrument having effect by virtue of any enactment other than this Ordinance.

56. No suit, prosecution or other legal proceeding shall lie against the Central Government or a State Government or any officer or authority of the Central Government or State Government or any other authority on whom powers have been conferred under this Ordinance, for anything which is in good faith done or purported to be done in pursuance of this Ordinance:

Provided further that no suit, prosecution or other legal proceedings shall lie against any serving member or retired member of the armed forces or other para-military forces in respect, of any action taken or purported to be taken by him in good faith, in the course of any operation directed towards combating terrorism.

57. (1) Any police officer who exercises powers corruptly or maliciously, knowing that there are no reasonable grounds for proceeding under this Ordinance, shall be punishable with imprisonment which may extend to two years, or with fine, or with both.

(2) If the Special Court is of opinion that any person has been corruptly or maliciously proceeded against under this Ordinance, the court may award such compensation as it deems fit to the person, so proceeded against

and it shall be paid by the officer, person, authority or Government, as may be specified in the order.

58. Notwithstanding anything contained in any other law for the time being in force, the passport and the arms license of a person, who is charge sheeted for having committed any offence under this Ordinance, shall be deemed to have been impounded for such period as the Special Court may deem fit.

59, (1) The Central Government and each State Government shall, whenever necessary, constitute one or more Review Committees for the purposes of this Ordinance.

(2) Every such Committee shall consist of a Chairperson and such other members not exceeding three and possessing such qualifications as may be prescribed.

(3) A Chairperson of the Committee shall be a person who is, or who has been a Judge of a High Court, who shall be appointed by the Central Government, or as the case may be, the State Government, so however, that the concurrence of the Chief Justice of the High Court shall be obtained in the case of a sitting Judge:

Provided that in the case of a Union territory, the appointment of a person who is a Judge of the High Court of a State shall be made as a Chairperson with the concurrence of the Chief Justice of the concerned High Court.

60. The High Courts may, by notifications in the Official Gazette, make such rules, if any, as they may deem necessary for carrying out the provisions of this Ordinance relating to Special Courts within their territories.

61. (1) Without prejudice to the powers of the High Courts to make rules under section 60, the Central Government may, by notification in the Official Gazette, make rules for carrying out the provisions of this Ordinance.

(2) In particular, and without prejudice to the generality of the foregoing power, such rules may provide for all or any of the following matters, namely:

- (a) Regulating the conduct of persons in respect of areas the control of which is considered necessary or expedient and the removal of such persons from such areas;
- (b) The entry into and search of,
  - (i) Any vehicle, vessel or aircraft; or
  - (ii) Any place, whatsoever, reasonably suspected of being used for committing the offences referred to in section 3 or section 4 or for manufacturing or storing anything for the commission of any such offence;

(c) Conferring powers upon,
   (i) The Central Government;
   (ii) A State Government;
   (iii) An Administrator of a Union territory under article 239 of the Constitution;
   (iv) An officer of the Central Government not lower in rank than that of a Joint Secretary; or
   (v) An officer of a State Government not lower in rank than that of a District Magistrate, to make general or special orders to prevent or deal with terrorist acts;

(d) The arrest and trial of persons contravening any of the rules or any order made thereunder;

(e) The punishment of any person who contravenes or attempts to contravene or abets or attempts to abet the contravention of any rule or order made thereunder with imprisonment for a term, which may extend to one year or fine or both.

(f) Providing for the seizure and detention of any property in respect of which such contravention, attempt or abetment as is referred to in clause (e) has been committed and for the adjudication of such seizure and detention, whether by any court or by any other authority.

(g) Determination of the price of the forfeited property under sub-section (2) of section 10;

(h) The procedure of making application under sub-section (3) of section 19;

(i) The qualifications of the members of the Review Committee under sub-section (2) of section 59.

SCHEDULE
(SEE SECTION 18)

Terrorist Organisations

1. Babbar Khalsa international.
2. Khalistan commando force.
3. Khalistan Zindabad force.
4. International Sikh youth federation.
5. Lashkar-e-Taiba/Pasban-e-Ahle Hadis.
6. Jaish-e-Mohammed/Tahrik-e-Furqan.
7. Harkat-ul-mujahideen/Harkat-ul-Ansar/Harkat-ul-jehad-e-Islami.
8. Hizb-ul-Mujahideen/Hizb-ul-Mujahideen Pir Panjal regiment.
9. Al-Umar Mujahideen.
10. Jammu and Kashmir Islamic front.

11. United liberation front of Asom (ULFA).
12. National democratic front of Bodoland (NDFB).
13. Peoples' liberation Army (PLA).
14. United National Liberation Front (UNLF).
15. Peoples' Revolutionary Party of Kangleipak (PREPAK).
16. Kangleipak Communist Party (KCP)
17. Kanglei Yaol Kanba Lup (KYKL).
18. Manipur peoples' Liberation Front (MPLF).
19. All Tripura Tiger Force.
20. National Liberation Front of Tripura.
21. Liberation Tigers of Tamil Eelam (LTTE).
22. Students Islamic Movement of India.
23. Deedar anjuman.

K.R. Narayanan
President

Subhash C. Jain
Secy. to the Govt. of India

The Prevention of Terrorism Act

[*The Prevention of Terrorism Act, enacted on 28 March 2002, replaced the Prevention of Terrorism Ordinance 2001. The UPA Government passed a Bill that repealed the Act*]

THE PREVENTION OF TERRORISM ACT, 2002
ACT NO. 15 OF 2002

An Act to make provisions for the prevention of, and for dealing with, terrorist activities and for matters connected therewith.

BE it enacted by Parliament in the Fifty-third Year of the Republic of India as follows:

CHAPTER I
PRELIMINARY

1. Short Title, Application, Commencement, Duration and Savings: (1) This Act may be called the Prevention of Terrorism Act, 2002.

(2) It extends to the whole of India.

(3) Every person shall be liable to punishment under this Act for every act or omission contrary to the provisions thereof, of which he is held guilty in India.

(4) Any person who commits an offence beyond India, which is punishable under this Act, shall be dealt with according to the provisions of this Act in the same manner as if such act had been committed in India.

(5) The provisions of this Act apply also to

(a) citizens of India outside India;
(b) persons in the service of the Government, wherever they may be; and
(c) persons on ships and aircrafts, registered in India, wherever they may be.

(6) Save as otherwise provided in respect of entries at serial numbers 24 and 25 of the Schedule to this Act, it shall be deemed to have come into force on the 24th day of October, 2001 and shall remain in force for a period of three years from the date of its commencement, but its expiry under the operation of this sub-section shall not affect

(a) the previous operation of, or anything duly done or suffered under this Act, or
(b) any right, privilege, obligation or liability acquired, accrued or incurred under this Act, or
(c) any penalty, forfeiture or punishment incurred in respect of any offence under this Act, or
(d) any investigation, legal proceeding or remedy in respect of any such right, privilege, obligation, liability, penalty, forfeiture or punishment as aforesaid, and, any such investigation, legal proceeding or remedy may be instituted, continued or enforced and any such penalty, forfeiture or punishment may be imposed as if this Act had not expired.

2. Definitions: (1) In this Act, unless the context otherwise requires,

(a) "Code" means the Code of Criminal Procedure, 1973 (2 of 1974);
(b) "Designated Authority" shall mean such officer of the Central Government not below the rank of Joint Secretary to the Government, or such officer of the State Government not below the rank of Secretary to the Government, as the case may be, as may be specified by the Central Government or, as the case may be, the State Government, by a notification published in the Official Gazette;
(c) "proceeds of terrorism" shall mean all kinds of properties which have been derived or obtained from commission of any terrorist act or have been acquired through funds traceable to a terrorist act, and shall include cash irrespective of person in whose name such proceeds are standing or in whose possession they are found;
(d) "property" means property and assets of every description, whether corporeal or incorporeal, movable or immovable, tangible or intangible and deeds and instruments evidencing title to, or interest in, such property or assets and includes bank account;
(e) "Public Prosecutor" means a Public Prosecutor or an Additional Public Prosecutor or a Special Public Prosecutor appointed under section 28 and includes any person acting under the directions of the Public Prosecutor;
(f) "Special Court" means a Special Court constituted under section 23;
(g) "terrorist act" has the meaning assigned to it in sub-section (1) of section 3, and the expression "terrorist" shall be construed accordingly;
(h) "State Government", in relation to a Union territory, means the Administrator thereof;

(i) words and expressions used but not defined in this Act and defined in the Code shall have the meanings respectively assigned to them in the Code.

(2) Any reference in this Act to any enactment or any provision thereof shall, in relation to an area in which such enactment or such provision is not in force, be construed as a reference to the corresponding law or the relevant provision of the corresponding law, if any, in force in that area.

CHAPTER II
PUNISHMENT FOR, AND MEASURES FOR DEALING WITH, TERRORIST ACTIVITIES

3. Punishment for terrorist acts: (1) Whoever,

(a) with intent to threaten the unity, integrity, security or sovereignty of India or to strike terror in the people or any section of the people does any act or thing by using bombs, dynamite or other explosive substances or inflammable substances or firearms or other lethal weapons or poisons or noxious gases or other chemicals or by any other substances (whether biological or otherwise) of a hazardous nature or by any other means whatsoever, in such a manner as to cause, or likely to cause, death of, or injuries to any person or persons or loss of, or damage to, or destruction of, property or disruption of any supplies or services essential to the life of the community or causes damage or destruction of any property or equipment used or intended to be used for the defense of India or in connection with any other purposes of the Government of India, any State Government or any of their agencies, or detains any person and threatens to kill or injure such person in order to compel the Government or any other person to do or abstain from doing any act;

(b) is or continues to be a member of an association declared unlawful under the **Unlawful Activities (Prevention) Act, 1967** (37 of 1967), or voluntarily does an act aiding or promoting in any manner the objects of such association and in either case is in possession of any unlicensed firearms, ammunition, explosive or other instrument or substance capable of causing mass destruction and commits any act resulting in loss of human life or grievous injury to any person or causes significant damage to any property, commits a terrorist act.

Explanation: For the purposes of this sub-section, "a terrorist act" shall include the act of raising funds intended for the purpose of terrorism.

(2) Whoever commits a terrorist act, shall,

(a) if such act has resulted in the death of any person, be punishable with death or imprisonment for life and shall also be liable to fine;

(b) in any other case, be punishable with imprisonment for a term which shall not be less than five years but which may extend to imprisonment for life and shall also be liable to fine.

(3) Whoever conspires or attempts to commit, or advocates, abets, advises or incites or knowingly facilitates the commission of, a terrorist act or any act preparatory to a terrorist act, shall be punishable with imprisonment for a term which shall not be less than five years but which may extend to imprisonment for life and shall also be liable to fine.

(4) Whoever voluntarily harbors or conceals, or attempts to harbour or conceal any person knowing that such person is a terrorist shall be punishable with imprisonment for a term which shall not be less than three years but which may extend to imprisonment for life and shall also be liable to fine:

Provided that this sub-section shall not apply to any case in which the harbour or concealment is by the husband or wife of the offender.

(5) Any person who is a member of a terrorist gang or a terrorist organisation, which is involved in terrorist acts, shall be punishable with imprisonment for a term which may extend to imprisonment for life or with fine which may extend to rupees ten lakh or with both.

Explanation: For the purposes of this sub-section, "terrorist organisation" means an organisation, which is concerned with or involved in terrorism.

(6) Whoever knowingly holds any property derived or obtained from commission of any terrorist act or has been acquired through the terrorist funds shall be punishable with imprisonment for a term which may extend to imprisonment for life or with fine which may extend to rupees ten lakh or with both.

(7) Whoever threatens any person who is a witness or any other person in whom such witness may be interested, with violence, or wrongfully restrains or confines the witness, or any other person in whom the witness may be interested, or does any other unlawful act with the said intent, shall be punishable with imprisonment which may extend to three years and fine.

4. Possession of Certain Unauthorized Arms, etc.: Where any person is in unauthorised possession of any

(a) arms or ammunition specified in columns (2) and (3) of Category I or Category III (a) of Schedule I to the Arms Rules, 1962, in a notified area,

(b) bombs, dynamite or hazardous explosive substances or other lethal weapons capable of mass destruction or biological or chemical substances of warfare in any area, whether notified or not, he shall be guilty of terrorist act notwithstanding anything contained in any other law for the time being in force, and be punishable with imprisonment for a term which may extend to imprisonment for life or with fine which may extend to rupees ten lakh or with both.

Explanation: In this section, "notified area" means such area as the State Government may, by notification in the Official Gazette, specify.

5. Enhanced Penalties: (1) If any person with intent to aid any terrorist contravenes any provision of, or any rule made under the Explosives Act, 1884 (4 of 1884), the Explosive Substances Act, 1908 (6 of 1908), the Inflammable Substances Act, 1952 (20 of 1952) or the Arms Act, 1959 (54 of 1959), he shall, notwithstanding anything contained in any of the aforesaid Acts or the rules made thereunder, be punishable with imprisonment for a term which may extend to imprisonment for life and shall also be liable to fine.

(2) For the purposes of this section, any person who attempts to contravene or abets, or does any act preparatory to the contravention of any provision of any law, rule or order, shall be deemed to have contravened that provision, and the provisions of sub-section (1) shall, in relation to such person, have effect subject to the modification that the reference to "imprisonment for life" shall be construed as a reference to "imprisonment for ten years".

6. Holding of Proceeds of Terrorism Illegal: (1) No person shall hold or be in possession of any proceeds of terrorism.

(2) Proceeds of terrorism, whether held by a terrorist or by any other person and whether or not such person is prosecuted or convicted under this Act, shall be liable to be forfeited to the Central Government or the State Government, as the case may be, in the manner provided under this Chapter.

7. Powers of Investigating Officers and Appeal against Order of Designated Authority: (1) If an officer (not below the rank of Superintendent of Police) investigating an offence committed under this Act, has reason to believe that any property in relation to which an investigation is being conducted, represents proceeds of terrorism, he shall, with the prior approval in writing of the Director General of the Police of the State in which such property is situated, make an order seizing such property and where it is not practicable to seize such property, make an order of attachment directing that such property shall not be transferred or otherwise dealt with except with the prior permission of the officer making such order, or of the Designated Authority before whom the properties seized or attached are produced and a copy of such order shall be served on the person concerned.

(2) For the removal of doubts, it is hereby provided that where an organisation is declared as a terrorist organisation under this Act and the investigating officer has reason to believe that any person has custody of any property which is being used or is intended to be used for the purpose of such terrorist organisation, he may, by an order in writing, seize or attach such property.

(3) The investigating officer shall duly inform the Designated Authority within forty-eight hours of the seizure or attachment of such property.

(4) It shall be open to the Designated Authority before whom the seized or attached properties are produced either to confirm or revoke the order of attachment so issued:

Provided that an opportunity of making a representation by the person whose property is being attached shall be given.

(5) In the case of immovable property attached by the investigating officer, it shall be deemed to have been produced before the Designated Authority, when the investigating officer notifies his report and places it at the disposal of the Designated Authority.

(6) The investigating officer may seize and detain any cash to which this Chapter applies if he has reasonable grounds for suspecting that

(a) it is intended to be used for the purposes of terrorism;

(b) it forms the whole or part of the resources of an organisation declared as terrorist organisation under this Act:

Provided that the cash seized under this sub-section by the investigating officer shall be released not later than the period of forty-eight hours beginning with the time when it is seized unless the matter involving the cash is before the Designated Authority and such Authority passes an order allowing its retention beyond forty-eight hours.

Explanation: For the purposes of this sub section, "cash" means

(a) coins and notes in any currency;

(b) postal orders;

(c) traveler's cheques;

(d) banker's drafts; and

(e) such other monetary instruments as the Central Government or, as the case may be,

the State Government may specify by an order made in writing.

(7) Any person aggrieved by an order made by the Designated Authority may prefer an appeal to the Special Court and the Special Court may either confirm the order of attachment of property or seizure so made or revoke such order and release the property.

8. Forfeiture of Proceeds of Terrorism: Where any property is seized or attached on the ground that it constitutes proceeds of terrorism and the Special Court is satisfied in this regard under sub-section (7) of section 7, it may order forfeiture of such property, whether or not the person from whose possession it is seized or attached, is prosecuted in a Special Court for an offence under this Act.

9. Issue of Show cause Notice before Forfeiture of Proceeds of Terrorism: (1) No order forfeiting any proceeds of terrorism shall be made under section 8 unless the person holding or in possession of such proceeds is given a notice in writing informing him of the grounds on which it is proposed to forfeit the proceeds of terrorism and such person is given an opportunity of making a representation in writing within such reasonable time as may be specified in the notice against the grounds of forfeiture and is also given a reasonable opportunity of being heard in the matter.

(2) No order of forfeiture shall be made under sub-section (1), if such person establishes that he is a bona fide transferee of such proceeds for value without knowing that they represent proceeds of terrorism.

(3) It shall be competent for the Special Court to make an order in respect of property seized or attached,

(a) directing it to be sold if it is a perishable property and the provisions of section 459 of the Code shall, as nearly as may be practicable, apply to the net proceeds of such sale;

(b) nominating any officer of the Central or State Government, in the case of any other property, to perform the function of the Administrator of such property subject to such conditions as may be specified by the Special Court.

10. Appeal: (1) Any person aggrieved by an order of forfeiture under section 8 may, within one month from the date of the receipt of such order, appeal to the High Court within whose jurisdiction, the Special Court, who passed the order appealed against, is situated.

(2) Where an order under section 8 is modified or annulled by the High Court or where in a prosecution instituted for the contravention of the provisions of this Act, the person against whom an order of forfeiture has been made under section 8 is acquitted, such property shall be returned to him and in either case if it is not possible for any reason to return the forfeited property, such person shall be paid the price therefore as if the

property had been sold to the Central Government with reasonable interest calculated from the day of seizure of the property and such price shall be determined in the manner prescribed.

11. Order of Forfeiture not to Interfere with Other Punishments: The order of forfeiture made under this Act by the Special Court, shall not prevent the infliction of any other punishment to which the person affected thereby is liable under this Act.

12. Claims by Third Party: (1) Where any claim is preferred, or any objection is made to the seizure of any property under section 7 on the ground that such property is not liable to seizure, the Designated Authority before whom such property is produced, shall proceed to investigate the claim or objection:

Provided that no such investigation shall be made where the Designated Authority considers that the claim or objection is designed to cause unnecessary delay.

(2) In case claimant or objector establishes that the property specified in the notice issued under section 9 is not liable to be forfeited under the Act, the said notice shall be withdrawn or modified accordingly.

13. Powers of Designated Authority: The Designated Authority, acting under the provisions of this Act, shall have all the powers of a civil court required for making a full and fair enquiry into the matter before it.

14. Obligation to Furnish Information: (1) Notwithstanding anything contained in any other law, the officer investigating any offence under this Act, with prior approval in writing of an officer not below the rank of a Superintendent of Police, may require any officer or authority of the Central Government or a State Government or a local authority or a bank, or a company, or a firm or any other institution, establishment, organisation or any individual to furnish information in their possession in relation to such offence, on points or matters, where the investigating officer has reason to believe that such information will be useful for, or relevant to, the purposes of this Act.

(2) Failure to furnish the information called for under sub-section (1), or deliberately furnishing false information shall be punishable with imprisonment for a term, which may extend to three years or with fine or with both.

(3) Notwithstanding anything contained in the Code, the offence under sub-section (1) shall be tried as a summary case and the procedure prescribed in Chapter XXI of the said Code [except sub-section (2) of section 262] shall be applicable thereto.

15. Certain Transfers to be Null and Void: Where, after the issue of an order under section 7 or issue of a notice under section 9, any property referred to in the said order or notice is transferred by any mode whatsoever, such transfer shall, for the purpose of the proceedings under this Act, be ignored and if such property is subsequently forfeited, the transfer of such property shall be deemed to be null and void.

16. Forfeiture of Property of Certain Persons: (1) Where any person is accused of any offence under this Act, it shall be open to the Special Court trying him to pass an order that all or any of the properties, movable or immovable or both belonging to him, shall, during the period of such trial, be attached, if not already attached under this Act.

(2) Where a person has been convicted of any offence punishable under this Act, the Special Court may, in addition to awarding any punishment, by order in writing, declare that any property, movable or immovable or both, belonging to the accused and specified in the order, shall stand forfeited to the Central Government or the State Government, as the case may be, free from all encumbrances.

17. Company to Transfer Shares to Government: Where any shares in a company stand forfeited to the Central Government or the State Government, as the case may be, under this Act, then, the company shall, on receipt of the order of the Special Court, notwithstanding anything contained in the Companies Act, 1956 (1 of 1956), or the articles of association of the company, forthwith register the Central Government or the State Government, as the case may be, as the transferee of such shares.

CHAPTER III
TERRORIST ORGANISATIONS

18. Declaration of an Organization as a Terrorist Organization: (1) For the purposes of this Act, an organisation is a terrorist organisation if

(a) it is listed in the Schedule, or

(b) it operates under the same name as an organisation listed in that Schedule.

(3) The Central Government may by order, in the Official Gazette,

(a) add an organisation to the Schedule;

(b) remove an organisation from that Schedule;

(c) amend that Schedule in some other way.

(3) The Central Government may exercise its power under clause (a) of sub-section (2) in respect of an organisation only if it believes that it is involved in terrorism.

(4) For the purposes of sub-section (3), an organisation shall be deemed to be involved in terrorism if it

(a) commits or participates in acts of terrorism,

(b) prepares for terrorism,
(c) promotes or encourages terrorism, or
(d) is otherwise involved in terrorism.

19. Denotification of a Terrorist Organization: (1) An application may be made to the Central Government for the exercise of its power under clause (b) of sub-section (2) of section 18 to remove an organisation from the Schedule.

(2) An application may be made by

(a) the organisation, or
(b) any person affected by inclusion of the organisation in the Schedule as a terrorist organisation.

(3) The Central Government may make rules to prescribe the procedure for admission and disposal of an application made under this section.

(4) Where an application under sub-section (1) has been refused, the applicant may apply for a review to the Review Committee constituted by the Central Government under sub-section (1) of section 60 within one month from the date of receipt of the order by the applicant.

(5) The Review Committee may allow an application for review against refusal to remove an organisation from the Schedule, if it considers that the decision to refuse was flawed when considered in the light of the principles applicable on an application for judicial review.

(6) Where the Review Committee allows review under sub-section (5) by or in respect of an organisation, it may make an order under this sub-section.

(7) Where an order is made under sub-section (6), the Central Government shall, as soon as the certified copy of the order is received by it, make an order removing the organisation from the list in the Schedule.

20. Offence Relating to Membership of a Terrorist Organization: (1) A person commits an offence if he belongs or professes to belong to a terrorist organisation:

Provided that this sub-section shall not apply where the person charged is able to prove

(a) that the organisation was not declared as a terrorist organisation at the time when he became a member or began to profess to be a member; and
(b) that he has not taken part in the activities of the organisation at any time during its inclusion in the Schedule as a terrorist organisation.

(2) A person guilty of an offence under this section shall be liable, on conviction, to imprisonment for a term not exceeding ten years or with fine or with both.

21. Offence Relating to Support Given to a Terrorist Organization: (1) A person commits an offence if

(a) he invites support for a terrorist organisation, and
(b) the support is not, or is not restricted to, the provision of money or other property within the meaning of section 22.

(2) A person commits an offence if he arranges, manages or assists in arranging or managing a meeting which he knows is

(a) to support a terrorist organisation, or
(b) to further the activities of a terrorist organisation, or
(c) to be addressed by a person who belongs or professes to belong to a terrorist organisation.

(3) A person commits an offence if he addresses a meeting for the purpose of encouraging support for a terrorist organisation or to further its activities.

(4) A person guilty of an offence under this section shall be liable on conviction, to imprisonment for a term not exceeding ten years or with fine or with both.

Explanation: For the purposes of this section, the expression "meeting" means a meeting of three or more persons whether or not the public are admitted.

22. Fund Raising for a Terrorist Organization to be an Offence: (1) A person commits an offence if he

(a) invites another to provide money or other property, and
(b) intends that it should be used, or has reasonable cause to suspect that it may be used, for the purposes of terrorism.

(2) A person commits an offence if he

(a) receives money or other property, and
(b) intends that it should be used, or has reasonable cause to suspect that it may be used, for the purposes of terrorism.

(3) A person commits an offence if he

(a) provides money or other property, and
(b) knows or has reasonable cause to suspect that it will or may be used for the purposes of terrorism.

(4) In this section, a reference to the provision of money or other property is a reference to its being given, lent or otherwise made available, whether or not for consideration.

(4) A person guilty of an offence under this section shall be liable on conviction, to imprisonment for a term not exceeding fourteen years or with fine or with both.

CHAPTER IV
SPECIAL COURTS

23. Special Courts: (1) The Central Government or a State Government may, by notification in the Official Gazette, constitute one or more Special Courts for such area or areas, or for such case or class or group of cases, as may be specified in the notification.

(2) Where a notification constituting a Special Court for any area or areas or for any case or class or group of cases is issued by the Central Government under sub-section (1), and a notification constituting a Special Court for the same area or areas or for the same case or class or group of cases has also been issued by the State Government under that sub-section, the Special Court constituted by the Central Government, whether the notification constituting such Court is issued before or after the issue of the notification constituting the Special Court by the State Government, shall have, and the Special Court constituted by the State Government shall not have, jurisdiction to try any offence committed in that area or areas or, as the case may be, the case or class or group of cases and all cases pending before any Special Court constituted by the State Government shall stand transferred to the Special Court constituted by the Central Government.

(3) Where any question arises as to the jurisdiction of any Special Court, it shall be referred to the Central Government whose decision in the matter shall be final.

(4) A Special Court shall be presided over by a judge to be appointed by the Central Government or, as the case may be, the State Government, with the concurrence of the Chief Justice of the High Court.

(5) The Central Government or, as the case may be, the State Government may also appoint, with the concurrence of the Chief Justice of the High Court, additional judges to exercise jurisdiction of a Special Court.

(6) A person shall not be qualified for appointment as a judge or an additional judge of a Special Court unless he is, immediately before such appointment, a sessions judge or an additional sessions judge in any State.

(7) For the removal of doubts, it is hereby provided that the attainment, by a person appointed as a judge or an additional judge of a Special Court, of the age of superannuation under the rules applicable to him in the service to which he belongs, shall not affect his continuance as such judge or additional judge.

(8) Where any additional judge or additional judges is or are appointed in a Special Court, the judge of the Special Court may, from time to time, by general or special order, in writing, provide for the distribution of

business of the Special Court among all judges including himself and the additional judge or additional judges and also for the disposal of urgent business in the event of his absence or the absence of any additional judge.

24. Place of Sitting: A Special Court may, on its own motion, or on an application made by the Public Prosecutor and if it considers it expedient or desirable so to do, sit for any of its proceedings at any place other than its ordinary place of sitting:

Provided that nothing in this section shall be construed to change the place of sitting of a Special Court constituted by a State Government to any place outside that State.

25. Jurisdiction of Special Courts: (1) Notwithstanding anything contained in the Code, every offence punishable under any provision of this Act shall be triable only by the Special Court within whose local jurisdiction it was committed or, as the case may be, by the Special Court constituted for trying such offence under section 23.

(2) If, having regard to the exigencies of the situation prevailing in a State,

(a) it is not possible to have a fair, impartial or speedy trial; or

(b) it is not feasible to have the trial without occasioning the breach of peace or grave risk to the safety of the accused, the witnesses, the Public Prosecutor and a judge of the Special Court or any of them; or

(c) it is not otherwise in the interests of justice, the Supreme Court may transfer any case pending before a Special Court to any other Special Court within that State or in any other State and the High Court may transfer any case pending before a Special Court situated in that State to any other Special Court within the State.

(3) The Supreme Court or the High Court, as the case may be, may act under this section either on the application of the Central Government or a party interested and any such application shall be made by motion, which shall, except when the applicant is the Attorney-General of India, be supported by an affidavit or affirmation.

26. Power of Special Courts with Respect to Other Offences: (1) When trying any offence, a Special Court may also try any other offence with which the accused may, under the Code, be charged at the same trial if the offence is connected with such other offence.

(2) If, in the course of any trial under this Act of any offence, it is found that the accused person has committed any other offence under this Act or under any other law, the Special Court may convict such person of such other offence and pass any sentence or award punishment authorised by this Act or such rule or, as the case may be, under such other law.

27. Power to Direct for Samples, etc.: (1) When a police officer investigating a case requests the Court of a Chief Judicial Magistrate or the Court of a Chief Metropolitan Magistrate in writing for obtaining samples of handwriting, finger-prints, foot-prints, photographs, blood, saliva, semen, hair, voice of any accused person, reasonably suspected to be involved in the commission of an offence under this Act, it shall be lawful for the Court of a Chief Judicial Magistrate or the Court of a Chief Metropolitan Magistrate to direct that such samples be given by the accused person to the police officer either through a medical practitioner or otherwise, as the case may be.

(2) If any accused person refuses to give samples as provided in sub-section (1), the Court shall draw adverse inference against the accused.

28. Public Prosecutors: (1) For every Special Court, the Central Government or, as the case may be, the State Government, shall appoint a person to be the Public Prosecutor and may appoint one or more persons to be the Additional Public Prosecutor or Additional Public Prosecutors:

Provided that the Central Government or, as the case may be, the State Government, may also appoint for any case or class or group of cases, a Special Public Prosecutor.

(2) A person shall not be qualified to be appointed as a Public Prosecutor or an Additional Public Prosecutor or a Special Public Prosecutor under this section unless he has been in practice as an Advocate for not less than seven years or has held any post, for a period of not less than seven years, under the Union or a State, requiring special knowledge of law.

(3) Every person appointed as a Public Prosecutor or an Additional Public Prosecutor or a Special Public Prosecutor under this section shall be deemed to be a Public Prosecutor within the meaning of clause (u) of section 2 of the Code, and the provisions of the Code shall have effect accordingly.

29. Procedure and Powers of Special Courts: (1) Subject to the provisions of section 50, a Special Court may take cognizance of any offence, without the accused being committed to it for trial, upon receiving a complaint of facts that constitute such offence or upon a police report of such facts.

(2) Where an offence triable by a Special Court is punishable with imprisonment for a term not exceeding three years or with fine or with both, the Special Court may, notwithstanding anything contained in sub-section (1) of section 260 or section 262 of the Code, try the offence in a summary way in accordance with the procedure prescribed in the Code and the provisions of sections 263 to 265 of the Code, shall so far as may be, apply to such trial:

Provided that when, in the course of a summary trial under this sub-section, it appears to the Special Court that the nature of the case is such that it is undesirable to try it in a summary way, the Special Court shall recall any witnesses who may have been examined and proceed to re-hear the case in the manner provided by the provisions of the Code for the trial of such offence and the said provisions shall apply to and in relation to a Special Court as they apply to and in relation to a Magistrate:

Provided further that in the case of any conviction in a summary trial under this section, it shall be lawful for a Special Court to pass a sentence of imprisonment for a term not exceeding one year and with fine, which may extend to rupees five lakh.

(3) Subject to the other provisions of this Act, a Special Court shall, for the purpose of trial of any offence, have all the powers of a Court of Session and shall try such offence as if it were a Court of Session so far as may be in accordance with the procedure prescribed in the Code for the trial before a Court of Session.

(4) Subject to the other provisions of this Act, every case transferred to a Special Court under section 25 shall be dealt with as if such case had been transferred under section 406 of the Code to such Special Court.

(5) Notwithstanding anything contained in the Code, but subject to the provisions of section 299 of the Code, a Special Court may, if it thinks fit and for reasons to be recorded by it, proceed with the trial in the absence of the accused or his pleader and record the evidence of any witness, subject to the right of the accused to recall the witness for cross-examination.

30. Protection of Witnesses: (1) Notwithstanding anything contained in the Code, the proceedings under this Act may, for reasons to be recorded in writing, be held in camera if the Special Court so desires.

(2) A Special Court, if on an application made by a witness in any proceeding before it or by the Public Prosecutor in relation to such witness or on its own motion, is satisfied that the life of such witness is in danger, it may, for reasons to be recorded in writing, take such measures as it deems fit for keeping the identity and address of such witness secret.

(3) In particular, and without prejudice to the generality of the provisions of sub-section (2), the measures, which a Special Court may take under that sub-section, may include:

(a) the holding of the proceedings at a place to be decided by the Special Court;

(b) the avoiding of the mention of the names and addresses of the witnesses in its orders or judgments or in any records of the case accessible to public;

(c) the issuing of any directions for securing that the identity and address of the witnesses are not disclosed;
(d) a decision that it is in the public interest to order that all or any of the proceedings pending before such a Court shall not be published in any manner.

(4) Any person who contravenes any decision or direction issued under sub-section (3) shall be punishable with imprisonment for a term, which may extend to one year and with fine which may extend to one thousand rupees.

31. Trial by Special Courts to have Precedence: The trial under this Act of any offence by a Special Court shall have precedence over the trial of any other case against the accused in any other court (not being a Special Court) and shall be concluded in preference to the trial of such other case and accordingly the trial of such other case shall remain in abeyance.

32. Certain Confessions made to Police Officers to be Taken into Consideration: (1) Notwithstanding anything in the Code or in the Indian Evidence Act, 1872 (1 of 1872), but subject to the provisions of this section, a confession made by a person before a police officer not lower in rank than a Superintendent of Police and recorded by such police officer either in writing or on any mechanical or electronic device like cassettes, tapes or sound tracks from out of which sound or images can be reproduced, shall be admissible in the trial of such person for an offence under this Act or the rules made thereunder.

(2) A police officer shall, before recording any confession made by a person under sub-section (1), explain to such person in writing that he is not bound to make a confession and that if he does so, it may be used against him:

Provided that where such person prefers to remain silent, the police officer shall not compel or induce him to make any confession.

(3) The confession shall be recorded in an atmosphere free from threat or inducement and shall be in the same language in which the person makes it.

(4) The person from whom a confession has been recorded under sub-section (1), shall be produced before the Court of a Chief Metropolitan Magistrate or the Court of a Chief Judicial Magistrate along with the original statement of confession, written or recorded on mechanical or electronic device within forty-eight hours.

(5) The Chief Metropolitan Magistrate or the Chief Judicial Magistrate, shall, record the statement, if any, made by the person so produced and get his signature or thumb impression and if there is any

complaint of torture, such person shall be directed to be produced for medical examination before a Medical Officer not lower in rank than an Assistant Civil Surgeon and thereafter, he shall be sent to judicial custody.

33. Power to Transfer Cases to Regular Courts: Where, after taking cognizance of any offence, a Special Court is of the opinion that the offence is not triable by it, it shall, notwithstanding that it has no jurisdiction to try such offence, transfer the case for the trial of such offence to any court having jurisdiction under the Code and the Court to which the case is transferred may proceed with the trial of the offence as if it had taken cognizance of the offence.

34. Appeal: (1) Notwithstanding anything contained in the Code, an appeal shall lie from any judgment, sentence or order, not being an interlocutory order, of a Special Court to the High Court both on facts and on law.

Explanation: For the purposes of this section, "High Court" means a High Court within whose jurisdiction, a Special Court which passed the judgment, sentence or order, is situated.

(2) Every appeal under sub-section (1) shall be heard by a bench of two Judges of the High Court.

(3) Except as aforesaid, no appeal or revision shall lie to any court from any judgment, sentence or order including an interlocutory order of a Special Court.

(4) Notwithstanding anything contained in sub-section (3) of section 378 of the Code, an appeal shall lie to the High Court against an order of the Special Court granting or refusing bail.

(5) Every appeal under this section shall be preferred within a period of thirty days from the date of the judgment, sentence or order appealed from:

Provided that the High Court may entertain an appeal after the expiry of the said period of thirty days if it is satisfied that the appellant had sufficient cause for not preferring the appeal within the period of thirty days.

35. Transitional Provisions and Transfer of Pending Proceedings: (1) The jurisdiction conferred by this Act on a Special Court, shall, until a Special Court is constituted under section 23, in the case of any offence punishable under this Act, notwithstanding anything contained in the Code, be exercised by the Court of Session of the division in which such offence has been committed and it shall have all the powers and follow the procedure provided under this Chapter.

(2) On and from the date when the Special Court is constituted under section 23, every trial under the provisions of this Act, which would have

been required to be held before the Special Court, shall stand transferred to that Court on the date on which it is constituted.

CHAPTER V
INTERCEPTION OF COMMUNICATION IN CERTAIN CASES

36. Definitions: In this Chapter, unless the context otherwise requires,

(a) "electronic communication" means any transmission of signs, signals, writings, images, sounds, data or intelligence of any nature transmitted in whole or in part by a wire, radio, electromagnetic, photo electronic or photo optical system that affects inland or foreign commerce but does not include

  (i) the radio portion of a cordless telephone communication that is transmitted between the wireless telephone hand-set and the base unit; or

  (ii) any wire or oral communication; or

  (iii) any communication made through a tone only paging device; or

  (iv) any communication from a tracking device;

(b) "intercept" means the aural or other acquisition of the contents by wire, electronic or oral communication through the use of any electronic, mechanical or other device;

(c) "oral communication" means any oral communication uttered by a person exhibiting an expectation that such communication is not subject to interception under circumstances justifying such expectation but such term does not include any electronic communication;

(d) "wire communication" means any aural transmission made in whole or part through the use of facilities for the transmission of communications by the aid of wire, cable or other like connection between the point of origin and the point of connection, between the point of origin and the point of reception (including the use of such connection in switching station) and such term includes any electronic storage of such communication.

37. Appointment of Competent Authority: The Central Government or the State Government, as the case may be, may appoint an officer not below the rank of Secretary to the Government in the case of State Government and not below the rank of Joint Secretary to the Government in the case of Central Government, to be the Competent Authority for the purposes of this Chapter.

38. Application for Authorization of Interception of Wire, Electronic or Oral communication: (1) A police officer not below the rank of Superintendent of Police supervising the investigation of any terrorist act under this Act may submit an application in writing to the Competent Authority for an order authorising or approving the interception of wire, electronic or oral communication by the investigating officer when he believes that such interception may provide, or has provided evidence of any offence involving a terrorist act.

(2) Each application shall include the following information:

(a) the identity of the investigating officer making the application, and the head of the department authorising the application;

(b) a statement of the facts and circumstances relied upon by the applicant to justify his belief that an order should be issued, including

(i) details as to the offence of terrorist act that has been, is being, or is about to be committed;

(ii) a particular description of the nature and location of the facilities from which or the place where the communication is to be intercepted;

(iii) a particular description of the type of communications sought to be intercepted; and

(iv) the identity of the person, if known, committing the terrorist act whose communications are to be intercepted;

(c) a statement of the period of time for which the interception is required to be maintained, if the nature of the enquiry is such that the authorisation of interception should not automatically terminate after the described type of communication has been first obtained;

(d) a particular description of facts establishing probable cause to believe that additional communications of the same type will occur thereafter; and

(e) where the application is for the extension of an order, a statement setting forth the results thus far obtained from the interception, or a reasonable explanation of the failure to obtain such results.

(3) The Competent Authority may require the applicant to furnish additional oral or documentary evidence in support of the application.

39. Decision by Competent Authority on Application for Interception: (1) Upon such application, the Competent Authority may reject the application, or issue an order, as requested or as modified, authorising or approving interception of wire, electronic or oral communications, if the Competent Authority determines on the basis of the facts submitted by the applicant that

(a) there is a probable cause for belief that an individual is committing, has committed, or is about to commit, a particular offence described and made punishable under sections 3 and 4 of this Act;

(b) there is a probable cause of belief that particular communications concerning that offence may be obtained through such interception;

(c) there is probable cause of belief that the facilities from which, or the place where, the wire, electronic or oral communications are to be intercepted are being used or are about to be used, in connection with the commission of such offence, leased to, or are listed in, the name of or commonly used by such person.

(2) Each order by the Competent Authority authorising or approving the interception of any wire, electronic or oral communication under this section shall specify

(a) the identity of the person, if known, whose communications are to be intercepted;

(b) the nature and location of the communication facilities as to which, or the place where, authority to intercept is granted;

(c) a particular description of the type of communication sought to be intercepted, and a statement of the particular offence to which it relates;

(d) the identity of the agency authorised to intercept the communications, and the person authorising the application; and

(e) the period of time during which such interception is authorised, including a statement as to whether or not the interception shall automatically terminate after the described communication has been first obtained.

40. Submission of Order of Interception to Review Committee: (1) The Competent Authority shall, immediately after passing the order under sub-section (1) of section 39, but in any case not later than seven days from the passing of the order, submit a copy of the same to the Review Committee constituted under section 60 along with all the relevant underlying papers, record and his own findings, in respect of the said order, for consideration and approval of the order by the Review Committee.

(2) An order authorising the interception of a wire, electronic or oral communication under this section shall, upon request of the applicant, direct that a provider of wire or electronic communication service, landlord, custodian or other person shall furnish to the applicant forthwith all information, facilities and technical assistance necessary to accomplish

the interception unobtrusively and with a minimum of interference with the services that such service provider, landlord, custodian or person is providing to the person whose communications are to be intercepted.

41. Duration of an Order of Inception, etc.: (1) No order issued under this section may authorise or approve the interception of any wire, electronic or oral communication for any period longer than is necessary to achieve the objective of the authorisation, nor in any event longer than sixty days and such sixty days period shall begin on the day immediately preceding the day on which the investigating officer first begins to conduct an interception under the order or ten days after order is issued whichever is earlier.

(2) The extension of an order may be granted, but only upon an application for an extension made in accordance with sub-section (1) of section 38 and the Competent Authority making the findings required by sub-section (1) of section 39, and the period of such extension shall be no longer than the Competent Authority deems necessary to achieve the purposes for which it was granted and in no event for longer than sixty days at a time.

(3) Every order and extension thereof shall contain a provision that the authorisation to intercept shall be executed as soon as practicable and shall be conducted in such manner as to minimise the interception of communications not otherwise subject to interception under this section and shall terminate upon attainment of the authorised objective, or in any event on the expiry of the period of said order or extension thereof.

42. Authority Competent to Carry Out Interception: (1) An interception under this Chapter may be conducted in whole or in part by a public servant, acting under the supervision of the investigating officer authorised to conduct the interception.

(2) Whenever an order authorising an interception is issued pursuant to this section, the order may require reports to be made to the Competent Authority who issued the order showing that progress has been made towards achievement of the authorised objective and the need for continued interception and such report shall be made at such intervals as the Competent Authority may require.

43. Interception of Communication in Emergency: (1) Notwithstanding anything contained in any other provision of this Chapter, an officer not below the rank of Additional Director General of Police or a police officer of equivalent rank who reasonably determines that

(a) an emergency situation exists that involves,

(i) immediate danger of death or serious physical injury to any person; or

(ii) conspiratorial activities threatening the security or interest of the State; or

(iii) conspiratorial activities, characteristic of a terrorist act, that requires a wire, electronic or oral communication to be intercepted before an order from the Competent Authority authorising such interception can, with due diligence, be obtained; and

(b) there are grounds on which an order should be issued under this section to authorise such interception,

may authorise, in writing, the investigating officer to intercept such wire, electronic or oral communication, if an application for an order approving the interception is made in accordance with the provisions of sub-sections (1) and (2) of section 38 within forty-eight hours after the interception has occurred, or begins to occur.

(2) In the absence of an order approving the interception made under sub-section (1), such interception shall immediately terminate when the communication sought is obtained or when the application for the order is rejected, whichever is earlier; and in the event of an application for permitting interception being rejected under sub-section (1) of section 39 or an application under sub-section (1) of this section for approval being rejected, or in any other case where the interception is terminated without an order having been issued, the contents of any wire, electronic or oral communication intercepted shall be treated as having been obtained in violation of this section.

44. Protection of Information Collected: (1) The contents of any wire, electronic or oral communication intercepted by any means authorised by this Chapter shall, as far as possible, be recorded on tape or wire or other comparable device and shall be done in such manner as to protect the recording from editing or other alterations.

(2) Immediately upon the expiration of the period of order, or extension thereof, such recording shall be made available to the Competent Authority issuing such order and shall be sealed under his directions and kept in the custody of such person or authority as the Competent Authority orders, and such recordings shall not be destroyed except upon an order of the Competent Authority and in any event shall be kept for ten years

(3) Applications made and orders issued under this Chapter shall be sealed by the Competent Authority and custody of the applications and orders shall be kept in such manner as the Competent Authority directs, and shall not be destroyed except on an order of the Competent Authority, and in any event shall be kept for ten years.

45. Admissibility of Evidence Collected through the Interception of Communications: Notwithstanding anything in the Code or in any other law for the time being in force, the evidence collected through the interception of wire, electronic or oral communication under this Chapter shall be admissible as evidence against the accused in the Court during the trial of a case:

Provided that, the contents of any wire, electronic or oral communication intercepted pursuant to this Chapter or evidence derived therefrom shall not be received in evidence or otherwise disclosed in any trial, hearing or other proceeding in any court unless each accused has been furnished with a copy of the order of the Competent Authority, and accompanying application, under which the interception was authorised or approved not less than ten days before trial, hearing or proceeding:

Provided further that, the period of ten days may be waived by the judge trying the matter, if he comes to the conclusion that it was not possible to furnish the accused with the above information ten days before the trial, hearing or proceeding and that the accused will not be prejudiced by the delay in receiving such information.

46. Review of Authorization Order: (1) The Review Committee constituted by the Central Government or the State Government, as the case may be, shall review every order passed by the Competent Authority under section 39.

(2) Every order passed by the Competent Authority under section 39, or disapproved by the officer under section 43, shall be placed before the Review Committee, which shall be considered by the Review Committee within ten days after its receipt, to decide whether the order was necessary, reasonable and justified.

(3) The Review Committee, after examining the entire record and holding such enquiry, if any, deemed necessary may, by order in writing, either approve the order passed by the Competent Authority or may issue order disapproving the same.

(4) On issue of an order of disapproval by the Review Committee, the interception, if any, already commenced shall be forthwith discontinued and the intercepted communication, if any, in the form of tape, wire or other device shall, thereupon, not be admissible as evidence in any case and shall be directed to be destroyed.

47. Interception and Disclosure of Wire, Electronic or Oral Communications Prohibited: Except as otherwise specifically provided in section 39, any police officer who

(a) intentionally intercepts, endeavours to intercept, or procures any other person to intercept or endeavour to intercept any wire, electronic or oral communication;

(b) intentionally uses, endeavours to use, or procures any other person to use or endeavours to use any electronic, mechanical or other device to intercept any oral communication when

(i) such device is affixed to, or otherwise transmits a signal through a wire, cable, or other like connection used in wire communication; or

(ii) such device transmits communications by radio, or interferes with the transmission of such communication;

(c) intentionally discloses, or endeavours to disclose, to any other person the contents of any wire, electronic or oral communication, knowing or having reason to know that the information was obtained through the interception of a wire, electronic or oral communication in violation of this Chapter;

(d) intentionally uses, or endeavours to use, the contents of any wire, electronic or oral communication, knowing or having reason to know that the information was obtained through the interception of a wire, electronic or oral communication in violation of this Chapter;

(e) intentionally discloses, or endeavours to disclose, to any other unauthorised person the contents of any wire, electronic or oral communication, intercepted by means authorised by section 39;

(f) intentionally continues the interception of wire, electronic or oral communication after the issue of an order of rejection by the Competent Authority under this Chapter;

(g) intentionally continues the interception of wire, electronic or oral communication after the issue of an order of disapproval by the Review Committee under sub-section (3) of section 46, shall for such violation be punishable with imprisonment for a term which may extend to one year and with fine up to rupees fifty thousand.

48. Annual Report of Interceptions: (1) The Central Government and the State Government, as the case may be, shall cause an annual report to be prepared giving a full account of

(a) the number of applications for authorisation of interceptions received by the Competent Authority from the Police Department in which prosecutions have been launched;

(b) the number of such applications permitted or rejected;

(c) the number of interceptions carried out in emergency situations and the number of approvals granted or rejected in such matters;

(d) the number of prosecutions launched based on such interceptions and convictions resulting from such interceptions, along with an explanatory memorandum giving general assessment of the utility and importance of the interceptions authorised.

(2) An annual report shall be laid by the State Government before the State Legislature within three months of the completion of every calendar year:

Provided that, if the State Government is of the opinion that the inclusion of any matter in the annual report would be prejudicial to the security of the State or to the prevention or detection of any terrorist act, the State Government may exclude such matter from being included in such annual report.

(3) An annual report shall be laid by the Central Government before each House of Parliament within three months of the completion of every calendar year:

Provided that, if the Central Government is of the opinion that the inclusion of any matter in the annual report would be prejudicial to the security of the country or to the prevention or detection of any terrorist act, the Central Government may exclude such matter from being included in such annual report.

CHAPTER VI
MISCELLANEOUS

49. Modified Application of Certain Provisions of the Code: (1) Notwithstanding anything contained in the Code or any other law, every offence punishable under this Act shall be deemed to be a cognizable offence within the meaning of clause (c) of section 2 of the Code, and "cognizable case" as defined in that clause shall be construed accordingly.

(2) Section 167 of the Code shall apply in relation to a case involving an offence punishable under this Act subject to the modification that in sub-section (2),

(a) the references to "fifteen days", "ninety days" and "sixty days", wherever they occur, shall be construed as references to "thirty days", "ninety days" and "ninety days", respectively; and

(b) after the proviso, the following provisos shall be inserted, namely: "Provided further that if it is not possible to complete the investigation within the said period of ninety days, the Special Court shall extend the said period up to one hundred and eighty days, on the report of the Public Prosecutor indicating the progress of the investigation and the specific reasons for the detention of the accused beyond the said period of ninety days:

Provided also that if the police officer making the investigation under this Act, requests, for the purposes of investigation, for police custody from judicial custody of any person from judicial custody, he shall file an affidavit stating the reasons for doing so and shall also explain the delay, if any, for requesting such police custody.".

(3) Section 268 of the Code shall apply in relation to a case involving an offence punishable under this Act subject to the modification that

(a) the reference in sub-section (1) thereof

(i) to "the State Government" shall be construed as a reference to "the Central Government or the State Government",

(ii) to "order of the State Government" shall be construed as a reference to "order of the Central Government or the State Government, as the case may be"; and

(b) the reference in sub-section (2) thereof, to "the State Government" shall be construed as a reference to "the Central Government or the State Government, as the case may be".

(4) Sections 366, 367 and 371 of the Code shall apply in relation to a case involving an offence triable by a Special Court subject to the modification that the reference to "Court of Session", wherever occurring therein, shall be construed as the reference to "Special Court".

(5) Nothing in section 438 of the Code shall apply in relation to any case involving the arrest of any person accused of having committed an offence punishable under this Act.

(6) Notwithstanding anything contained in the Code, no person accused of an offence punishable under this Act shall, if in custody, be released on bail or on his own bond unless the Court gives the Public Prosecutor an opportunity of being heard.

(7) Where the Public Prosecutor opposes the application of the accused to release on bail, no person accused of an offence punishable under this Act or any rule made thereunder shall be released on bail until the Court is satisfied that there are grounds for believing that he is not guilty of committing such offence:

Provided that after the expiry of a period of one year from the date of detention of the accused for an offence under this Act, the provisions of sub-section (6) of this section shall apply.

(8) The restrictions on granting of bail specified in sub-sections (6) and (7) are in addition to the restrictions under the Code or any other law for the time being in force on granting of bail.

(9) Notwithstanding anything contained in sub-sections (6), (7) and (8), no bail shall be granted to a person accused of an offence punishable under this Act, if he is not an Indian citizen and has entered the country unauthorisedly or illegally except in very exceptional circumstances and for reasons to be recorded in writing.

50. Cognizance of Offences: No court shall take cognizance of any offence under this Act without the previous sanction of the Central Government or, as the case may be, the State Government.

51. Officers Competent to Investigate Offences under this Act: Notwithstanding anything contained in the Code, no police officer,

(a) in the case of the Delhi Special Police Establishment, below the rank of a Deputy Superintendent of Police or a police officer of equivalent rank;
(b) in the metropolitan areas of Mumbai, Kolkata, Chennai and Ahmedabad and any other metropolitan area notified as such under sub-section (1) of section 8 of the Code, below the rank of an Assistant Commissioner of Police;
(c) in any other case not relatable to clause (a) or clause (b), below the rank of a Deputy Superintendent of Police or a police officer of an equivalent rank,

shall investigate any offence punishable under this Act.

52. Arrest: (1) Where a police officer arrests a person, he shall prepare a custody memo of the person arrested.

(2) The person arrested shall be informed of his right to consult a legal practitioner as soon as he is brought to the police station.

(3) Whenever any person is arrested, information of his arrest shall be immediately communicated by the police officer to a family member or in his absence to a relative of such person by telegram, telephone or by any other means and this fact shall be recorded by the police officer under the signature of the person arrested.

(4) The person arrested shall be permitted to meet the legal practitioner representing him during the course of interrogation of the accused person:

Provided that nothing in this sub-section shall entitle the legal practitioner to remain present throughout the period of interrogation.

53. Presumption as to Offences under Section 3: (1) In a prosecution for an offence under sub-section (1) of section 3, if it is proved

(a) that the arms or explosives or any other substances specified in section 4 were recovered from the possession of the accused and there is reason to believe that such arms or explosives or other substances of a similar nature, were used in the commission of such offence; or
(b) that the finger-prints of the accused were found at the site of the offence or on anything including arms and vehicles used in connection with the commission of such offence,

the Special Court shall draw adverse inference against the accused.

(2) In a prosecution for an offence under sub-section (3) of section 3, if it is proved that the accused rendered any financial assistance to a person, having knowledge that such person is accused of, or reasonably suspected of, an offence under that section, the Special Court shall draw adverse inference against the accused.

54. Bar of Jurisdiction of Courts, etc.: No civil court or other authority shall have or, be entitled to, exercise any jurisdiction, powers or authority in relation to the matters referred to in sections 19 and 40 of the Act.

55. Saving: (1) Nothing in this Act shall affect the jurisdiction exercisable by, or the procedure applicable to, any court or other authority under any law relating to the naval, military or air forces or other armed forces of the Union.

(2) For the removal of doubts, it is hereby declared that for the purposes of any such law as is referred to in sub-section (1), a Special Court shall be deemed to be a court of ordinary criminal justice.

56. Overriding Effect: The provisions of this Act shall have effect notwithstanding anything inconsistent therewith contained in any enactment other than this Act or in any instrument having effect by virtue of any enactment other than this Act.

57. Protection of Action Taken in Good Faith: No suit, prosecution or other legal proceeding shall lie against the Central Government or a State Government or any officer or authority of the Central Government or State Government or any other authority on whom powers have been conferred under this Act, for anything which is in good faith done or purported to be done in pursuance of this Act:

Provided that no suit, prosecution or other legal proceedings shall lie against any serving member or retired member of the armed forces or other para-military forces in respect of any action taken or purported to be taken by him in good faith, in the course of any operation directed towards combating terrorism

58. Punishment and Compensation for Malicious Action: (1) Any police officer who exercises powers corruptly or maliciously, knowing that there are no reasonable grounds for proceeding under this Act, shall be punishable with imprisonment which may extend to two years, or with fine, or with both.

(2) If the Special Court is of the opinion that any person has been corruptly or maliciously proceeded against under this Act, the Court may award such compensation as it deems fit to the person, so proceeded against and it shall be paid by the officer, person, authority or Government, as may be specified in the order.

59. Impounding Passport and Arms License of Person Charge-Sheeted under the Act: Notwithstanding anything contained in any other law for the time being in force, the passport and the arms license of a person, who is charge-sheeted for having committed any offence under this Act, shall be deemed to have been impounded for such period as the Special Court may deem fit.

60. Review Committees: (1) The Central Government and each State Government shall, whenever necessary, constitute one or more Review Committees for the purposes of this Act.

(2) Every such Committee shall consist of a Chairperson and such other members not exceeding three and possessing such qualifications as may be prescribed.

(3) A Chairperson of the Committee shall be a person who is, or has been, a Judge of a High Court, who shall be appointed by the Central Government, or as the case may be, the State Government, so however, that the concurrence of the Chief Justice of the High Court shall be obtained in the case of a sitting Judge:

Provided that in the case of a Union territory, the appointment of a person who is a Judge of the High Court of a State shall be made as a Chairperson with the concurrence of the Chief Justice of the concerned High Court.

61. Power of High Courts to Make Rules: The High Court may, by notification in the Official Gazette, make such rules, if any, as they may deem necessary for carrying out the provisions of this Act relating to Special Courts within their territories.

62. Power to Make Rules: (1) Without prejudice to the powers of the High Courts to make rules under section 61, the Central Government may, by notification in the Official Gazette, make rules for carrying out the provisions of this Act.

(2) In particular, and without prejudice to the generality of the foregoing powers, such rules may provide for all or any of the following matters, namely:

(a) regulating the conduct of persons in respect of areas the control of which is considered necessary or expedient and the removal of such persons from such areas;

(b) the entry into, and search of
  (i) any vehicle, vessel or aircraft; or
  (ii) any place, whatsoever,
  Reasonably suspected of being used for committing the offences referred to in section 3 or section 4 or for manufacturing or storing anything for the commission of any such offence;

(c) conferring powers upon
  (i) the Central Government;
  (ii) a State Government;
  (iii) an Administrator of a Union territory under article 239 of the Constitution;
  (iv) an officer of the Central Government not lower in rank than that of a Joint Secretary; or

(v) an officer of a State Government not lower in rank than that of a District Magistrate,

to make general or special orders to prevent or deal with terrorist acts;

(d) the arrest and trial of persons contravening any of the rules or any order made thereunder;

(e) the punishment of any person who contravenes or attempts to contravene or abets or attempts to abet the contravention of any rule or order made thereunder with imprisonment for a term which may extend to one year or fine or both;

(f) providing for the seizure and detention of any property in respect of which such contravention, attempt or abetment as is referred to in clause (e) has been committed and for the adjudication of such seizure and detention, whether by any court or by any other authority;

(g) determination of the price of the forfeited property under sub-section (2) of section 10;

(h) the procedure of making application under sub-section (3) of section 19; and

(i) the qualifications of the members of the Review Committee under sub-section (2) of section 60.

63. Orders and Rules to be Laid before Houses of Parliament: Every order and every rule made by the Central Government under this Act shall be laid, as soon as may be after it is made, before each House of Parliament, while it is in session, for a total period of thirty days which may be comprised in one session or in two or more successive sessions, and if, before the expiry of the session immediately following the session or the successive sessions aforesaid, both Houses agree in making any modification in the order or rule or both Houses agree that the order or rule should not be made, the order or rule shall thereafter have effect only in such modified form or be of no effect, as the case may be; so, however, that any such modification or annulment shall be without prejudice to the validity of anything previously done under that order or rule.

64. Repeal and Saving: (1) The Prevention of Terrorism (Second) Ordinance, 2001 is hereby repealed.

(2) Notwithstanding the repeal of the said Ordinance, anything done or any action taken under the said Ordinance shall be deemed to have been done or taken under the corresponding provisions of this Act.

THE SCHEDULE
(See Section 18)

Terrorist Organisations

1. Babbar Khalsa International.
2. Khalistan Commando Force.
3. Khalistan Zindabad Force.
4. International Sikh Youth Federation.
5. Lashkar-e-Taiba/Pasban-e-Ahle Hadis
6. Jaish-e-Mohammed/Tahrik-e-Furqan
7. Harkat-ul-Mujahideen/Harkat-ul-Ansar/Harkat-ul-Jehad-e-Islami.
8. Hizb-ul-Mujahideen/Hizb-ul-Mujahideen Pir Panjal Regiment.
9. Al-Umar-Mujahideen.
10. Jammu and Kashmir Islamic Front.
11. United Liberation Front of Assam (ULFA).
12. National Democratic Front of Bodoland (NDFB).
13. People's Liberation Army (PLA).
14. United National Liberation Front (UNLF).
15. People's Revolutionary Party of Kangleipak (PREPAK).
16. Kangleipak Communist Party (KCP).
17. Kanglei Yaol Kanba Lup (KYKL).
18. Manipur People's Liberation Front (MPLF).
19. All Tripura Tiger Force.
20. National Liberation Front of Tripura.
21. Liberation Tigers of Tamil Eelam (LTTE).
22. Students Islamic Movement of India.
23. Deedar anjuman.
24. Communist Party of India (Marxist-Leninist): Peoples' War, all its formations and front organisations
25. Maoist Communist Centre (MCC), All its formations and front organisations.
26. Al Badr
27. Jamiat-Ul-Mujahidden
28. Al-Qaeda.
29. Dukhtaran-e-Millat (DEM)
30. Tamil Nadu Liberation Army (TNLA)
31. Tamil National Retrieval Troops (TNRT)
32. Akhil Bharat Nepali Ekta Samaj (ABNES)

Explanation: For the purposes of this Schedule, serial numbers 24 and 25 shall be deemed to have been included with effect from the date of publication of S.O. No. 1194(E), dated the 5th December 2001.

K.N. Chaturvedi,
Addl. Secy. to the Govt. of India

The Arunachal Pradesh Control of Organised Crime Act, 2002

[*The Arunachal Pradesh Legislative Assembly enacted an Act known as Arunachal Pradesh Control of Organised Crime Act on 23 August 2002. The Act's primary aim was to prevent and control, and also to cope with, criminal activities perpetrated by organised crime syndicates or gangs, and matters or incidents related to such activities. This Act was enacted under the Chief Ministership of Mukut Mithi. The Act was repealed after Gegong Apang dislodged the Mithi ministry*]

To make special provisions for prevention and control of, and for coping with, criminal activities by organised crime syndicates or gangs and matters connected therewith or incidental thereto.

Where as it was expedient to make special provisions for prevention and control of, and for coping with, criminal activities by organised crime syndicates or gangs and matters connected therewith or incidental thereto;

And whereas it was considered necessary to immediately make a law for the same;

And whereas the Arunachal Pradesh Legislative Assembly is not in session;

And whereas the Governor of Arunachal Pradesh was satisfied that circumstances existed which rendered it necessary for him to make immediate action to make law for the purposes aforesaid and, therefore, promulgated the Arunachal Pradesh Control of Organised Crime Ordinance, 2002 on 3rd April, 2002

And whereas it is expedient to replace the said Ordinance by an Act of the State Legislature; it is hereby enacted in the Fifty Third Year of the Republic of India as follows:

1. Short Title Extent and Commencement: (1) This Act may be called the Arunachal Pradesh Control of Organised Crime Act, 2002.

(2) It extends to the whole of the State of Arunachal Pradesh.

(3) It shall be deemed to have come into force on 3rd April 2002.

2. Definition: (1) In this, Act, unless the context otherwise requires,

(a) "Abet" with its grammatical variations and cognate expressions, includes,

(i) The communication or association with any person with

actual knowledge or having reason to believe that such person is engaged in assisting in any manner, an organised crime syndicate;

(ii) The passing on or publication of, without any lawful authority, any information likely to assist the organised crime syndicate and the passing on or publication of or distribution of any document or matter obtained from the organised crime syndicate; and

(iii) The tendering of any assistance, whether financial or otherwise, to the organised crime syndicate;

(b) "Code" means the Code of Criminal Procedure, 1973;

(c) "Competent Authority" means the Competent Authority appointed under section 13;

(d) "Continuing unlawful activity" means an activity prohibited by law for the time being in force, which is a cognisable offence punishable with imprisonment of three years or more, undertaken either singly of jointly, as a member of an organised crime syndicate of on behalf of such syndicate in respect of which more than within the preceding period of ten years and that Court has taken cognisance of such offence;

(e) "Organised crime" means any continuing unlawful activity by an individual, singly or jointly, either as a member of an organised crime syndicate or on behalf of such syndicate, by use of violence or threat of violence or intimidation or coercion or other unlawful means, with the objective of gaining pecuniary benefits or gaining undue economic or other advantage for himself or any other person or promoting insurgency;

(f) "Organised crime syndicate" means a group of two or more persons who acting either singly or collectively, as a syndicate or gang indulge in activities of organised crime.

(g) "Special Court" means the Special Court constituted under section 5

(2) Words and expressions used but not defined in this Act and defined in the Code shall have the meaning respectively assigned to them in the Code.

3. Punishment for Organised Crime: (1) Whoever commits an offence of organised crime shall:

(i) If such offence has resulted in the death of any person be punishable with death or imprisonment for life and shall also be liable to a fine, subject to a minimum fine of rupees one lakh.

(ii) In any other case, be punishable with imprisonment for a team which shall not be less than five years but which may extend to imprisonment for life and shall also liable to a fine, subject to a minimum fine of rupees five lakh.

(2) Whoever conspires or attempts to commit or advocates, abets of knowingly facilities the commission of an organised crime or an acts preparatory to organised crime, shall be punishable with imprisonment for a term which shall be not less than live years but which may extend to imprisonment for life and shall also be liable a fine subject to a minimum fine of Rupees five lakh.

(3) Whoever harbours or conceals or attempts to harbour of conceal, any member of an organised crime syndicate shall be punishable with imprisonment for a term which shall not be less than five years but which may extend to imprisonment for life, and shall also be liable to a fine, subject to a minimum fine of Rupees five lakh.

(4) Any person who is a member of an organised crime syndicate shall be punishable with imprisonment for a term which shall not be less than five years but which may extend to imprisonment for life and shall also be liable to a fine, subject to a minimum fine of Rupees two lakh.

(5) Whoever holds any property derived or obtained from commission of an organised crime or which has been acquired through the organised crime syndicate funds shall be punishable with a term which shall not be less than three years but which may extend to imprisonment for life and shall also be liable to a fine subject to a minimum fine of Rupees two lakh.

4. Punishment for Possessing Unaccountable Wealth on Behalf of Member of Organised Crimes Syndicate: If any person on behalf of a member of an organised crime syndicate is, or at any time has been, in possession of movable or immovable properly which he cannot satisfactorily account for, he shall be punishable with imprisonment for a tern which shall not be less than three years but which may extend to ten years and shall also be liable to a fine, subject to a minimum fine of Rupees one lakh and such property shall also be liable for attachment and forfeiture, as provided by section 20.

5. Special Courts: (1) The State Government may, by notification in the Official Gazette, constitute one or more Special Courts for such area or areas or for such case or class or group of cases, as may be prescribed in the notification.

(2) Where any question arises as to the jurisdiction of any Special Court, it shall be referred to the State Government whose decision shall be final.

(3) A Special Court shall be presided over by a judge to be appointed by the State Government, with the concurrence of the Chief Justice of the

Gauhati High Court. The State Government may also appoint with the concurrence of the Chief Justice of the Gauhati High Court, additional judges to exercise jurisdiction in a Special Court.

(4) A person shall not be qualified for appointment as a judge or an additional judge of a special Court, unless he immediately before such appointment is a session judge or an additional session judge.

(5) Where any additional judge is or additional judges are appointed in a Special Court, the judge of the Special Court may, from time to time, by general or special order in writing, provide for the distribution of the business of the Special Court among himself and the additional judge or additional judges and also for the disposal of urgent business in the event of his absence or the absence of any additional judges.

6. Jurisdiction of Special Court: Notwithstanding anything contained in the Code, every offence punishable under this Act shall be friable only by the Special Court within whose local jurisdiction it was committed, or as the case may be, by the Special Court constituted for trying such offence under sub-section (1) of section 5.

7. Power of Special Courts with Respect to Other Offences: (1) When trying any offence punishable under this Act, a Special Court may also try any other offence with which the accused may, under the code, be charged at the same trial, if the offence is connected with such other offence.

(2) If, in the course of any trial of any offence under this Act, it is found that the accused person has committed any other offence under this Act or under any other law, the Special Court may convict such person of such other offence and may pass any sentence authorised by this Act, or, as the case may be, such other law, for the punishment thereof.

8. Public Prosecutor: (1) For every Special Court, the State Government shall appoint a person to be the Public Prosecutor and may appoint one or more persons to be the Additional Public Prosecutor or Additional Public Prosecutors;

Provided that, the State Government may also appoint for any case or group of cases, a Special Public Prosecutor.

(2) A person shall not be qualified to be appointed as a Public Prosecutor, an Additional Public Prosecutor or a Special Public Prosecutor unless he has been in practice as an advocate for not less than ten years.

(3) Every person appointed as a Public Prosecutor or Additional Public Prosecutor or Special Public Prosecutor under this section shall be deemed to be Public Prosecutor within the meaning of clause (u) of section 2 of the Code, and the provisions of the Code shall have effect accordingly.

9. Procedures and Powers of Special Court: (1) A Special Court may take cognisance of any offence without the accused being committed to it for trial, upon receiving a complaint of facts, which constitute such offence or upon a police report of such facts.

(2) Where an offence triable by a Special Court is punishable with imprisonment for a term not exceeding three years or with fine or with both, the Special Court may, notwithstanding anything contained in sub-section (1) of section 260 or section 262 of the Code, try the offence in a summary way in accordance with the procedure prescribed in this Code and the provisions of sections 263 of the Code shall, as far as may, be apply to such trial.

Provided that, where in the course of a summary trial under this sub-section, it appears to the Special Court that the nature of the case is such that it is undesirable to try in summary way, the Special Court shall recall any witnesses who may have been examined and proceed to rehear the case in the manner provided by the provisions of the Code for the trial of such offence and the said provisions shall apply to and in relation, to a Special Court as they apply to and in relation, to a Magistrate.

Provided further that, in case of any conviction in a summary trial under this section, it shall be lawful for Special Court to pass a sentence of imprisonment for a term not exceeding two years.

(3) A Special Court may, with a view to obtaining the evidence of any person, supposed to have been directly or indirectly concerned in or privy to an offence, tender a pardon to such person on condition of his making a full and true disclosure of the whole circumstances within his knowledge relative to the offence and to every other person concerned, whether as principal or abettor, in the commission thereof, and any pardon so tendered shall, for the purposes of section 308 of the Code, be deemed to have been tendered under section 307 thereof.

(4) Subject to other provisions of this Act, a Special Court shall for the purpose of trial of any offence, have all the powers of a Court of session, and shall try such offence as if it were a court of session, so far as may be, in accordance with the procedure prescribed in the Code for the trial before a court of session.

10. Trial by Special Courts to have Precedence: The trial of any offence under this Act by a Special Court shall have precedence over the trial of any other case against the accused in any other Court (not being a Special Court) and shall be concluded in preference of the trial of such other case and accordingly the trial of such other cases shall remain in abeyance.

11. Power to Transfer Cases to Regular Courts: Where, after taking cognisance of an offence, a Special Court is of the opinion that the offence is not triable by it, it shall notwithstanding that it has no jurisdiction to try such offence, transfer the case for trial of such offence to any Court having jurisdiction under the Code and the Court to which the case is transferred may proceed with the trial of the offence as if it had taken cognisance of the offence.

12. Appeal: (1) Notwithstanding anything contained in the Code, an appeal shall lie from any judgment, sentence or order, not being an interlocutory order, of a Special Court in the High Court.

(2) Every appeal under this section shall be preferred within thirty days from the date of the judgment, sentence or order.

13. Appointment of Competent Authority: The State Government may appoint any of its officers, in Home Department, not below the rank of Secretary to the Government, to be the Competent Authority for the purposes of Section 14.

14. Authorisation of Interception of Wire, Electronic or Oral Communication: (a) (1) A police officer not below the rank of Superintendent of Police supervising the investigation of an organised crime under this Act may submit an application in writing to the Competent Authority for an order authorising or approving the interception of wire, electronic or oral communication by the investigating officer when such interception may provide or has provided evidence of any offence involving an organised crime.

(2) Each application shall include the following information:

(a) The identity of the investigative or law enforcement officer making the application, and the head of the department authorising the application;

(b) A statement of the facts and circumstances relief upon by the applicant, to justify his belief that an order should be issued, including

  (i) Details as to the offence of organised crime that has been, is being or is about to be committed;

  (ii) A particular description of the nature and location of the facilities from which or the place where the communication is to be intercepted,

  (iii) A particular description of the type of communications sought to be intercepted; and

  (iv) The identity of the person, if known, committing the offence of organised crime whose communications are to be intercepted;

(c) A statement as to whether or not other modes of enquiry or intelligence gathering have been tried and failed or why they reasonably appear to be unlikely to succeed if tried or to be too dangerous or is likely to expose the identity of those connected with the operation of interception;

(d) A statement of the period of time for which the interception is required to be maintained. If the nature of the enquiry is such that the authorisation for interception should not automatically terminate when the described type of communication has been first obtained, a particular description of facts establishing probable cause to believe that additional communications of the same type will occur thereafter;

(e) A statement of the facts concerning all previous applications known to the individual authorising and making the application, made to the Competent Authority for authorisation to intercept, or for approval of interception of, wire, electronic or oral communications involving any of the same persons, facilities or places specified in the application and the action taken by the Competent Authority on each such application; and

(f) Where the application is for the extension of an order, a statement setting forth the results thus obtained from the interception, or a reasonable explanation of the failure to obtain such results.

(3) The Competent Authority may require the applicant to furnish additional oral or documentary evidence in support of the application.

(4) Upon such application, the Competent Authority may after recording the reasons in writing reject the application, or issue an order, as requested or as modified, authorising or approving interception of wire, electronic or oral communications, if the Competent Authority determines on the basis of the facts submitted by the applicant that:

(a) There is a probable cause for belief that an individual is committing, has committed or is about to commit a particular offence described and made punishable under sections 3 and 4 of this Act;

(b) There is a probable cause for belief that particular communications concerning that offence will be obtained through such interception;

(c) Normal modes of enquiry and intelligence gathering have been tried and have failed or reasonably appear to be unlikely to succeed if tried or to be too dangerous or is likely to expose the identity of those connected with the operation of interception;

(d) There is probable cause for belief that the facilities from which, or the place where, the wire, electronic or oral communications are to be intercepted or be used or are about to be used, in connection with the commission of such offence, leased to, or are listed in the name of or commonly used by such person.

(5) Each order by the Competent Authority authorising or approving the interception of any wire, electronic or oral communication under this section shall specify:

(a) The identity of the person, it known, whose communications are to be intercepted;

(b) The nature and location of the communication facilities as to which, or the place where, authority to intercept is granted;

(c) A particular description of the type of communication sought to be intercepted, and a statement of the particular offence to which it relates;

(d) The identity of the agency authorised to intercept the communications and of the person authorising the application; and

(e) The period of time during which such interception is authorised, including a statement as to whether or not the interception shall automatically terminate when the described communication has been first obtained.

(6) The Competent Authority shall immediately after passing the order under sub-section (4), but in any case not later than seven days from the passing of the order, submit a copy of the same to the Review Committee constituted under section 15 along with all the relevant underlying papers, record and his own findings, etc. in respect of the said order, for consideration and approval of the order by the Review Committee.

(7) An order authorising the interception of a wire, electronic or oral communication under this section shall, upon request of the applicant, direct that a provider of wire or electronic communication service, landlord, custodian or other person shall furnish to the applicant forthwith all information, facilities, and technical assistance necessary to accomplish the interception unobtrusively and with a minimum of interference with the services that such service provider, landlord, custodian or person is providing to the person whose communications are to be intercepted.

(8) No order issued under this section may authorise or approve the interception of any wire, electronic or oral communication for any period longer than is necessary to achieve the objective of the authorisation, nor in any event longer than sixty days. Such sixty days period shall begin on the day immediately proceeding the day or which the investigative or law enforcement officer first begins to conduct an interception under the order or ten days after the order is issued, whichever is earlier. Extension of an order may be granted, but only upon an application for an extension is made in accordance with sub-section (1) and the Competent Authority making the findings required by sub-section (4). The period of extension shall be no longer than the Competent Authority deems necessary to achieve

the purposes for which it was granted and in no event for longer than sixty days at a time. Every order and extension thereof shall contain a provision that the authorisation to intercept shall be executed as soon as practicable and shall be conducted in such a way or manner as to minimise the interception of communications not otherwise subject to interception under this section and must terminate upon attainment of the authorised objective or in any event on expiry of the period of order. In the event the intercepted communication is in a code or foreign language, and an expert in that foreign language or code is not reasonably available during the interception period minimisation may be accomplished as soon as practicable after such interception. An interception under this section may be conducted in whole or in part by public servant, or by an individual operating under a contract with the State Government acting under the supervision of the investigative or law enforcement officer authorised to conduct the interception.

(9) Whenever an order authorising interception is issued pursuant to this section, the order may require reports to be made to the Competent Authority who issued the order showing that progress has been made towards achievement of the authorised objective and the need for continued interception. Such reports shall be made at such intervals as the Competent Authority may require.

(10) Notwithstanding anything contained in any other provision of this section, an Officer not below the rank or Inspector General of Police who reasonably determines that

(a) An emergency situation exists that involves
  (i) Immediate danger of death or serious physical inquiry to any person;
  (ii) Conspiratorial activities threatening the security or interest of the State; or
  (iii) Conspiratorial activities, characteristic of organised crime, that requires a wire, electronic or oral communication to be intercepted before an order from the Competent Authority authorising such interception, can with due diligence, be obtained, and

(b) There are grounds upon which an order could be issued under this section to authorise such interception, may authorise, in writing, the investigating Police Officer to intercept such wire, electronic or oral communication, if an application for an order approving the interception is made in accordance with the provisions of sub-section (1) and (2) within forty-eight hours after the interception has occurred, or beings to occur.

(11) In the absence of an order approving the interception made under sub-section (10), such interception shall immediately terminate when the communication sought is obtained or when the application for the order is rejected, whichever is earlier, in the event where an application for permitting interception is rejected under sub-section (4) or an application under sub-section (1)) for approval is rejected, or in any other case where the interception is terminated without an order having been issued, the contents of any wire, electronic or oral communication intercepted shall be treated as having been obtained in violation of this section.

(12) (a) The contents of any wire, electronic or oral communication intercepted by any means authorised by this section shall, if possible, be recorded on tape of wire or other comparable device. Recording of the contents of any wire electronic or oral communication under this sub-section shall be done in such a way as will protect the recording from editing or other alterations. Immediately upon the expiration of the period of order, or extension thereof, such recordings shall be made available to the Competent Authority issuing such order age shall be sealed under his directions. Custody of the recordings shall be where of the Competent Authority orders. They shall not be destroyed except upon an order of the Competent Authority and in any event shall be kept for ten years.

(b) Applications made and order issued under this section shall be sealed by the Competent Authority Custody of the applications and order shall be wherever the Competent Authority directs, and shall not be destroyed except on an order of the Competent Authority and in any event shall be kept for ten years.

The Competent Authority upon the filing of a motion, may in his discretion make available to such person or his counsel for inspection such portion of the intercepted communication, applications and orders as the Competent Authority determines to be in the interest of justice.

(13) Notwithstanding anything in the Code or in any other law for the time being in force, the evidence collected through the interception of wire, electronic or oral communication under this section shall be admissible as evidence against the accused in the Court during the trial of a case:

Provided that the contents of any wire, electronic or oral communication intercepted pursuant to this section or evidence derived therefrom shall not be received in evidence or otherwise disclosed in any trial, hearing or other proceeding in any court unless each party, not less than ten days before trial, hearing or proceeding, has been furnished with a copy of the order of the Competent Authority, and accompanying application, under which the interception was authorised or approved.

Provided further that, this ten days period may be waived by the judge, trying the matter, if he finds that it was not possible to furnish the party with the above information ten days before the trial, hearing or proceeding and that the party will not be prejudiced by the delay in receiving such information.

Explanation: For the purposes of this section

(a) "Wire communication means" any aural transfer made in whole or part through the use of facilities for the transmission of communications by the aid of wire, cable or other like connection between the point of origin and the point of connection, between the point of origin and the point of reception (including the use of such connection in switching a station and such term includes any electronic storage of such communication.

(b) "Oral communication" means any oral communication uttered by a person exhibition on expectation that such communication is not subject to interception under circumstances justifying such expectation trial such term dues not includes any electronic communication.

(c) "Electronic communications" means any transfer of signs, signals, writings images sounds data of inelegance of any nature transmitted in whole or in part by a wire radio electronic magnate photo, electronic photo optical system that affects inland or foreign commerce but does not include:

(i) The radio portion of cordless telephones communication that is transmitted between the wireless telephone handset and the base unit,

(ii) Any wire or oral communication;

(iii) Any communication made through a tone of paging device; or

(iv) Any communication from a tracking device;

(d) "Intercept" means the aural or other acquisition of the contents by wire, electronic or oral communication through the use of any electronic, mechanical or other device.

15. Constitution of Review Committee for Review of Authorisation Orders: (1) There shall be a Review Committee to review any order passed by the Competent Authority under section 14.

(2) The Review Committee shall consist of the following ex officio members namely:

(i)	The Chief Secretary to the Government	Chairman
(ii)	The Communication or the Joint Secretary, as the case may be, of the Home Department	Member
(iii)	Secretary (Law and Judicial)	Member

(3) Every order passed by the Competent Authority under section 14, placed before the Review Committee, shall be considered by the Review Committee within ten days after its receipt, to decide, whether the order, authorising or approving the application under sub-section (4) of section 14 for interception or disapproving the interception made under sub-section (10) of that section in emergency situation, passed by the Competent Authority was necessary, reasonable and justified.

(4) The Review Committee after examining the entire record and holding such enquiry, if any, deemed necessary may, by order in writing, either approve the order passed by the Competent Authority or may issue order disapproving the same. On issue of an order of disapproval by the Review Committee, the interception, if any, already commenced shall be forthwith discontinued. The intercepted communication, it any, in the form of tape, wire or other device shall, thereupon, not be admissible as evidence in any case and shall be directed to be destroyed.

16. Interception and Disclosure of Wire, Electronic or Oral Communications Prohibited: Except as otherwise specification provided in section 14, any police officer who:

(a) Intentionally intercepts, endeavours to intercept, or procures any other person to intercept or endeavour to intercept any wire, electronic or oral communication;

(b) Intentionally uses, endeavours to use, or procures any other person to use or endeavours to use any electronic, mechanical or other device to intercept any oral communication when

  (i) Such device is affixed to, or otherwise transmits a signal through a wire cable, or other like connection used in wire communication; or

  (ii) Such device transmits communications by radio, or interferes with the transmission of such communication;

(c) Intentionally discloses, of endeavours to disclose, to any other person the contents of any wire, electronic or oral communication, knowing or having reason to know that the information was obtained through the interception of a wire, electronic or oral communication in violation of this sub-section;

(d) Intentionally users, or endeavours to use the contents of any wire, electronic or oral communication, knowing or having reason to know that the information was obtained through the interception of a wire, electronic or oral communication in violation of this sub-section; or

(e) (i) Intentionally discloses, or endeavours to disclose, to any other person the contents of any wire, electronic or oral communication intercepted by means authorised by section 14;

(ii) Knowing or having reason to know that the information was obtained through the interception of such a communication in connection with a criminal investigation under this Act;

(iii) Having obtained or received the information in connection with a criminal investigation; and

(iv) With intent to improperly obstruct, impede, or interfere with a duly authorised criminal investigation; or

(f) Intentionally continues the interception of wire, electronic or oral, communication after the issue of an order of disapproval by the Review Committee under sub-section (4) of section 15 shall for such violation be punishable with imprisonment for a term which may extend to one year and with fine up to rupees fifty thousand.

17. Special Rules of Evidence: (1) Notwithstanding anything to contrary contained in the Code or the Indian Evidence Act 1872, for the purpose of trial and punishment for offences under this Act or connected offences, the Court may take into consideration as having probative value, the fact that the accused was, —

(a) On any previous occasion bound under section 107 or section 110 of the Code;

(b) Detained under any law relating to preventive detention; or

(c) On any previous occasion was prosecuted in the Special Court under this Act.

(2) Where it is proved that any person involved in an organised crime to any person on his behalf is or has at any time been in possession of movable on immovable property which he cannot satisfactorily account for the Special Court shall unless contrary is proved presume that such property or pecuniary resources have been acquired or derived by his illegal activities.

(3) Where it is proved that he accused has kidnapped or abducted any person the Special Court shall presume that it was for ransom.

18. Certain Confessions made to Police Officer to be Taken into Consideration: (1) Notwithstanding anything in the Code or in the Indian Evidence Act, 1872, but subject to the provisions of this section, a confession made by person before a police officer, not below the rank of the Superintendent of Police and recorded by such police officer either in writing or on any mechanical device like cassettes, tape or sound tracks from which sounds or images can be reproduced shall be admissible in the trial of such person or co-accused, abettor of conspirator

Provided that the co-accused, abettor or conspirator is charged and tried in the same case together with the accused.

(2) The confession shall be recorded in a free atmosphere in the same language in which the person is examined and as narrated by him.

(3) The police other shall, before recording any confession under sub-section (1), explain to the person making it that he is not bound to make a confession and that, if he does, so, it may be used as evidence against him and such police officer shall not record any such confession unless upon questioning the person making it, he is satisfied that it is being made voluntarily. The concerned police officer shall, after recording such voluntary confession, certify in writing below the confession about his personal satisfaction of the voluntary character of such confession, putting the date and time to the same.

(4) Every confession recorded under sub-section (1) shall be sent forthwith to the Chief Judicial Magistrate having jurisdiction over the area in which such confession has been recorded and such Magistrate shall forward the recorded confession, so received, to the Special Court which may take cognisance of the offence.

(5) The person, from whom a confession has been recorded under sub-section (1), shall also be produced before the Chief Justice Magistrate to whom the confession is required to be sent under sub-section (4) along with the original statement of confession, written or recorded on mechanical device without unreasonable delay.

(6) The Chief Judicial Magistrate shall scrupulously record the statement, if any, made by the accused so produced and get his signature and in case of any complaint of torture, the person shall be directed to be produced for medical examination before a Medical Officer not lower in rank than of an District Medical Officer.

19. Production of Witnesses: (1) Notwithstanding anything contained in the Code, the proceedings under this Act may be held in Camera, if the special Court so desires.

(2) A Special Court may, on an application made by a witness in any proceeding before it or by the Public Prosecutor in relation to such witness or on its own motion, take such measures as it deems fit for keeping the identity and address of any witness secret.

(3) In particular, and without prejudice to the generality of the provisions of sub-section (2), the measures which Special Court may take under that sub-section may include:

(a) The holding of the proceedings at a place to be decided by the Special Court;

(b) The avoiding of the mention of the name and addresses of the witnesses in its order or judgments or in any records of the case accessible to public;

(c) The issuing of any directions for securing that the identity and addresses of the witnesses are not disclosed;

(d) The, it is in the public interest to order that all or any of the proceedings pending before such a Court shall not be published in any manner.

(4) Any person who contravenes any direction issued under sub-section (3) shall be punishable with imprisonment for a term, which may extend to one year and with fine, which may extend to one thousand rupees.

20. Forfeiture and Attachment of Property: (1) Where a person has been convicted of any offence punishable under this Act, the Special Court may, in addition to awarding any punishment, by order in writing, declare that any property, movable or immovable or both, belonging to the accused and special in the order, shall stand forfeited to the State Government, tree from all encumbrances.

(2) Where any person is accused of any offence under this Act, it shall be open to the Special Court trying him, to pass an order that all or any properties, movable or immovable or both, belonging to him shall, during the period of such trial, be attached and when such trial ends in conviction, the properties so attached shall stand forfeited to the State Government, free from all encumbrances.

(3) (a) If, upon a report in writing made by an investigating police officer with the approval of the supervision officer, referred to in sub-section (1) of section 14, any Special Court has reason to believe that any person, who has committed an offence punishable under this Act, has absconded or is concealing himself, so that he may not be apprehended, such Court may, notwithstanding anything contained in section 82 of the Code, publish a written proclamation requiring him to appear at a specified place and at a specified time not less than fifteen days but not more than thirty days from the publication of such proclamation:

Provided that, if the investigation police officer concerned fails to arrest the accused, who has absconded or is concealing himself, within a period of three months from the date of registering the offence against such persons, the officer shall, on the expiry of the said period, make a report to the Special Court for issuing the proclamation.

(b) The special Court issuing a proclamation under clause (a) may, at any time, order the attachment of any property, movable or immovable or both, belonging to the proclaimed person, and thereupon the provisions of section 83 to 85 of the Code shall apply to such attachment as if such attachment were made under that Code.

(c) If within six months from the date of attachment any person whose ...(illegible) before the special court by whose order the property was attached or the court to which such Court is subordinate, and proves to the satisfaction of such Court that he did not abscond or conceal himself for the purpose of avoiding apprehension and that he had not received such notice of the proclamation as to enable him to attend within the specified time therein, such property or, if the same has been sold, the net proceeds of the same and the residue of the property, shall, after satisfying therefrom all costs incurred in consequence of the attachment.

21. Application of Certain Provisions of the code: (1) Notwithstanding anything contained in the Code or any other law, every offence punishable under this Act, shall be deemed to be a cognizable offence within the meaning of clause (c) of section 2 of the Code and "cognizable case" as defined in that clause shall be construed accordingly.

(2) Section 167 of the Code shall apply in relation to a case involving an offence punishable under this Act subject to the modifications that, in sub-section (2):

(a) The references to "fifteen days", and "sixth days", wherever they occur shall be construed as references to "thirty days" and "ninety days" respectively:

"Provided further that if it is not possible to complete the investigation within the said period of ninety days, the Special Court shall extend the said period up to one hundred and eighty days, on the report of the Public Prosecutor indicating the progress of the investigation and the specific reasons for the detention of the accused beyond the said period of ninety days."

(3) Nothing in section 438 of the Code shall apply in relation as any case involving the arrest of any person on an accusation of having committed an offence punishable under this Act.

(4) Notwithstanding anything contained in the code, no person accused of an offence punishable under this Act shall, if in custody, be released on bail or his own bond, unless:

(a) The Public Prosecutor has been given an opportunity to oppose the application of such release; and

(b) Where the Public Prosecutor opposes the application, the court is satisfied that there are reasonable grounds for believing the he is not guilty of such offence and that he is not likely to commit any offence while on bail.

(5) Notwithstanding anything contained in the Code, the accused shall not be granted bail if it is noticed by the Court that he was on bail in an offence under this Act, or under this Act, or under any other Act, on the date of the offence in question.

(6) The limitations on granting of bail specified in sub-section (4) are in addition to the limitations under the code or any other law for the time being in force on the granting of bail.

(7) The police officer seeking the custody of any person for pre-indictment or pre-trial interrogation from the judicial custody shall file a written statement explaining the reason for seeking such custody and also for the delay, if any, in seeking the police custody.

22. Presumption to as Offences under Section 3: (1) In a prosecution of offence of organised crime punishable under section 3, if it is proved:

(a) That unlawful arms and other material including documents or papers were recovered from the possession of the accused and there is reason to believe that such unlawful arms and other material including documents or papers were used in the commission of such offence; or

(b) That by the evidence of an expert, the finger prints of the accused was found at the site of the offence or on anything including unlawful arms and other material including documents or papers and vehicle used in connection with the commission of such offence, the Special Court shall presume, unless the contrary is proved, that the accused had committed such offence.

(2) In a prosecution for an offence of organised crime punishable under sub-section (2) of section 3, if it is proved that the accused rendered any financial assistance to a person accused of, or reasonably suspected of, an offence of organised crime, the Special Court shall presume, unless the contrary is proved, that such person has committed the offence under the said sub-section (2).

23. Cognisance of, and Investigation into an Offence: (1) Notwithstanding anything contained in the code:

(a) No information about the commission of an offence of organised crime under this Act shall be recorded by a police officer without the prior approval of the police officer not below the rank of the Deputy Inspector General of Police;

(b) No investigation of an offence under the provision of this Act shall be carried out by a police officer below the rank of the Deputy Superintendent of Police;

(2) No Special Court shall take cognisance of any offence under this Act without the previous sanction of the police officer not below the rank of Inspector General of Police.

24. Punishment for Public Servants Failing in the Discharge of Their Duties: Whoever being a public servant renders any help or support in any manner in the commission of organised crime as defined in clause (e) of section 2 whether before or after the commission of any in offence by a member of an organised crime syndicate or abstains from taking lawful measures under this Act or intentionally avoids to carry out the direction of any Court or of the superior police officers in this respect, shall be punished with imprisonment of either description for a term which may extend to three years and also with fine.

25. Overriding Effect: The provisions of this Act or any rule made there under or any order made under any such rule shall, have effect notwithstanding anything inconsistent therewith contained in any other law for the time being in force or in any instrument having the force of law.

26. Protection of Action Taken in Good Faith: No suit, prosecution or other legal proceeding shall lie against the State Government or any officer or authority of the State Government for anything which is in good faith done or intended to be done in pursuance of this Act or any rule made there under or any order issued under any such rule.

27. Annual Report of Interceptions: (1) The State Government shall cause an annual report to be prepared giving a full accounts of:

(i) The number of applications for authorisation of interceptions received by the Competent Authority from the Police Department in which prosecutions have been launched;
(ii) The number of such applications permitted or rejected;
(iii) The number of interceptions carried out in emergency situations and the number of ex-post-facto authorisations or approvals granted or rejected in such matter;
(iv) The number of prosecutions launched, based on such interceptions and convictions resulting form such interceptions, along with an explanatory memorandum giving general assessment of the utility and importance of the interceptions authorised.

(2) Such annual report shall be laid by the State Government before the House of the State Legislature within three months of the completion of every calendar year:

Provided that, if the State Government is of the opinion that the inclusion of any matter in the annual report would be prejudicial to the security of the State or to the prevention or detection of any organised crime, the State Government may exclude such matter from being included in such annual report.

28. Power of High Court to Make Rules: The High Court may, by notification in the Official Gazette, make such rules, as it may deem necessary for carrying out the provisions of this Act relating to the Special Courts.

29. Powers of State Government to Make Rules: Without prejudice to the powers of the High Court to make rules under section 28, the State Government may, by notification in the Official Gazette, make rules for carrying out the purposes of this Act.

30. Repealing and Saving: (1) The Arunachal Pradesh Control of Organised Crime Ordinance, 2002 is hereby repealed.

(2) Notwithstanding such repeal, anything done or any action taken under the said Ordinance shall be deemed to have been done or taken as the case may be under the corresponding provisions of this Act.

31. Statement of Object and Reasons: Government of Arunachal Pradesh have felt it necessary to make a Law to make special provisions for prevention and control of, and for coping with, criminal activities by organised crime syndicates of gangs and matters connected therewith or incidental thereto.

Hence the Government of Arunachal Pradesh had decided to promulgate an Ordinance namely Arunachal Pradesh Control of Organised Crime Ordinance, 2002 which was approved by the Cabinet in its meeting held on 1st April 2002 and came in to force from 3rd April 2002.

The ordinance promulgated shall have the same force and effect as an Act of State Legislature assented to by the Governor, but such ordinance is required to be placed before the ensuing Assembly Session to replace the said Ordinance by an Act.

Hence the Bill.
(Mukut Mithi)
Chief Minister, Arunachal Pradesh.

Memorandum of Settlement on Bodoland Territorial Council

[*On 10 February 2003, the Government of India, the Government of Assam and the Bodo Liberation Tigers signed the Memorandum of Settlement on Bodoland Territorial Council in New Delhi. The jurisdiction of the BTC shall extend over 3082 villages and it has been given legislative powers over 40 subjects. The accord provides for an Executive Council comprising of a maximum of 12 Executive Members, including a Chief and a Deputy Chief, with adequate representation to the non-tribal population*]

1. The Government of India and the Government of Assam have been making concerted efforts to fulfill the aspirations of the Bodo people relating to their cultural identity, language, education and economic development. Towards this end, a series of talks were held between Government of India, Government of Assam and Bodo Liberation Tigers (BLT) since March, 2000. As a result, it is agreed to create a self-governing body for the Bodo Areas in the State of Assam as follows:

2. Objectives: The objectives of the agreement are: to create an Autonomous self governing body to be known as Bodoland Territorial Council (BTC) within the State of Assam and to provide constitutional protection under Sixth Schedule to the said Autonomous Body; to fulfill economic, educational and linguistic aspirations and the preservation of land-rights, socio-cultural and ethnic identity of the Bodos; and speed up the infrastructure development in BTC area.

3. Area: 3.1. The area of proposed BTC shall comprise all the 3082 villages and areas to be so notified by the State Government. The above mentioned villages and areas shall be divided into 4 contiguous districts after reorganisation of the existing districts of Assam within a period of 6 months of the signing of the agreement on the lines of the proposal given by BLT subject to clearance of the Delimitation Commission.

3.2 A committee comprising one representative each from Governments of India and Assam and BLT will decide by consensus on the inclusion of additional villages and areas in the BTC from out of 95 villages and areas on the basis of the criteria of tribal population being not less than 50 per cent, contiguity or any other agreed relevant criteria within a period of three months of signing of this MoS.

4. Status of Bodoland Territorial Council: The provision of the Sixth schedule and other relevant Articles of the Constitution of India will apply to BTC, mutatis mutandis in terms of this agreement. The safeguards/ modifications for the non-tribals in BTC area, inter-alia, will include the following:

4.1. Provision of para 1(2) of Sixth Schedule regarding Autonomous Regions will not be applicable to BTC.

4.2. A provision will be made in para 2(1) of the Sixth Schedule for increasing the number of members for BTC up to 46 out of which 30 will be reserved for Scheduled Tribes, 5 for non-tribal communities, 5 open for all communities and 6 to be nominated by Governor of Assam from the unrepresented communities for BTC area of which at least two should be women. Nominated members will have the same rights and privileges as other members, including voting rights. Election from the 40 constituencies of BTC shall be on the basis of adult franchise. The term of the elected members of BTC shall be for 5 years.

4.3. Safeguards for the settlement rights, transfer and inheritance of property etc. of non-tribals will be suitably incorporated in para 3 of the Sixth Schedule. Any such law as may be made by the BTC in this regard will not, in particular:

(a) Extinguish the rights and privileges enjoyed by an citizen of India in respect of their land at the commencement of BTC, and
(b) Bar any citizen from acquiring land either by way of inheritance, allotment, settlement or by way of transfer if such citizens were eligible for such bonafide acquisition of land within the BTC area.

4.4. Provision will be added in para 6 of Sixth Schedule that in BTC area, language and medium of instruction in educational institutions will not be changed without approval of the State Government.

4.5. Provision of para 8 of Sixth Schedule regarding power to assess and collect land revenue and impose taxes shall be applicable to BTC.

4.6. Para 10 of the Sixth Schedule will not be applicable to BTC area.

4.7. Provision of Article 332(6) of the Constitution will be so modified that the existing status of representation of BTC area in the State Assembly is kept intact. After the creation of BTC, the Parliamentary and Assembly Constituencies shall be delimited by the Delimitation Commission in accordance with the provisions of the Constitution.

4.8. In the event, Panchayati Raj system ceases to be in force in the council area, the powers of the Panchayati Raj Institutions in such matters shall be vested with the Council.

The Amendments to the Sixth Schedule shall include provisions in such a manner that non-tribals are not disadvantaged in relation to the rights enjoyed by them at the commencement of BTC and their rights and privileges including land rights are fully protected.

5. Power and Functions:

5.1. The Council shall have legislative powers in respect to subjects transferred to it as enumerated below. All laws made under this paragraph shall be submitted forthwith to the Governor and until assented to by him, shall have no effect. The BTC shall have executive, administrative and financial powers in respect of subjects transferred to it.

SUBJECTS TO BE ENTRUSTED TO BTC BY
ASSAM GOVERNMENT

1. Small, Cottage and Rural Industry; 2. Animal Husbandry and Veterinary; 3. Forest; 4. Agriculture; 5. PWD; 6. Sericulture; 7. Education (Primary Education, Higher Secondary Including vocational training, Adult Education, College Education (General); 8. Cultural Affairs; 9. Soil Conservation; 10. Co-operation; 11. Fisheries; 12. Panchayat and Rural Development; 13. Handloom and Textile; 14. Health and Family Welfare; 15. Public Health Engineering; 16. Irrigation; 17. Social Welfare; 18. Flood Control; 19. Sports and Youth Welfare; 20. Weights and Measures; 21. Library Services; 22. Museum and Archaeology; 23. Urban Development—Town and Country Planning; 24. Tribal Research Institute; 25. Land and Revenue; 26. Publicity/Public Relations; 27. Printing and Stationery; 28. Tourism; 29. Transport; 30. Planning and Development; 31. Municipal Corporation, Improvement Trust, District Boards and other local authorities; 32. Welfare of Plan Tribes and Backward Classes; 33. Markets and fairs; 34. Lotteries, Theatres, Dramatic performance and cinema; 35. Statistics; 36. Food and Civil supply; 37. Intoxicating liquors, opium and derivatives etc.; 38. Labour and employment; 39. Relief and Rehabilitation; 40. Registration of Births and Deaths.

5.2. There shall be an Executive Council comprising of not more than 12 Executive Members, one of whom shall be the Chief and another one the Deputy Chief of the said Executive Council. There shall be adequate representation for the non-tribal members in the Executive Council. The Chief and the Deputy Chief of the Council shall have the status equivalent to the Cabinet Minister and the other Executive Members equivalent to the Minister of the State of Assam for protocol purposes in BTC area.

5.3. The BTC shall have the full control over the officers and staff connected with the delegated subjects working in the BTC area and shall be competent to transfer officers and staff within the BTC area. ACRs of these officers shall also be written by the appropriated BTC authority.

5.4. BTC shall also be competent to make appointments for all posts under its control in accordance with the rules of appointment followed by the Government of Assam. However, the posts, where recruitment is made on the recommendation of APSC, shall not be covered under this provision. The Council may constitute a Selection Board for appointments to be made by it and may also make rules, with the approval of the Governor of Assam to regulate appointments and to ensure adequate representation for all communities living in the Council area.

5.5. No posts shall be created by BTC without concurrence of the Government of Assam and it shall also abide by the decision of the Government of Assam in respect of abolition of/temporarily keeping vacant any post.

5.6. Development functions and bodies within the competence of BTC shall be transferred to BTC. In respect of DRDA, concurrence of Government of India will be obtained.

5.7. The offices of the Dy. Commissioner and Superintendent of Police will be outside the superintendence and control of BTC.

5.8. The State Government would provide an amount, to be decided every year on population ratio basis, as grants-in-aid in two equal installments to the BTC for executing development works. The proportionate share for the BTC shall be calculated on the basis of the plan funds available after setting aside the funds required for earmarked sectors and the salary. This amount may be reduced proportionately if the state plan allocation is reduced or there is plan cut due to resource problem. In addition, the Council will be paid a suitable amount of plan funds and non-plan funds to cover the office expenses and the salaries of the staff working under their control. The BTC shall disburse the salaries of the staff under their control and would ensure strict economy in the matter.

5.9. BTC authority shall prepare a plan with the amounts likely to be available for development works, both under State share and Central share, covering any or all the activities of the departments under their control. The Council shall have full discretion in selecting the activities and choosing the amount for the investment under the same in any year covering all groups of people in a fair and equitable manner. This plan will be a sub set of the State plan and would be treated as its integral part. Once the plan of the State, including BTC plan, gets the approval of the Planning Commission the BTC authority will start execution of their plan in the BTC area. Modifications, if any, made by the Planning Commission in the BTC proposal, shall be binding on the BTC authority. The State Government shall not divert the funds allocated to the BTC to other heads and also ensure its timely release. BTC may have Planning Department to prepare the plans for BTC area to be submitted to Planning Commission through the Government of Assam.

5.10. The executive functions of the BTC shall be exercised through its Principal Secretary who shall be an officer of the rank not below of Commissioner/Secretary to Government of Assam. The sanctioning powers of the Government of Assam shall be vested with the Principal Secretary of BTC and sanctioning powers of head(s) of the Department(s) including for technical sanction shall be conferred on the senor most officer of that Department preferably not below the rank of Additional Director, who may be designated as Director of BTC for that department. The Principal Secretary and other officers shall exercise their powers under the overall guidance and supervision of BTC.

6. Law and Order: To strengthen the Police Administration, Government of Assam shall appoint an IGP for 4 districts of BTC and the jurisdiction of the DIG Kokrajhar shall also be modified to cover these 4 districts.

7. Revision of List of ST: Consequent to the inclusion of BTC area into the Sixth Schedule, the list of ST for the State of Assam shall be so modified so as to ensure that the tribal status of Bodos and other tribals living outside the BTC are does not get affected adversely.

8. Grant of ST Status of Bodo Kacharis of Karbi Anglong and NC Hills Districts: The Government of India agrees to consider sympathetically the inclusion of the Bodo Kacharis living in Karbi Anglong and NC Hills Autonomous Council area in the ST (Hill) List of State of Assam.

9. Development of Bodo Language:

9.1. The Government of India agrees to consider favourably the inclusion of Bodo Language in Devnagri Script in the Eighth Schedule of the Constitution.

9.2. Bodo language shall be the official language of BTC subject to the condition that Assamese and English shall also continue to be used for official purpose

10. Additional Development Package for BTC:

10.1. The State Government, within the limitation of financial and other constraints, may offer or allow the Council to offer, possible and sustainable additional incentives for attracting private investment in the Council area and would also support projects for external funding.

10.2. In order to accelerate the development of the region and to meet the aspirations of the people, the Government of India will provide financial assistance of Rs. 100 crore per annum for 5 years for projects to develop the socio-economic infrastructure in BTC areas over and above the normal plan assistance to the State of Assam. The size of the Corpus will be reviewed after a period of 5 years. Suitable mechanism will be built in the system to ensure that the funds are transferred to BTC in time and at regular intervals. An illustrative list of projects which may be considered to be taken up in BTC given below:

List of Projects

1. To establish a centre for development and research of Bodo language; 2. Upgradation of existing educational infrastructure by way of renovation/addition of buildings, providing modern facilities for teaching such as computers, science laboratories etc. from primary level to college level in BTC area; 3. A cultural complex to be established at Kokrajhar to promote and develop Bodo tradition and cultural heritage; 4. To establish a super-speciality hospital with all modern facilities at Kokrajhar Government Hospitals shall be established in all district, sub-divisional and block headquarter; 5. To establish sports complexes in all the district headquarters; 6. Food processing plants and clod storage facilities at Kokrajhar, Kajolgaon, Udalguri and Tamulpur; 7. Construction of a bridge over river Aai to connect Koilamoila, Amguri etc. with the rest of the district; 8. To build a Bodoland Bhawan in Delhi; 9. To set up integrated agro-processing park and textile-cum-apparel park; 10. Revitalisation of Kokilabari Agricultural Farm; 11. To develop adequate infrastructure to promote Manas sanctuary as an international tourist spot; 12. To complete Champa, Suklai and Dhansiri irrigation projects; 13. To construct a highway on the Indo-Bhutan border from Jamduar to Bhairabkunda to connect remote places located adjacent to the border; 14. To set up model dairy, fishery, horticulture and poultry farms/training centres at different places in all the 4 districts to encourage youth for self-employment; 15. To enhance the existing facilities in veterinary hospitals in BTC area.

10.3. Government of India will provide necessary one time financial assistance required for development of administrative infrastructure in the newly created district headquarters, sub-divisional headquarters and book headquarters, besides the BTC Secretariat Complex at Kokrajhar

11. Centrally Funded University:

11.1. A centrally funded Central Institute of Technology (CIT) will be set up to impact education in various technological/vocational disciplines such as Information Technology, Bio-Technology, Food Processing, Rural Industries, Business Management, etc.

11.2. The CIT will be subsequently upgraded to a Centrally funded State University with technical and non-technical disciplines to be run by the BTC.

12. Relief and Rehabilitation:

12.1. The BLT would join the national mainstream and shun the path of violence in the interest of peace and development. After the formation of the interim council of BTC, BLT will dissolve itself as an organisation and surrender with arms within a week of swearing-in of the interim council. The State Government would provide full support to relief and rehabilitation of the members of BLT who would surrender with arms in this process in accordance with the existing policy of the State. Financial support in such cases, however shall be limited to be provisions of the scheme prepared and funded by the Government of India. Withdrawal of cases against such persons and those related to over ground Bodo movement since 1987 shall be considered according to the existing policy of the State of Assam.

12.2. The Government of India will initiate steps for review of action against the Bodo employees of Government of India and subordinate officers as well as in respect of Central Government Undertakings. Similar action would be taken by the Government of Assam.

12.3. Bodo youth will be considered for recruitment in Police, Army and Paramilitary forces to increase their representation in these forces.

13. Special Rehabilitation Programme for the People Affected by Ethnic Disturbances: The Special Rehabilitation Programme (SRP) for the people affected by ethnic disturbances in Assam, who are at present living at relief camps in Kokrajhar, Bongaigaon etc. shall be completed by the Government of Assam with active support of BTC. Necessary funds for their rehabilitation shall be provided by the Government of India and lands which are free from all encumbrances required for such rehabilitation shall be made available by the BTC.

14. Interim Council: Immediately after signing of the agreement, Interim Executive Council for BTC shall be formed by Governor of Assam from amongst the leaders of the present Bodo movement, including the signatories to this settlement, and shall include adequate representation to the non-tribal communities in BTC area. The Interim Council shall not continue for a period beyond 6 months during which period election to the Council shall be held. Government of Assam shall dissolve the Bodoland Autonomous Council (BAC) and repeal the BAC Act.

15. Government of Assam will consider inclusion of all tribals including Bodos in RHAC/MAC/LAC in consultation with leaders of these Councils.

16. The Implementation of the provision of the Memorandum of Settlement shall be periodically reviewed by a Committee comprising representatives of Government of India, Government of Assam and BTC.

Signed on 10 February 2003 at New Delhi in the presence of **Shri L.K. Advani**, Hon'ble Deputy Prime Minister of India and **Shri Tarun Gogoi**, **Chief Minister of Assam**.

(Hagrama Basumatary)	**(P.K. Dutta)**	**(R.C.A. Jain)**
Chairman	Chief Secretary	Secretary (BM)
Bodo Liberation Tigers	Govt. of Assam	Ministry of Home Affairs
Government of India		